Archaeological Sites of Britain

Archaeological Sites of Britain

Peter Clayton

WEIDENFELD AND NICOLSON
LONDON

192

DD (cca)

Designed by Sheila Sherwen
for George Weidenfeld and Nicolson Ltd
11 St John's Hill, London SW11

ISBN 0 297 77115 9

Printed in Great Britain by
Butler and Tanner Ltd
Frome and London

Contents

Preface

There are over 1500 visible archaeological sites in England, Scotland and Wales. They range in size from the faint indications of a partially ploughed-out barrow (ancient burial mound) to grand circuits of Roman walls like those at the Saxon Shore fort of Pevensey in Sussex. No matter how large or small each site is, it is an element in the history of our past, and its importance similarly varies, often bearing no relationship to its present size. Horrific tales abound in the daily press of well-known monuments threatened in the name of progress, and smaller ones pass away unsung. But the present generation is not new in extolling the virtues of so-called progress over all other considerations – at the time of the First World War it was suggested that Stonehenge should be demolished as it constituted a hazard to low-flying aircraft!

Nowadays the steady march of motorways across the countryside has bred a new and specialist form of archaeology – motorway archaeology – which entails being at least one step ahead of the planners and developers in order to record and save as much as possible from a site before it is sealed in its concrete tomb or bulldozed out of existence. Happy exceptions occur from time to time – for instance when, after much hard work and lobbying, local archaeologists managed to have a motorway raised slightly so that it would not totally destroy the recently found remains of the Saxon Shore fort at Dover. At Welwyn in Hertfordshire local archaeological society pressure resulted in a simple-plan Roman bath-house being preserved cocooned in concrete beneath the carriageway of the new road, for the benefit of school parties and other interested visitors who are going there in ever-increasing numbers.

Yet for every site that is saved – if only for a future generation to re-excavate as at Dover – hundreds are lost. Obviously it is impossible to pursue a policy that cries out that all archaeological sites must be preserved: important ones yes, if at all possible, but the essential thing is that they should all be fully recorded before they are swept away. We owe the future at least this much of the past.

To write about all the visible sites would be tedious in the extreme; many of them, although archaeologically important, are not visually attractive or have only a little to show on the ground. Similarly, to the uninitiated, and even at times to the keen archaeologist, too many barrows or hill forts can be highly indigestible. The greater number of visible monuments are in fact barrows, mostly of the Bronze Age, and hill forts, mainly of the Iron Age. A glance at almost any one-inch Ordnance Survey map, or the new 1 : 50,000 series, will immediately reveal a scatter of the tell-tale 'tumuli' or 'fort' notices in distinctive gothic lettering. These are followed in density by Roman remains, indicated on the maps in an appropriate type-face, and among these we find sections of town walls, buildings such as villas and, of course, the greatest site of that period in Britain – the remains of Hadrian's Wall, extending 73 miles from the mouth of the river Tyne across to the Solway Firth. Much could be written about all these sites, but there would be a great deal of repetition in the description of, say, one Bronze Age barrow after another throughout Wiltshire, or Iron Age hill fort after hill fort in Wessex.

The book has been divided into broad geographical regions, not even coming down into county divisions for, although some of them correspond amazingly closely at times to ancient British tribal areas, these boundaries are nevertheless the product of a modern administrative system. The county names mentioned in the text are the ones used prior to the 1974 reorganization, since these will be more familiar to the majority of readers. Within each area only selected monuments are described in detail – ones which it is hoped will prove to be of general interest as places to visit, enough to make a detour to see on a car journey. All these sites are given an Ordnance Survey map reference number so that they can be found easily. In trying to scale down the vast number of visible sites to manageable proportions it has meant that an element of personal preference has at times crept in; how else would it be possible to choose between a series of outstanding hill forts, such as one finds for instance in Sussex? I hope that the sites selected and the comments made about them will perhaps serve as a springboard towards more detailed accounts of individual areas or sites. The literature of British archaeology is vast, and this small addition to it is offered in the hope that it may stimulate a dormant interest in some readers and perhaps at the same time indicate a little of my own interest and personal preferences. My own 'archaeological bug' started active life when I was a schoolboy; that is one of the attractions of archaeology – you cannot really be too young and you are never too old for it to mean something to you. We are all living in what will be before very long someone else's past; our past should live for us, as that greatest of living British archaeologists Sir Mortimer Wheeler has so rightly observed: 'Dead archaeology is the dryest dust that blows.'

P.A.C.

Introduction

> In the beginning God created Heaven and Earth,
> *Gen. l.v.l.* Which beginning of time, according to
> our Chronologie, fell upon the entrance of the night
> preceding the twenty third day of *Octob.* in the year
> of the Julian Calendar, 710 ... 4004 before Christ.
>
> JAMES USSHER, *The Annals of the World Deduced from the Origin of Time . . .*
> *Containing the Historie of the Old and New Testament*, 1658.

In 1650 James Ussher, archbishop of Armagh, published his *Annales Veteris Testamenti A Prima Mundi Origine Deducti*, and eight years later his dogmatic assertion appeared translated into English. Such was his standing, and man's ignorance of his past, that the arch-bishop's dating became almost Holy Writ, and the date 4004 was even printed in the margins of the Authorized Version of the Bible. Little could the learned prelate have realized the influence his 'Chronologie' would have in retarding archaeological studies, even to the extent of causing a man of such integrity, learning and scholarship as Dean William Buckland to perjure himself over his excavation of the Red Lady of Paviland (p. 158). To query biblical authority was deemed heresy, and as learned men became more and more aware of the geo-logical implications of these early finds, so they became more and more disquieted. On the Continent men like Boucher de Perthes were find-ing and noting prehistoric axes in the gravels of the Somme and, despite the fact that his discoveries were ridiculed, he published in 1847 a book on his finds entitled *Antiquités Celtiques et Antédiluviennes*. To suggest that some of his finds were from before the Flood raised a storm of protest, but he weathered it and continued his work.

   In Denmark in the first half of the nineteenth century Christian Thomsen, acting as unpaid secretary of the National Museum, began to sort the collections into three basic groups of material made of stone, bronze and iron. Thus the Three-Age System – Stone, Bronze and

Iron Age – came about, and from humble beginnings was to be elaborated and refined, first by Thomsen's successor Jens Jacob Worsaae and then by others throughout Europe and beyond. Closely tied in with this basic outline of evolution was the invasion theory – that bronze-using technologies would obviously oust their stone-using predecessors by force of arms, and so on.

Archbishop Ussher had held undisputed sway for 200 years since his book was published, and at times it is rather hard to realize how recent in fact our archaeological knowledge is. In Britain true archaeological excavation, and therefore knowledge, appreciation and interpretation, begins with General Pitt Rivers who inherited vast estates at Cranborne Chase in Dorset in 1880. He recognized the basic precept that finds from undisturbed ground are older the deeper you dig – the stratigraphical method of excavation. British archaeology was founded on this precept, although intelligent interest in the monuments and sites scattered throughout the countryside can be traced back to John Leland, the King's Antiquary, in the early sixteenth century, and other famous antiquaries such as William Camden in the seventeenth and William Stukeley in the early eighteenth century. This base of antiquarian studies brought a fund of received knowledge to British archaeology.

It is a fairly obvious fact that the earlier the remains one seeks the more difficult they are to find because of their original widespread distribution and scarcity, as communities were so small. Remains in Britain from the Stone Age, lower or upper palaeolithic (*c.* 500,000–10,000 BC), are plentiful in terms of artifacts such as stone hand-axes and other flint implements, but sites are few and far between. Even when found and excavated they present little for the trained archaeologist, let alone the interested layman. This is why very few sites of

1 Three different types of Acheulean hand-axes, all found in England. British Museum

this period will be found described here: only major ones such as those in the area of Cheddar Gorge and Wookey Hole are of sufficent general interest to merit a detour and visit. The succeeding period of the hunter–fisher folk, called the mesolithic (*c.* 10,000–4000 BC) has left even fewer traces, as these people were nomadic, and although a number of mesolithic sites are known, notably that of Star Carr in east Yorkshire, there is nothing to see.

The New Stone Age, the neolithic (*c.* 4000–2000 BC), brought with it a rather crude form of pottery which reflects in its shape the leather containers that it copied. The neolithic period is divided into three parts – early, middle and late – and it is from the middle neolithic, which lasted about 1000 years from the mid-third to the mid-second millennium BC, that substantial monuments and sites become known and recognizable. In this period long barrows began to be built. These were burial mounds of great length, the early ones usually having an entrance at the front leading via a passage to a burial chamber. Many barrows of this kind were used for communal burial in southern England over a long period of time, and therefore may have remained open for a couple of generations before being finally closed and sealed (e.g. West Kennet, p. 82). Other barrows have produced evidence of a wooden hut or mortuary house where disarticulated bones were placed after the flesh had been allowed to disintegrate elsewhere. Obviously such timber structures soon rotted and collapsed within the body of the mound. It is only in recent years, with modern, refined excavation techniques, that such structures have been recognized for what they are, not only under neolithic long barrows but also under a number of Bronze Age barrows as well. Some of the long barrows have a forecourt and a stone structure in front of the broad end of the barrow. This, however, is not what it seems: it is a false entrance

2 Neolithic and Bronze Age pottery; left to right: 'Windmill Hill' type from Norton Bavant, 'Peterborough' type from Hedsor, and a typical Bronze Age beaker from Cholsey. British Museum

which might have had ritual significance but was more probably a
simple expedient against tomb robbers. The actual burials were made
in small chambers situated along the sides of the mound: Belas Knap
(p. 73), is a good example of this type. There are, of course, regional
variations in the mode of burial and in barrow construction which
are noted in archaeological terminology by descriptive titles that often
indicate the geographical region concerned, such as Clyde–Carl-
ingford- or Severn–Cotswold-type tombs. To explain all these variations in detail would involve going beyond the scope of this book, but
certain monuments in these categories will be described.

The neolithic period also saw the beginning of the hill forts that
are so much a feature of hill tops in the English countryside. In
archaeology, artifacts or types of monument are frequently named
after the site where they were first recognized; these are known as
eponymous sites. Palaeolithic Acheulean hand-axes, for instance, are
named after St Acheul on the Somme in France and, relevant to our
topic of the neolithic, Windmill Hill-type causewayed camps are
named after the classic site near Avebury (p. 80). These camps, rather
than forts, consist of an area encircled by banks and ditches with cross-
ing-places at intervals along causeways over the ditches. They certainly could not have fulfilled any defensive function, and must have
been used in some way as cattle corrals or gathering-places for barter
and exchange of crops, animals and other goods. More and better flint
and stone was required in the middle and late neolithic periods for
implement-making, and this led to the exploitation of rich seams made
accessible by mining in areas of Sussex and especially at the famous
site of Grimes Graves in Norfolk (p. 116). Where suitable stone could
be found on open sites, often high up on mountainsides such as at
Cwm Mawr (p. 131), this was worked on the spot and then often traded
over long distances. At the time of writing, an extensive programme
of research is being carried out which involves taking thin sections
from stone axes with known provenances which can then be matched
against known factory sites. Distribution maps of the finds are then
built up, which can indicate the routes along which the axes were
traded.

Also involved in this trading, but not to such an extent as the axes,
was neolithic pottery. The basic types had by now changed into forms
much more satisfying than the early baggy shapes and were rather
more elegant, although still very thick-walled, and decorated with cord
impressions or stabbed decoration made with small sticks or even
thumb-nails. Distinctive types again take the names of their find spots,
such as Peterborough, Mortlake and Fengate.

To the neolithic period, also, belong a number of the stone circles
and alignments of stones found throughout Britain. Many of these
sites continued as sacred areas into the Bronze and Iron Ages, and
subsequently when another religion introduced its own symbol of
unity they were still a centre of worship – consider for instance the
Norman church in the centre of the henge monument at Knowlton
Circles in Dorset (p. 51). Some of the most outstanding monuments

in Britain have their early phases and constructions well bedded in the neolithic, as at Stonehenge (p. 87) and Avebury (p. 80).

Into all this activity some time shortly after the middle of the second millennium BC came a new people from the Rhineland area. At one time their advent was thought of in terms of a sudden influx around 2000 BC, but excavation now indicates a gradual introduction of the people and their new rituals over several hundred years. A number of sites show evidence of the gradual fusion of the newcomers with the neolithic natives. They had much to offer that was new, especially in the technological fields of metal-working and pottery. Theirs was the secret of bronze-working and their pottery is typified by a distinctive beaker – they are often referred to by this 'type fossil' as beaker folk. This vessel was a feature of the offerings placed in graves with their dead. They also introduced new shapes for the actual barrows: round barrows with a great variety of shapes – bell, bowl-, disc-, pond-, and saucer-barrows. Disc-barrows appear to have been used exclusively for female burials although there are a few known from saucer-barrows.

It was during the Bronze Age that a warrior aristocracy developed in Wessex, an area comprising large parts of the counties of Hampshire, Wiltshire and Dorset with some smaller parts of Somerset and Berkshire. The focal point of Wessex was the religious complex to be found on Salisbury Plain. Such was the power of the warrior chieftains of the Wessex Culture that not only could major engineering works be undertaken such as the later phases of the building of Stonehenge, but they could also command vast resources of wealth through trade that included gold from Ireland and amber from the Baltic. Much of this they took with them to the grave under their large bell- and bowl-barrows. Today we can see examples in finds such as those from the Bush Barrow on Normanton Down, the Rillaton gold cup and small drinking cups made of precious amber.

The pre-eminence gained by a people skilled in bronze-working gradually gave way before a superior technology that knew the secret of working iron. Again there was no distinct division but a gradual absorption over a number of years. The Iron Age started about 700 BC in Britain and advanced very slowly at first; then knowledge of the new material and its potential began to spread more widely. Iron Age peoples were basically farmers, but they needed to defend themselves from time to time and the hill fort developed and became more complex as it was found that more sophisticated weapons dictated more stringent methods of defence. The best of these military installations can be seen in sites such as Maiden Castle (p. 58) and the Stanwick fortifications (p. 144). Many hill forts had vain attempts made to refurbish them and enlarge their defences in the face of the Roman invasion of AD 43 and its aftermath. None managed to stand for long against the military machine of Rome – witness the east gate of Maiden Castle. Most of the forts that did attempt to withstand the *Pax Romana* were taken, their defences slighted and their population removed to a convenient centre, sometimes newly built, for romanization.

13

Fig.1 Basic types of Bronze Age round barrow
(long barrows are neolithic) See illus. 72

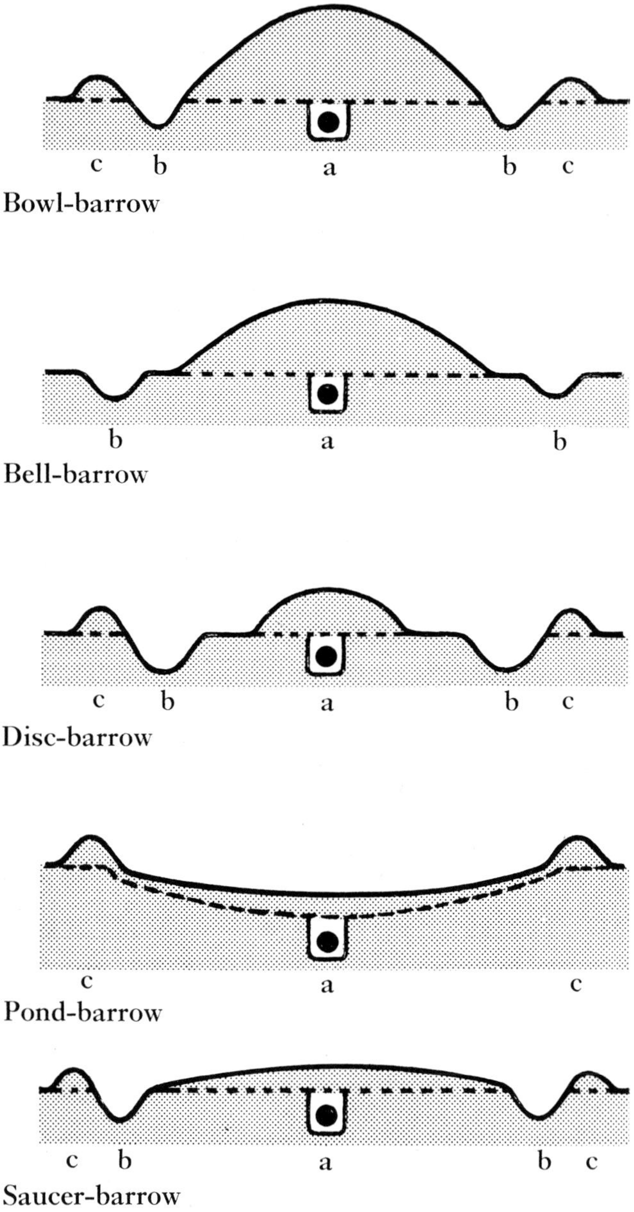

Bowl-barrow

Bell-barrow

Disc-barrow

Pond-barrow

Saucer-barrow

a burial   b outer ditch   c outer bank

The dotted line represents the natural ground level
within the solid earth barrow

3 Celtic torc of electrum, nearly 8 ins in diameter, from the Snettisham treasure found in 1950 and declared Treasure Trove. British Museum

As in the Bronze Age, and indeed with almost any society that has a point to it, there was a ruling aristocracy. Described in the late Iron Age by Caesar in rather critical and naturally biased terms, they nevertheless created, or rather had created for them, some of the most magnificent works of art, generally in metalwork, that have come down to us from early times in Britain. The Celtic warrior chieftains of the late Iron Age and their men must indeed have been a fearsome sight in battle as the Roman chronicles described them. Much of the surviving Celtic art tends to be part of a warrior's accoutrements or decoration on them, or vessels for the great drinking sessions that were the mark of the warrior's world. As Professor Stuart Piggott has aptly remarked, 'Celtic art owed much to Celtic thirst.' Yet this society could also command the creation of objects of great beauty and superb design such as the Snettisham torc, the Battersea shield and the Desborough mirror. It is sad that the great majority of these magnificent pieces come to us as the result of chance finds and not from excavated archaeological contexts that could tell us so much more about them.

Under the Roman occupation *Britannia* became just another province in a growing empire, but the way of life of the Iron Age farmer did not die out. It was merely overlaid by the new economic stresses and strains of a literate administration backed initially by the force of a military system that was rendered highly mobile as a network of major roads, legionary fortresses, towns and settlements was laid down. The province went through several vicissitudes that reflected problems elsewhere in the empire, and not least the troubles of several usurper emperors in the course of three centuries in Britain itself. Ever-present, too, was the threat of invasion by hostile elements beyond this last frontier of Rome, a threat that did from time to time materialize as hordes swept down on unsuspecting towns or swift pirate raids erupted out of the sea. The Roman way of life set a pattern that spread out across downlands the villas of the wealthy, situated in ideal locations and made opulent with warm air central heating systems, colourful and intricate mosaics and tastefully painted plastered walls (e.g. the villas at Bignor, Chedworth, Lullingstone etc.). Great civic works were undertaken, not only huge temples to the living god – the emperor – as at Colchester, but buildings that in their grandeur spoke of Mediterranean civilization and its way of life – baths, the forum and the basilica. When, at the end of the fourth century, Roman troops were recalled to try and save the crumbling centre of the empire, the light was not extinguished as suddenly as many books of a few years ago would have us believe. There is even evidence in towns such as St Albans (*Verulamium*) of new work and buildings going on into the fifth century.

The decline of Roman Britain was a gradual one; evidence from cemeteries indicates the merger of Germanic peoples and their individual style of pottery into a unity that was to become Anglo-Saxon England. Many of the Roman ruins were to be partially inhabited by squatters. Most of the towns served as ready and easily accessible quarries; Bede records the bricks and stonework of *Verulamium* being removed by the cartload: much of it went towards the construction of the cathedral, as evidenced by the Roman tiles visible in its fabric, and, as he records, 'When the peace of Christian times was restored, a beautiful church worthy of his [St Alban's] martyrdom was built.'

In parts of Britain beyond the immediate sphere of Roman influence and new ideas brought by visitors from the Continent at various times, change took longer to come about. In some areas an earlier way of life continued long into a period of time that elsewhere had been subject to great advancement and a subsequent change of name. The Stone Age existence of the inhabitants of Skara Brae is a case in point, when in areas to the south much more advanced technology was in use. Similarly, the division between Iron Age and Roman Britain is not one that can be closely defined; where there was no Roman impact obviously the Iron Age continued, native forts continued to be built and perhaps a few Roman trinkets might make their way through trade beyond the frontiers, the *limes*, of Rome.

It is salutary to remember that while the Iron Age started about 700 BC in Britain it only ended with the recent advent of atomic power that inaugurated the Atomic Age. To future archaeologists we are the children of our time and the transition from Iron Age to Atomic Age was, for us, relatively painless if not unnoticed; so to a degree must have been those transitions in earlier ages where archaeologists can at times get terribly dogmatic about dates, almost as if the change came about overnight – even Archbishop Ussher was very definite that not only did the world begin in 4004 BC, but it was actually on the evening of 23 October!

1 The South-East

Since Roman times the focus of communication in the South-East has been at the lowest crossing point on the river Thames. This area where two spurs of gravel faced each other across the river so that it could be forded was to become the site of *Londinium*. First trackways, then roads, and eventually the iron roads of the railway converged here, and still do; so it is logical to start at London in seeking out some of the more interesting archaeological sites and remains in south-east England.

Before the Roman invasion under the emperor Claudius in AD 43 there is little evidence for any settlement on the present site of London. Further up the river at Brentford the remains of huts with wattle floors apparently of Romano–British date were found in 1929 and 1955, and it has been suggested that it was in this area of the river that Caesar forced his way across against native British opposition during his second foray into Britain in 54 BC.

Within the City of London (TQ 513281) the most substantial Roman remains visible are sections of the wall surrounding *Londinium*. The wall dates from the late third century AD, and before that date the city was protected only by a military fort to the north-west of the settlement. A convenient place from which to start looking at some of the more accessible parts of the Roman wall is within the Tower of London: close to the south-east side of the dominating White Tower are a few courses of the Roman wall, incorporated in the ruins of the base of the Wardrobe Tower. The distinctive red Roman bonding tiles are easily seen in these foundation levels where they occur at regularly spaced intervals, often in triple lines.

Across the other side of Tower Hill, in Trinity Place, is a most impressive piece of the wall now preserved in a public garden. Roman work with its red tiles can be clearly seen at the base, above which are courses of Kentish ragstone running into medieval renewal of the wall rising to the sentry's catwalk over 20 ft above the Roman courses. Close to the wall are the outline foundations of a Roman guard turret. Modern copies of two pieces of inscribed stone are set in a twentieth-century brick wall in the public garden: these pieces were once part of a funerary monument originally located, in accordance with Roman law, outside the city walls. The fragments of this monument, found during building operations in 1852 and 1935, were re-used as filling in the base of a bastion on the Roman city wall. They comprise one of the most important historical inscriptions from Roman Britain, since they were part of the tomb of Julius Classicianus who is known to us from other sources to be the procurator sent by the emperor Nero to restore the fortunes of a shattered province after the revolt of Boudicca (Boadicea), the warrior queen of the Iceni, in AD 61. His humanitarian approach to the problem, instead of instituting extreme punitive measures, did much to restore the prosperity of the province. The monument was erected, as the inscription goes on to tell us, by his wife Julia Pacata. The original inscribed stones, together with a portion of the ornament from the top of the monument, have been restored and are now in the British Museum.

A little to the north of Trinity Place, in the headquarters of the Toc H Club, a magnificent portion of the wall can be seen at one end of the dining-room. It may be viewed at convenient times, on application.

Still close to Tower Hill, in Cooper's Row, another long, tall stretch of the wall is preserved. This has been consolidated and turned into a feature of a pleasant little court with a fountain. Most of the wall here is medieval, as are the windows cut in it, but Roman courses can be seen right at the base.

From this point the Roman wall continued north for a while before turning westwards to continue encircling the city. Over the years many pieces of it have been found during building operations, but the next sections worth seeing are over in the Moorgate area in the aptly named street, London Wall. Above ground is a section which still stands quite high, again preserved in a public garden, which was used in the Middle Ages as the wall of St Alphage's churchyard. It is topped by battlements added in the late fifteenth century. Somewhat unexpectedly there is a fine stretch in the underground car park, and in a room near one of the exits the foundations of the north turret and central piers of a double gate excavated in 1956–8 can be seen. This was not a major city gate, but a gate in the west wall of the fort which preceded the city wall and which was later incorporated within it. The existence of this earlier fort had not been suspected until excavations in the area after the Second World War by Professor W. F. Grimes revealed the evidence in the deep cellars of bombed Victorian warehouses.

In the area of Cripplegate a substantial amount of the wall can be seen, notably the Cripplegate bastion standing high beside the church of St Giles; several other bastions on the line of the wall, one of them incorporating early medieval arrow slits and then later windows; and the foundations of wall turrets and the 'double' wall where the narrower wall of the early fort was made wider when it became part of the city wall. This can best be seen in the gardens which run alongside in Noble Street.

4 Section of the Roman and medieval city wall in Wakefield Gardens, Trinity Place. Only the lower courses with the horizontal lines of red bonding tiles are of Roman date

One last piece of the wall remains to be mentioned, and this is the great horseshoe-shaped bastion which is now preserved under the General Post Office yard in St Martin's-le-Grand. This imposing portion, known as bastion 19, stands about 25 ft high. It can only be viewed after writing to the Post Office for an appointment.

All the stone for building the wall – and it was about 2 miles in length – had to be brought by barge from quarries on the river Medway near Maidstone, Kent, as there is no suitable building stone available nearer London. One of these barges, which had sunk with part of its cargo, was found deep in the river mud in 1962 during construction work for a new underpass by Blackfriars Station.

A purely imaginative view of the walls of Roman London appears on the reverse of a large gold medallion of Constantius Chlorus found at Arras in northern France in 1922. It shows Constantius on horseback armed with a spear approaching a female figure who kneels to

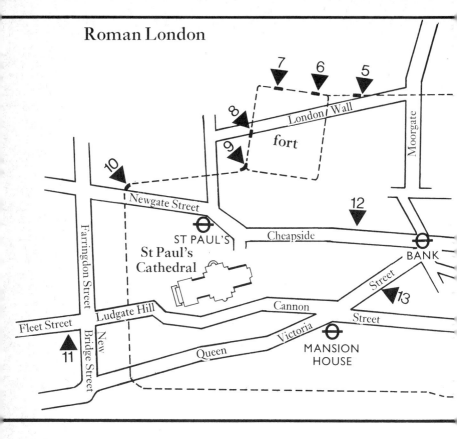

Roman London

Fig. 2 Outline map of some of the remains of Roman London that can still be seen.
1 Wardrobe Tower, Tower of London; 2 Wakefield Gardens, Tower Hill (*Illus. 4*); 3 Toc H; 4 8–10 Cooper's Row; 5 Underground car park, London Wall; 6 St Alphage's Churchyard, London Wall; 7 Cripplegate bastion beside St Giles Church, Cripplegate; 8 West gate of fort, London Wall; 9 Noble Street, wall and turret foundations; 10 Newgate bastion, beneath GPO yard, St Martin's-le-Grand; 11 St Bride's Church, Fleet Street; 12 11 Ironmonger Lane; 13 Reconstructed Mithraeum, Queen Victoria Street *(Illus. 8)*; 14 Lower Thames Street, hypocaust; 15 All Hallows by the Tower Church, two tessellated pavements

5 The Arras medallion showing the relief of London by Constantius Chlorus in AD 296

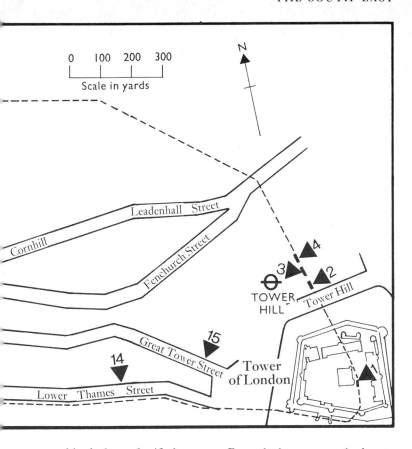

greet him before a fortified gateway. Beneath the gateway the letters
LON indicate that it is meant to represent *Londinium*, and the medallion
in fact commemorates Constantius' successful arrival at London in
AD 296 with his galleys (one of which is shown beneath the horse's
feet) after he had defeated the usurper emperor Allectus. The letters
PTR at the bottom of the design show that the medallion was struck
at the mint of Trier in Germany, so in all probability the die-engraver
had never seen *Londinium* and only had the great Roman gate that
still stands at Trier, the *Porta Nigra*, as his model for a gateway to
represent Roman London.

   Despite all the rebuilding that has gone on over the centuries in
London, and the destruction of earlier remains that this has involved,
it has been possible to preserve some traces of the Roman city within
the city wall. Retracing our steps to Tower Hill, a notable landmark
is the church of All Hallows, Barking. Most of the nave of the church
was destroyed during the last war, and during rebuilding operations
evidence was found of a seventh-century unaisled church, fragments
of two Saxon crosses and some even earlier remains. In the crypt are
two Roman tessellated pavements: one is *in situ* and the other has been
moved slightly from its original location; the wall of a Roman house
can also be seen, and several antiquities from the area of Roman date,

AN SORREL
1957

including a small tombstone inscribed in Greek to Demetrius (but
this may have been brought to the area at a later date). A fine model
of Roman London is on display, together with blackened ashes and
remains of buildings dating from Boudicca's destruction of the city.
The famous nineteenth-century bronze statue at the foot of West-
minster Bridge shows her driving a fast, two-horse Celtic chariot with
her two daughters crouched beside her.

Not far away in Lower Thames Street a hypocaust – the hot air heating system of a Roman house – was found in 1848 when the Coal
Exchange was built. That remarkable Victorian building has in its turn
succumbed to planners and redevelopment, but the Roman remains –
the piers made of red tiles that supported the floor, and a brick seat –
are still intact and are scheduled eventually to be open to inspection
in the basement of the new building to be erected on the site.

Preserved in another basement to the north, under Selborne House,
11 Ironmonger Lane, near the Guildhall, is a small section of a Roman
mosaic pavement with a geometric pattern in red, yellow, blue and
black tesserae. It dates from the second half of the second century
AD, and its juxtaposition with the metal filing cabinets of a modern
business firm, Messrs Peat, Marwick, Mitchell, is a most curious one!
This company saved the pavement, and other finds from the building
of the offices in 1949 are displayed in their entrance hall.

6–8 Artist's impression of the interior of the Walbrook Mithraeum, by Alan Sorrell. The head of Mithras, found in the Walbrook Mithraeum, shows him wearing his typical Phrygian cap (Museum of London). *Below* the Walbrook Mithraeum reconstructed in Queen Victoria Street

One of the most exciting discoveries from Roman London during the excavation of war-damaged sites was made by W. F. Grimes in 1953–4 on the west side of Walbrook on the site of Bucklersbury House. The modern street name is that of the small river that once flowed here and joined the Thames at Dowgate. On the east bank of the old river bed foundations appeared that were the remains of a small temple to the sun-god Mithras. The temple was of basilican plan with two narrow aisles, an entrance at the east end and an apse at the western end on a slightly higher level than the floor of the nave.

The cult of Mithras was Persian in origin, and its promise of a happy afterlife appealed most strongly to soldiers and merchants, exactly the people one would expect to find in a busy commercial and administrative centre such as *Londinium*. The dedication of the temple to Mithras was proved by the large amount of statuary, all of fine Italian marble, found concealed near the eastern end of the temple. As well as a head of Mithras other deities represented included Serapis, Minerva, Dionysus and Hermes, all connected in one way or another with the underworld. (Serapis is not the only representative of the Oriental cults found in London: a pottery wine jug found in Southwark has an inscription LONDINI AD FANUM ISIDIS scratched on it, which indicates there was a temple or shrine to the Egyptian goddess Isis somewhere in London at one time.) The temple was built during the second century AD and the sculptures probably date from the late second century. They had been deliberately and carefully concealed to save them from being destroyed by zealous Christians during the reign of Constantine the Great in the fourth century, when Christianity became the official religion of the Roman empire. The sculptures were until recently in the Guildhall Museum which has now amalgamated with the London Museum to form the Museum of London in the Barbican. So now those finds from the area of the temple made during the nineteenth century and put into the London Museum collection are once again united with their more recently discovered companions. After the excavation the temple was removed and reconstructed some 60 yards away in Queen Victoria Street where it can be seen in front of the appropriately named Temple Court building.

Just outside the old city wall on the west side (it runs near or beneath St Martin's Church, halfway down Ludgate Hill), at the foot of Ludgate Hill and the bottom of Fleet Street, is Sir Christopher Wren's incomparable church of St Bride, known as the 'wedding cake' church because of its ornamental spire. This is one of the many city churches heavily damaged by bombs in the Second World War, and now magnificently restored. During the work of restoration the remains of a Roman house were found and they can now be seen in the crypt of the church, along with pottery and other finds from the excavations.

Twenty miles north of London lies **St Albans,** the Roman city of *Verulamium* (TL 136071). The Roman road which made its way there in an almost direct straight line was Watling Street, which the modern A5 follows quite faithfully up the Edgware Road from Marble Arch. Several years ago during extensive roadworks at Marble Arch the surface of the Roman road was found aiming directly towards the A5; it is now lost beneath the ornamental fountains on the traffic island!

St Albans takes its modern name from Alban, a Christian soldier martyred in AD 304 during the reign of Diocletian and now commemorated in the proud cathedral that dominates the town, and which incorporates in its fabric much brickwork from the Roman town that

9 Sea god mosaic. Verulamium
Museum

lay near the river Ver. So much easily available building material was
too great a temptation, and many early Hertfordshire churches in the
area have the tell-tale red Roman tiles showing here and there in their
walls or towers. In the tenth century Abbot Ulsinus had St Michael's
church built in the centre of the old Roman town and placed it in
the ruin of the largest building, the basilica. Opposite St Michael's
is the Verulamium Museum which is the best place to begin a visit
to the site. It contains finds made over many years, including magnificent mosaics such as the sea god, the scallop shell, and the lion carrying
a stag; also painted wall plaster, objects of everyday life, realistic
models of the town, the London Gate and soldiers, and actual burials
found nearby.

Most of the remains of *Verulamium* lie beneath the playing fields
around the museum. In the middle of them is a low bungalow inside
which two rooms of a large Roman house have been preserved. Beneath a very big expanse of mosaic pavement, at one end, is the arched
stoke-hole leading down to the hypocaust system beneath the floor
which was supported in the usual way on piers of flat bricks or tiles.
Warm air from the furnace circulated between them and was ducted
through box tiles to the rooms above. Some of the box tiles are set
in the floor near the edge of the pavement. On the far side of the playing fields – the south side – is a very fine and long stretch of the city
wall. Outlined at one end are the foundations of the great London
Gate which faced down Watling Street, and to the side of the gravel
path in front of the wall is the now overgrown but still substantial ditch
that protected the approach to the wall. At intervals along the front
of the wall are round bastions that could be used as the base for
ballistae – catapults – and there are guardhouses at intervals behind the
wall.

The other major part of the site to visit at St Albans is the Roman
theatre (TL 134074), on the other side of the A414 from the museum.
This is the only Roman theatre in Britain that can be visited, although
at least five other examples are known to have existed. Walk along

the top of the semi-circular bank of earth round the stage to get a good impression of the site; the bank itself is not a feature of the original building, but is composed of soil from the excavations carried out by Dame Kathleen Kenyon in 1933. The theatre is of a type that appears in northern Gaul and Britain, but nowhere else in the Roman empire. Its stage area is quite small and it is obvious from the way the rows of seats are positioned that many of the audience would not have faced the stage, but would have been directed more to the centre of the orchestra in front of the stage where some kind of wild beast show or possibly cock-fighting could take place. The theatre went through several building phases and alterations and ended up being ignominiously used in the late fourth century as the town's rubbish dump. Gradually the interior was filled up with masses of broken pottery and literally thousands of low denomination bronze coins. Nearby are the remains of houses and shops excavated by Professor Sheppard Frere in the 1950s. One of the houses had an underground shrine with an apsidal end: it can be seen near the fence on the verge of the A414.

About 4 miles north of St Albans along Watling Street (the A5) at **Redbourn,** in the grounds of Rothamsted Experimental Station (TL 119136), is a small Roman mausoleum excavated in 1937. Only the foundations are visible and they clearly show a circular building set within a square enclosure wall about 100 ft square. The excavators found an alcove in the circular building with a plinth in front of it which might have supported a life-size statue, pieces of which were found nearby. Permission is needed to visit this site as it is on private property.

To the north-east of St Albans along the B651 is **Wheathampstead,** the site of a Belgic settlement (TL 185132) which, it has been suggested, was the headquarters of the British chieftain Cassivellaunus when he was attacked by Julius Caesar in 54 BC. Along the west side of the site is a deep ditch known, like so many of its kind throughout Britain, as the Devil's Dyke. The companion ditch on the east side does not bear comparison with its greater counterpart which is just over a quarter of a mile in length, nearly 40 ft deep and 120 ft wide at the top. Even today it is still a formidable obstacle; although a charming glen when covered in bluebells, it must have been very daunting to a heavily armed Roman soldier faced by defending Britons on top of the bank and with such a deep V-shaped ditch to cross.

Just outside the village of Welwyn in the grounds of **Lockleys Park** a Roman villa was excavated on top of the hill in 1937, and in recent years a large complex of Roman buildings and a Roman canal have been discovered down in the valley. Among the buildings was a small bath-house built early in the third century AD (TL 522316). It has a simple plan and, together with the rest of the buildings, was scheduled to be swept away in an extension of the A1 (M) motorway. However, after a lot of local pressure it was decided to preserve the bath-house in a concrete vault beneath the motorway, where the remains can be seen together with exhibits of material from the excavations. It is accessible by means of a tunnel.

10 Roman theatre at St Albans, looking towards the stage area and across the arena

11 The Six Hills, Roman barrows at Stevenage New Town

One does not generally expect to find ancient sites in the middle of a new town like Stevenage but, curiously enough, there beside the Roman road to the north (now the A1(M)) are six barrows. They are known as the **Six Hills,** have an average diameter of 60 ft and are around 10 ft high. Of Roman date, it is known that some of them at least were opened in 1741 by Dr Ducarel, who only found some wood and pieces of iron. Their interest really lies in their strange juxtaposition with modern blocks of glass and concrete: they form an oasis of calm in the centre of heavy traffic (TL 237237)

Near Royston in North Hertfordshire on **Therfield Heath** (TL 342402) is the largest barrow cemetery in the Chiltern Hills. The barrows stand out on the skyline above the old prehistoric trackway, the Icknield Way, which the modern A505 follows into Royston. The Way then continues into East Anglia, where we shall meet it again

27

(p. 123), and terminates at Castle Rising. One group consists of a small long barrow of neolithic date and ten round barrows of the Bronze Age, and half a mile away to the west is another Bronze Age round barrow, Pen Hills, standing at the termination of an Iron Age boundary ditch known as Mile Ditches which now only shows as faint crop marks. Several cremations and inhumations were found in this cemetery, and one mound is recorded as producing nine disarticulated skeletons. The finds are in the Museum of Archaeology, Cambridge. The Heath is open parkland but in visiting the barrows you will encounter the hazards of flying golfballs, galloping horses and a rifle-range!

Moving out of London to the south-east and into Kent the remains of a Roman cemetery can be found at Warbank, **Keston,** 4 miles south of Bromley west of the A233 in the grounds of Keston Foreign Bird Farm (TQ415634). Two main tombs are preserved: the largest is circular, about 29 ft in diameter with six large buttresses running out from it. Originally it was covered with earth and the ring wall would have acted as a retaining wall to help the piled-up cone of earth maintain its shape. The buttresses, which were covered in stucco and painted bright red, may have supported columns or pilasters and

12 Therfield Heath barrow cemetery. There is a neolithic long barrow in the foreground and a group of Bronze Age barrows beyond it

would have helped to counteract the thrust of the earth from the mound. There is a similar but larger tomb of this type at West Mersea (p. 112), and several examples in northern France and Germany around Trier. Between two of the buttresses, in a pit, a second tomb had been built of tiles; it was also roofed with tiles and can be seen through a modern trap-door. This tomb contained a lead casket inside which were the cremated remains of an adult. Beside the circular tomb is a rectangular one which contained a stone coffin. This was taken from the site in 1800 and served various functions including that of a horse-trough! It was shattered in an air-raid in 1941 and has since been restored and returned to the site. In the immediate area a dozen poor graves were found, and it seems that this may have been the private cemetery of the owner of a nearby house who buried his relatives and servants there.

The valley of the river Darent attracted a number of wealthy people who built villas in the area. One of the most important in Roman Britain is at **Lullingstone** just to the west of the village of Eynsford (TQ 530650). It was originally noted in 1788, but full excavation was not undertaken until 1949 when its importance was realized. Some of the walls still stand up to 8 ft high, which is very rare in Roman villas in Britain, but it is the finds within the villa that have created wide interest. The villa had a long history of over 300 years of occupation, and the floor mosaics that were laid down in the early fourth century are amongst the finest extant from Roman Britain. The reception room mosaic has a central panel showing the hero Bellerophon, mounted on his winged horse Pegasus, spearing the fabulous Chimaera. Dolphins surround the central motif, and outside the cable border that encircles them are representations of the four seasons (one in each corner) – these are a popular decoration for mosaics and will be seen in villas elsewhere (see pp. 44, 49, 70, 71). All the designs are carried out in brightly coloured tesserae and beyond them are geometric patterns of rather inferior work.

The second major mosaic, in the apsidal dining-room which leads off from the reception room, represents Europa wearing a transparent gown being carried off by the great white bull that was Jupiter in disguise. A cupid precedes the bull, waving him forward, and another holds on to the bull's tail. The mosaic is one of the few known that incorporate an inscription, and it shows both the owner's personal interest in the design and his education, as it is a couplet based on

13 The principal mosaics in the
Lullingstone villa showing
Europa and the bull and, in the
background, Bellerophon
killing the Chimaera

14 Reconstruction painting by
Alan Sorrell of the Roman villa
at Lullingstone c. AD 360. In
the background are a temple–
mausoleum and a small circular
temple

15 Wall painting of praying figures from the Lullingstone villa. British Museum

16 Wall painting of the *Chi Rho* monogram flanked by *alpha* and *omega*, from the Lullingstone villa. British Museum

a passage in Virgil's *Aeneid*. The two-line inscription reads: INVIDA SI [TAVRI] VIDISSET IVNO NATATVS/IVSTIVS AEOLIAS ISSET AD VSQUE DOMOS. It is a most curious comment to find on a dining-room floor as it refers to Juno's anger at her husband's amorous escapades, and says that if she had seen Jupiter thus she would have been justified in seeking out Aeolus in his cavern of the winds. Bright-coloured tesserae again pick out the design and it is set within a pavement of red tesserae.

The other point of major interest at this villa is the evidence that it produced for early Christianity in Britain. The villa's owner in the late fourth century became a Christian and had a room converted into a small chapel. On the fresh plaster on the west wall were painted six figures with their arms open in the attitude of prayer – the *orans* posture which is well known from early Christian art in the Mediterranean. On the south wall were other figures, together with a large *Chi Rho* monogram, the Christian emblem that incorporates the first two letters of *Christos* in Greek, literally 'The Anointed One'. The wall plaster was in fragments but it has been restored and is now in the British Museum, together with the two marble busts found in the pagan shrine in a room below the chapel. Another shrine, of the late second century, had been dedicated to a local water nymph and decorated with a niche-painting on plaster of three nymphs. The villa's end came in the early fifth century when it burnt down and was abandoned.

At **Swanscombe** in north Kent lies one of the most important sites in the history of early man in Britain. It was here in the Barnfield Pit (TQ 596746), now a National Nature Reserve, that fragments of the Swanscombe Skull were found in 1935 and 1955. They are the earliest remains from this country of the forerunner of modern man, *homo sapiens sapiens*, whose cranial capacity appears to be around 1325cc, which is relatively close to the modern capacity of 1700cc. It seems that Swanscombe man was responsible for the thousands of hand-axes of the Acheulean period of about 200,000 years ago found in the gravel pits here. His skull fragments are now in the Natural History Museum, South Kensington.

A more recent prehistoric site is the neolithic chamber tomb at **Coldrum**, Trottiscliffe (TQ 654607). Originally it was a long mound of about 70 ft × 55 ft broad, orientated east to west with a burial chamber at the eastern end. The mound has disappeared and left four huge sarsen stones of the burial chamber standing with a scatter of two dozen other stones around. Because of a natural terrace the burial chamber stands some 17 ft above the other stones. Excavations in 1910 produced the remains of 22 skeletons and some pottery. The National Trust has the site in its care and it is now a monument to the Kentish prehistorian Benjamin Harrison who is named on a plaque.

Probably one of the most famous prehistoric sites in Kent is **Kits Coty House** at Aylesford (TQ 745608). It is a neolithic long barrow of which only three uprights and the capstone of the burial chamber now remain from a mound that was over 170 ft long. Apparently, according to William Stukeley's sketches in 1722, there had been a single large stone known as 'The General's Tomb' at the far end, but this was blown up in 1867 as it obstructed ploughing! At one time there also seems to have been a revetment of stones around the outer edge of the mound. Five hundred yards south of Kits Coty, under some trees, is a jumble of fallen and tilted stones called **Lower Kits Coty,** or the **Countless Stones** (TQ 744604). They are part of a burial chamber rather similar in form to Coldrum.

The great medieval city of **Canterbury** overshadows even the modern expanding town, and of its precursor, the Roman city of *Durovernum Cantiacorum* (TR 159577), tribal capital of the Cantii, very little remains to be seen. This is very commonly the case with the major towns of Roman Britain – they continue as important focal points and only odd fragments of their earlier periods turn up as yet more buildings fall, to be replaced by others. The few exceptions of any size that have not been built over since Roman times are St Albans, Silchester and Wroxeter. The medieval walls that encircle Canterbury are located on top of their Roman predecessors which were built about AD 280, and the only portion of the Roman walls now to be seen is part of a gateway behind a car park in Broad Street. Only some jamb-stones and a few courses of brick are visible. Two small mosaics

17 The Coldrum burial chamber

18 Kits Coty House, the remains of the burial chamber of a neolithic long barrow

decorated with a large floral pattern within rope or guilloche borders from a Roman town house are preserved under a modern shopping precinct, and can be visited via an entrance in Butchery Lane off Long-market. Canterbury could boast one of the few theatres in Roman Britain. It was built in wood at the end of the first century and subsequently considerably enlarged in stone in the classical tradition in the second century. Its remains were found below St Margaret's Street. Many of the finds from Roman Canterbury and the surrounding area can be seen in the Canterbury Royal Museum in the High Street.

Roman Canterbury was the hub of the roads that radiated out over Kent to the series of forts that lined the south-east coast. Their remains today vary considerably in extent. These forts were the southern continuation of a line known as the forts of the Saxon Shore that

35

started at Brancaster in Norfolk and came down and round the South Foreland to end at Carisbrooke on the Isle of Wight. On the north side of the Isle of Thanet, once guarding the entrance to the Wantsum Channel that separated it from the mainland, stands **Reculver** – *Regulbium* (TR 227693). Its most distinctive feature, apart from the acres of caravans around the site, are the twin twelfth-century towers of the church which are a landmark for miles out to sea. The Roman fort originally occupied some 8 acres, of which about half have been swept away by the sea, leaving the church, a Saxon foundation in the middle of the fort, precariously perched on the cliff edge (which has now been consolidated). Surviving parts of the south, east and west walls stand in places to 7 ft. Excavations in recent years have revealed the remains of the south and the east gates, each with a single guard chamber on the inside. The other two gates, the north and west, each in the centre of their respective walls, have long since disappeared under the sea. The fort appears to have been built about AD 210, 70 years before the majority of its Saxon Shore fellows, and abandoned around AD 360.

The southern end of the Wantsum Channel was guarded at **Richborough** near Sandwich by the far more important fort of *Rutupiae* (TR 325602). It was in this area that the first landings were made by the invasion force in AD 43 when the fort was established as a bridgehead and supply base and continued to act as the main entry to Britain. Some time around AD 85 the wooden buildings of the supply depot were swept aside and a huge four-way Triumphal Arch was set up, cased in fine marble and ornamented with bronze statues, to commemorate what was reckoned to be the final conquest of Britain under the general Gn. Julius Agricola. The arch was over 35 ft high with a roadway on its east–west axis 23 ft wide; today, only the great concrete foundation of the monument remains. It had been neglected in Roman times, when the fort went out of use in the early third century, and stripped of its statuary it served as a signal station. At the end of the third century Richborough's fortunes revived and this Saxon Shore fort was built, whose walls, standing up to 25 ft, are the distinctive feature of the site. There is evidence that it was built in the reign of Carausius (AD 287–93), the usurper emperor in Britain. The Triumphal Arch was then dismantled and the three ditches that surrounded it were filled in, although today they stand open as excavated. Evidence of many of the wooden buildings of various periods was found during the excavations but it is only the more substantial foundations of flint and brick that remain, largely on the north side of the Arch base. The pillars of a small hypocaust can be seen together with the outlined remains of an apsidal-ended building called the Chapel of St Augustine, after a legend which says that it was at Richborough that Augustine landed in 597 on his way to meet King Ethelbert. A very interesting small museum by the entrance displays much material from the site. Across the road outside the site a large depression on the hill marks the site of the amphitheatre that probably served both the occupants of the fort and the neighbouring town.

19 Aerial view of the Roman fort at Richborough, showing the great cruciform platform that formed the base of the four-way Triumphal Arch
20 Interior view of the walls of Richborough and the ditches that surrounded the Arch

21 The Roman *pharos* at Dover

Richborough has fared better than its companion Reculver which has been greatly eroded by the action of the sea. The silt has been deposited further down the coast at Richborough, which now lies 3 miles inland across mud flats.

The next Saxon Shore fort in the chain was at **Dover**, *Dubris* (TR 326418). Until very recently little or nothing was known of the Roman town except for the *pharos*, or lighthouse, standing on the hill within the castle. This is the only standing example of a Roman *pharos* in Britain (its companion on the hill on the other side of the harbour entrance is only fallen masonry). It stands close against the west end of the church of St Mary-in-Castro to a height of 62 ft, although only the lower 42 ft are Roman work, the rest being medieval. The exterior is octagonal and rose originally to a height of about 80 ft; there would have been a beacon alight at the top, shining out through protective arches. It is still an impressive monument, and so is the view over the edge across Dover harbour. In the central area of the modern town, west of Cannon Street, recent excavations during the building of a bypass road have revealed extensive remains of the fort that was the headquarters of the British fleet, the *Classis Britannica*, known also from the letters CL BR found stamped into the red tiles used for its official buildings. In the original plans for the bypass the remains would have been destroyed; some were, but new plans have ensured that those sections that have to be reburied will be preserved sealed beneath the roadway, as the road will be lifted high enough to pass over them and not through them. When the road eventually becomes obsolete some archaeologist of the future will once again have the opportunity of examining the fort's remains. An extensive Roman house found during the excavations, possibly that of the fort commander, is being preserved by the Dover Corporation as it revealed the largest area of Roman wall-paintings so far found in Britain. A new museum will be opened nearby so that the two may be viewed together.

On the cliff-top above East Wear Bay just outside **Folkestone** (TR 241370) are the remains of what was once quite a large villa and an annexe with, in all, 53 rooms. Very little exists now as the remains have been a prey to the cliff edge upon which they stand, but the view out to sea is magnificent and one can appreciate the owner's choice of site. The finds are in Folkestone Museum.

Stutfall Castle at Lympne (TR 117342) is the last of the Saxon Shore forts in Kent. Its name was *Portus Lemanis* and today it stands, or more accurately tumbles, on a hillside overlooking Romney Marsh. About the same size as Reculver, it has been abandoned by the sea where Reculver has been eaten by it. Only odd sections of the walls remain, cast at curious angles by their movement down the hill slope, but it is a delightfully peaceful spot with only a few sheep placidly wandering about. A much damaged altar dedicated to Neptune by the admiral Gaius Aufidius Pantera, now in the British Museum, was found in the main gateway and it may indicate that *Lemanis* was the headquarters of the British fleet for a short while in the middle of the second century when Aufidius Pantera was in command.

Crossing the county boundary into Sussex the next fort in line is the very impressive site of **Pevensey Castle**, *Anderida* (TQ 644048). This fort was built late in the third century on a low hill standing

22 Exterior of the West Gate at Pevensey Castle

above the marshes, which explains its irregular outline. The sea came up to the walls on the south and there was a small harbour on the east side. The complete circuit of the walls remains, although a stretch on the north side of about 200 ft has fallen outwards. Elsewhere the walls still stand up to 28 ft high and there is a massive gateway at the west end set well back from the wall and with square guard chambers on the inside. The typical lines of red bonding tiles are clearly visible in the construction. Some repairs are known to have been made during the reign of the emperor Honorius (AD 394–423) as some of the tiles found were stamped HON AVG ANDRIA. There are ten massive U-shaped bastions surviving out of a probable fifteen around the walls. The fort was obviously still a good site for a strong-hold 800 years after it was built, and at the Norman Conquest Count Robert de Mortain began to build an inner bailey in the eastern angle of the Roman fort. This eventually became the Norman castle with its keep that now dominates the site. The history of Pevensey Castle as a defensive site comes right down to modern times – in 1940 pill boxes for machine guns were built in the ruins against a possible German invasion. A disguised pill box can be seen on top of the north-west bastion of the Roman wall, and another amongst the ruins of the east wall of the keep.

Moving inland to the village of Wilmington, cut into the hillside above the priory is one of the three ancient chalk-cut figures of southern England, the **Long Man** (TQ 543095). He is a tall slim figure with arms outstretched on either side, each holding a long staff, almost as if he were skiing down the hillside. No attempt has been made to suggest any anatomical detail (as with the Cerne Abbas Giant, p. 62) except for turf-covered mounds that mark the eyes, nose and mouth. The figure is meant to be seen from a distance, from the Weald, because close to it is foreshortened. It is 231 ft high, the staves being 6 and 10 ft taller respectively, and they are 115 ft apart. There is no doubt that the figure is ancient – the question is, how ancient. It is certainly not later than the Saxon period of the seventh century AD and it has been suggested that it represents the pagan god Woden. Alternatively it might be Romano–British in date – the stance of the figure is certainly very much like the standing soldier holding two standards found on coins of the fourth century.

In this area of Sussex there are several hill forts: **Combe Hill** (TQ 574021) near Eastbourne and **Whitehawk** (TQ 330048) near Brighton are of neolithic date, while **Hollingbury** (TQ 322078) behind Brighton and the **Caburn** (TQ 444089) near Lewes are of Iron Age date. They all have in common an elevated situation commanding fine views of the countryside round about. The Caburn is an excellent example, and a clear idea of its history has been obtained from excavations going back to the father of modern archaeological excavation techniques in this country, General Pitt Rivers, in the late nineteenth century. The fort is circular, about 3 acres in area, and crowns the summit of Mount Caburn 500 ft above sea level. It has a huge outer rampart and a smaller inner rampart and ditch. Original occupation

23 The Long Man of Wilmington

24 Soldier holding a standard in either hand on the reverse of a bronze coin of the emperor Vetranio, struck in AD 350. Note the *Chi Rho* monogram at the head of each standard *(cf. Illus. 16)*

25 The Caburn hill fort near Lewes

of the hill started about 500 BC with a farming settlement, and then
around 150 BC a V-shaped ditch was dug and the spoil thrown up
to make an interior bank. An entrance remained on the north-east.
Inside the fort evidence was found of storage pits for grain. With the
Roman invasion, efforts were made to strengthen the fort by erecting
a 10-ft-high palisade along the edge of the ditch and another behind
it. The intervening space was filled with chalk from the recut ditch
and from another huge ditch 30 ft wide and 8 ft deep dug in front
of it. This ditch is still a prominent feature of the site. The gateway
was also strengthened, but it was all in vain. The fort was sacked and
the gateway burnt. Traces of the Roman attackers were found in the
debris.

Further inland, at **Holtye** (TQ461391) near East Grinstead just
south of the B2110, is a section of a Roman road that appears to have
been a link from Watling Street off towards Lewes. It served the area
of Ashdown Forest which had an important iron-smelting industry
in Roman and medieval times. The preserved section of the road is
mainly composed of iron slag so compacted down that its surface is
much like that of a modern road. The ruts in it were made by passing
Roman carts heavily laden with iron ore for London or the south coast.
Fairly close are three Iron Age hill forts: **Dry Hill Camp** (TQ432417),
High Rocks (TQ561382) and **Saxonbury** (TQ577330), which present
no special features except that at High Rocks the overhanging rocks
below the fort formed a rock shelter used by earlier mesolithic hunters.

2 Southern England

The river Adur cutting its way through a gap in the South Downs to reach the sea at Shoreham makes a convenient dividing line between the monuments of south-east and southern England. To the west of the Adur, up on the Downs, are several hill forts of which the two most important and interesting are Chanctonbury Ring and Cissbury.

Chanctonbury Ring (TQ 139121) is quite a small oval hill fort, just over 3 acres in area, but the beech trees planted within it in the mid-eighteenth century make it a very conspicuous landmark. Amongst the trees are the remains of a small rectangular Roman temple, a situation not unknown in Iron Age hill forts, as at Maiden Castle. The remains of the rampart surrounding the fort are not very high and just outside on the west and east sides are ancillary banks and ditches, part of the defensive system. The view from the fort is superb.

Not very far away is the much larger hill fort of **Cissbury** (TQ 139080). The fort had a long history from the neolithic period through the Iron Age and into Roman times. Neolithic man first came to the hill in his search for good quality flint for tools, and traces of his activity can be seen outside the south entrance and at the western end of the fort. A series of depressions indicate where ancient flint mines were sunk — over 200 of them, often 40 ft deep, and cutting through six seams of flint to extract the prized nodules of suitable quality flint. When the shafts were excavated two of them produced human remains; one was the body of a young man surrounded by chalk blocks in a bare grave, and the other that of a young woman who appears to have met her death by accidentally falling down the shaft. The neolithic activity on the site took place around the middle of the fourth millennium BC. It was just over 3000 years later that the Iron Age fort was built covering an area of 62 acres and surrounded by a large bank and ditch with entrances on the south and east sides. Though a lot of hill forts were hurriedly refortified in the Roman period, Cissbury seems to have been quietly domesticated: no new earthworks were thrown up and there is evidence that the interior of the fort was

26 Mosaic showing Ganymede being carried off by the eagle (Zeus in disguise). Bignor villa

ploughed at this time. The answer to this rather curious situation may lie in the fact that the area round about, centred on *Calleva Atrebatum* (Silchester, p. 84) and the territory of the Atrebates tribe, was friendly to Rome.

The area of the South Downs was obviously very desirable, as evidenced by the number of hill forts, and the Roman who had his villa sited at **Bignor** (SU 988147), in the lee of Bignor Hill facing south, had a good eye for a pleasant situation. The presentation of the site is one of the most charming in Britain, small thatched huts standing over individual examples of the rooms preserved. Found in 1811, its mosaic pavements deservedly make it one of the most famous villas of Roman Britain. Six mosaics can be seen, of which the first to be discovered was the Ganymede pavement, on 18 July 1811. This find set the excavations in progress under the direction of the leading antiquary of the day, Samuel Lysons, who produced in 1817 the monumental work *Reliquiae Britannico–Romanae*, and devoted volume 3 of it entirely to Bignor. Room 3, a large apsidal room, contains Venus in a medallion and an amusing scene with cupids dressed as gladiators with their trainers set in a long border. Room 7 has a hexagonal water basin sunk in its centre which is surrounded by mosaics in hexagons, all rather damaged, and contains the major scene – Ganymede, in a circular medallion, being carried off by Zeus in the guise of an eagle. The colours are bright and very well preserved. In room 33 is a central medallion with a Medusa head and busts of the seasons set round about, of which Winter is the finest. Another Medusa head occurs in a central medallion in room 56. The other mosaics are all of geometrical·patterns, sometimes incorporating various birds or fish in small panels. The villa was obviously at the height of its prosperity in the middle of the fourth century, when the best mosaics were laid down, and it must have been one of the largest in Britain at that time. What happened to its owner in the end is not known; the evidence seems to indicate that the villa was abandoned in the early fifth century and simply allowed to fall into ruin. A small site museum displays finds, photographs and engravings of the pavements.

To the west of Bignor are several prehistoric sites, the **Devil's Jumps** (SU 825173), which are six Bronze Age bell-barrows; **Bow**

Hill (SU 820111), another Bronze Age barrow group, and the important hill fort of **The Trundle** (SU 877111). This last site is 670 ft above
sea level and commands the countryside for some distance around,
as do the radio masts now sited, to its detriment, within it. Within
the Iron Age ramparts are the remains of an earlier neolithic causewayed camp. The classic example of such a camp was excavated at
Windmill Hill in the 1920s and again in 1957–8 (p. 80). The causewayed camp at The Trundle has two major banks and ditches, the
inner one 380 ft in diameter and the outer one 950 ft in diameter.
Between the two is a subsidiary bank and ditch that meanders about
around the inner one. The ditches are crossed at intervals by several
irregularly placed causeways left during the digging of the ditch, hence
the term 'causewayed camp'. The spoil from digging the ditches was
thrown up to form the inner bank on the lip of the ditch. Many sugges-
tions have been made as to the original use of the causewayed camps,
ranging from cattle pounds to sacred enclosures, and the evidence now
available from a number of excavated examples would seem to indicate
that they did serve some ceremonial purpose connected with the well-
being of the tribes of the surrounding area.

Radio-carbon tests on bone found in the ditches, together with the
style of pottery associated with it, give a date of *c.* 3000 BC for the

27 The Trundle hill fort

site. It was not until some 2500 years later, *c.* 250 BC, that the octagonal defences, a single ditch and rampart, of the Iron Age fort were erected. This fort covers a much larger area, $12\frac{1}{2}$ acres, and had entrances on the east and the west sides. Excavations carried out on the Iron Age remains of the east gate suggest at least three phases of rebuilding, the last of which took place around 50 BC. This final phase of remodelling included a gate intended for a wide dual carriageway which seems never to have been completed. Evidence from post holes suggests that it would have been a massive affair with a walkway over the entrance. This gate now overlooks the Goodwood racecourse.

One of the most remarkable finds from Roman Britain made in recent years has been the Roman palace at **Fishbourne** (SU 841047) just outside Chichester on the A27. The site originally came to light in 1960 during trenching to lay a water main, when a workman noticed in the trench quantities of red tile, which he reported. Eight years of excavation under Professor Barry Cunliffe gradually revealed the sumptuous palace of a Romano–British magnate, almost certainly Cogidubnus the Roman client king. He is commemorated in a first-century inscription found in 1723 and now to be seen set in the wall beneath the arcade of the Assembly Rooms in North Street, Chichester (SU 861047). It is a joint dedication of a temple to Neptune and Minerva, and hails Cogidubnus as 'Tiberius Claudius Cogidubnus, king and legate to the emperor'.

The palace began life as a simple military supply base with wooden buildings which were associated with the general Vespasian's (later the emperor of AD 69–79) troop movements against the Isle of Wight and the south-west. Then, about AD 75, work began on the great palace itself, built around a formal garden that measures 250×320 ft. A lot of the palace still remains to be excavated, especially the south wing which lies under adjacent houses. The site also contains a harbour that would be of great interest if it were possible to insert a coffer dam to prevent water seepage, and then drain and examine the organic material that must certainly be preserved in the mud. At present the palace garden has been laid out on the evidence produced by the excavation, even to the extent of replanting shrubs that were indicated by analysis of the remains as being originally present. It is the first formal garden to be discovered in Roman Britain and the only example known north of the Alps. The north wing of the palace has been roofed over and you can walk above the foundations, walls and mosaics on a raised catwalk. The site is entered through a well-designed museum that explains its history and displays the finds. Several decorative mosaics with geometric patterns were laid down in the first century, and then a great deal of remodelling took place that involved laying down a new mosaic with a Medusa head central medallion early in the second century. Because of damage done by ploughing, the earlier mosaic can be seen showing through breaks in the later one.

Around the middle of the second century further alterations took place, and the finest of the mosaics extant was laid down in what was

28 North wing of the Roman palace at Fishbourne. In the foreground is a heating duct running from a hypocaust; the Cupid and dolphin mosaic is in the middle distance

29 Cupid and dolphin mosaic, Fishbourne Roman palace

probably the principal room. This mosaic, within a squared geometric border, has a multicoloured central roundel that features a winged cupid holding a trident and seated on a dolphin. In the corner angles of the mosaic are fan-shaped ornaments supporting ornate urns, and along the sides are fabulous sea monsters in pairs opposite each other – above and below the cupid are a pair of sea horses and to right and left a pair of sea panthers. Three other mosaics were laid at about the same time as the cupid and dolphin mosaic but they were not as fine and are generally much damaged. One of them may have featured a peacock as its principal motif. Most of the plastered walls of the rooms appear to have had wall-paintings on them which, together with the fine mosaics, would have made the owner seem a very opulent man indeed. A lot of the materials used in the construction of the palace, various fine marbles, etc., had been imported from the Continent, and the excellent stucco work betrays the hand of specially imported foreign craftsmen who knew their job.

Some time about the end of the third century, around 280–90, there was a disastrous fire in the roof of the north wing – molten lead that dripped from the roof fittings was found on the tessellated floors. After this the palace seems to have been abandoned. Its walls were used as a convenient quarry for stone and a few burials were made in graves dug into the rubble of the forsaken building.

On the north shore at the head of Portsmouth Harbour stands **Porchester Castle** (su 625046), *Portus Adurni*, the finest of the Saxon Shore forts and with the most complete Roman walls in northern Europe. The outer walls of the castle are all Roman work, except where medieval gateways have been built to a narrower measure than the originals; they enclose an area virtually 590 ft square and stand 18 ft

30 The Roman walls of Porchester Castle, with a later Norman keep in the far corner, standing at the head of Portsmouth harbour

31 Porchester Castle walls

high to the catwalk. Various sections are so well preserved that you can still see where separate gangs built individual sections: where they met with the next piece of wall there are variations evident in the courses of red bonding tiles. Fourteen of the Roman bastions remain. They are hollow and were presumably originally floored with timber, in which event they would only have been strong enough to carry light *ballistae*, or catapults, in contrast with the solid bastions at Burgh Castle (p. 119). Unlike the natural conditions that have affected the other forts, which were either eroded or silted up by the action of the sea, Porchester seems to have maintained the same ground level and situation. The sea still washes its south wall, and the medieval sea-gate in its centre still lives up to its name; through it is a good view of Portsmouth harbour. Like Pevensey, Porchester's upstanding walls made a fine outer bailey wall when a Norman keep was built in the north-west corner in the 1120s (in the reign of Henry I), and subsequently when a palace replaced it under Richard II in 1396–9. In the opposite corner of the fort is a church, founded as a priory of Augustinian canons by Henry I, which was completed by 1133 and is a fine example of Romanesque architecture.

From Portsmouth harbour it is easy to cross to the Isle of Wight, *Vectis*. The island contains a number of prehistoric monuments, notably a series of Bronze Age barrow cemeteries that command fine views: **Michael Moorey's Hump** (SZ 536874), four barrows; **Gallibury Hump** round barrows (SZ 441854); **Shalcombe Down** barrow cemetery (SZ 391855), six barrows; **Five Barrows, Brook Down** (SZ 390852), actually eight barrows in all; and **Afton Down** (SZ 352857), 23 barrows.

The finest site on the island is the Roman villa at **Brading** (SZ 599853), discovered in 1879. The villa was the centre of a rich farming estate and built about AD 300. The west wing, where the mosaics are, is roofed over and also houses a small site museum. Amongst the mosaics are several with motifs found elsewhere in Roman Britain, but taken together their interrelated subjects indicate a very personal interest in their subject matter on the part of the owner. In the central roundel of the mosaic in room 1 Orpheus is represented playing his lyre and charming the animals, who surround him spellbound. This was a favourite motif in this part of Britain and is to be found predominantly amongst mosaicists of the Cirencester school, notably in the great mosaic at Woodchester (p. 70). A mosaic without parallel in the Roman world was laid in room 2. It represents Bacchus in the central medallion and around him, sadly rather damaged, are enigmatic scenes of gladiators fighting, a fox running towards a small domed building and, strangest of all, a small gabled house with a ladder going up to its door, with two winged gryphons or lions on the right and a cock-headed man on the left. The latter figure is found on the so-called gnostic (mystical) gemstones and may be the gnostic god Abraxes. A hypocaust was found beneath the floor of rooms 4 and 5, and room 11 has a simple mosaic with a diamond pattern in the centre surrounded by a border of red and white tesserae.

32 Medusa head mosaic, Brading villa

Room 12 was the principal room of the north wing. It is really two rooms as it is divided by two projecting pier bases and a major mosaic was laid in each half of the room. The mosaic in the western half of the room has been much damaged, but enough remains to indicate that it was divided into nine panels all having reference to classical mythology. Perseus rescuing Andromeda is represented in the single panel left sufficiently complete for its subject to be identified. He is shown holding aloft the Gorgon's head (Medusa) which he has just struck off using his polished shield as a mirror so that he need not actually see the dreaded head. Andromeda likewise looks away knowing that she will be turned to stone if she should catch sight of the head before Perseus can stow it in his pouch. The corners of the mosaic have representations of the four seasons (Autumn has been destroyed), and Winter is particularly like its counterpart in the villa at Bignor.

In the doorway between the two halves of the room is a rectangular panel of mosaic with a bearded, seated astronomer who points at a globe with a wand. Above the globe is a sundial resting on a column. A rather similar representation of a seated man with a sundial (or globe) on a column, who is identified by the legend as Pythagoras, appears on the bronze coins of Roman Samos.

The mosaic in the eastern half of the room is divided into eight panels around a central medallion with a Medusa head, a link with the mosaic next to it. The four major panels show a maenad and a shepherd boy; the goddess Ceres giving ears of corn to Triptolemus; a satyr pursuing a half-naked maenad; and Lycurgus armed with a double axe (*labrys*) attacking the nymph Ambrosia, who is in the process of changing herself into the vine which will eventually wind itself round him and throttle him. The whole series of scenes forms a curious group which seem to be chosen to illustrate aspects of the major elements of earth, air, water and the heavens by the astronomer located between the two mosaics. In the triangular gaps between the major panels are the winds blowing horns. At the foot of the Medusa mosaic, at the end furthest away from the astronomer panel, is a long panel with a twin-tailed merman in the centre holding a steering oar and, on either side of him, a facing sea centaur each with a sea nymph sitting on his tail, one with her back to the viewer and the other facing forwards.

Pottery and coin evidence show that the villa continued to be in active use until the early fifth century.

Other Roman remains on the island are part of a villa at **Newport** (SZ 500880); another villa with two poor geometric mosaic pavements open in the grounds of the **Robin Hill** country park (SZ 538878); some traces of the Roman fort wall in the lower courses of the castle at **Carisbrooke** (SZ 487878), located at moat level on the left of the bridge over the moat into the gatehouse; and a mosaic with a vase of flowers and geometric decoration under cover in the garden of the nearby vicarage.

Crossing back from the Isle of Wight across the Solent the great promontory hill fort of **Hengistbury Head** (SZ 169908) rises on the south side of Christchurch harbour. It had been occupied in the Bronze Age when seven bowl-barrows were erected on the Head itself and two more on lower ground to the north-west. In the Iron Age it was obviously a great stronghold and busy warehouse and trading centre, well protected by the double bank of earthworks thrown up across the neck of the headland which enclosed an area of about a square mile. During excavations on the site in 1911–12 some 3000 ancient British coins were found over quite a small area. They had been minted locally, and the majority were of the Durotriges tribe with others of the Dobunni. In recent years ancient British gold coins and bracelets have been found on the beach at the foot of the headland – they must have fallen from the cliff above.

To the north-west, over the county boundary in Dorset, lies **Badbury Rings** hill fort (ST 964030) in a commanding position. It has two main banks and ditches with a smaller, possibly later bank and ditch encircling these and entrances on the east and west sides. The interior of the fort covers 18 acres of fairly wooded ground and has never been excavated. A depression within the west gate might be the site of a large hut, or even a shaft, and it is presumed that there was Roman occupation in huts inside the Iron Age defences. Certainly the fort was a sighting point in the Roman road system as two main roads cross each other just to the north-east of the fort. One was the **Ackling Dyke** from Dorchester via Old Sarum to London, of which a good section is visible on the north side of the fort where it runs against the outer rampart; the other was the road from Bath to Poole Harbour. The Dyke can be followed for 8 miles to the north to Oakley Down (SU 022178) where it can be particularly well seen. On the Down it cuts across two Bronze Age disc-barrows and the Dorset Cursus.

The Bronze Age henge monument known as the **Knowlton Circles** (SU 025102) is a very good example of the early Christian Church following the instructions that Bede tells us were sent by Pope Gregory to Abbot Mellitus upon his departure for Britain in AD 601.

He said '... the temples of the idols in that country should on no account be destroyed. He is to destroy the idols, but the temples themselves are to be aspersed with holy water, altars set up, and relics enclosed in them ... we hope that the people, seeing that its temples are not destroyed, may abandon idolatry and resort to these places as before. ...' In the middle of the central circle of the three at Knowlton stands a ruined Norman church, silent sentinel in a pagan sanctuary. (An earlier, Saxon, church stands close beside the great circle at Avebury, p. 81.) There are three sites at Knowlton almost in a straight north-west/south-east line, together with several Bronze Age round-barrows nearby. Little can be seen of the remains of the north circle, although aerial photographs show it to be more properly a D-shaped enclosure with a longest diameter of 275 ft and an entrance on the south side. The central circle is the best preserved. It is 350 ft in diameter, with a well-defined bank and a ditch on the inside and the church in its centre. The south circle, the largest of the three,

33 Badbury Rings hill fort

34 View across the centre of the middle henge monument of the three at Knowlton Circles. The ruined Norman church now dominates the site and the interior ditch and outer bank of the henge monument sweep away behind it

is 800 ft in diameter, and the B3078 road cuts it in two. It has a ditch inside its bank and Knowlton Farm is situated in its western section. Between the central and the south circle, slightly to the north-east, is an enormous round-barrow covered with trees. It is 125 ft in diameter and still rises to 20 ft in height. Obviously the three henge monuments and their adjacent barrows must have been an important religious sanctuary, probably in use about 1800–1600 BC. Some idea of the sanctity of the site still prevailed when the Norman church was built to overlook the site in the twelfth century.

To the north of Knowlton on **Oakley Down** (SU 018173) lies one of the finest Bronze Age barrow cemeteries in southern England. The site contains over 25 barrows, mainly in a fairly compact group on the east side of the A354 to Salisbury, and north of where it crosses the B3081. Most of the barrows were opened in 1800–10 by Sir Richard Colt Hoare (1758–1838), one of the foremost antiquaries of his day. His method was to sink a shaft down through the centre to reach the primary burial which he then recorded, with his helper William Cunnington, for subsequent publication. In several of the barrows that he opened on Oakley Down he left a small lead plaque which was stamped 'Open'd 1804 W.C.', together with some of the new halfpennies then in circulation that had been struck by Matthew Boulton at the Soho Mint in Birmingham. A rich harvest of finds was made from these barrows, including various kinds of pottery, bronze daggers, necklace beads of shale and amber, and flint arrowheads, which are all in the museum at Devizes. Most of the several kinds of Bronze Age barrows can be seen here: bowl-, bell-, and disc-barrows. The Roman road Ackling Dyke (p. 51) runs close by, actually cutting its way through

53

35 The Dorset Cursus with its parallel banks shows up clearly from the air

the edge of two of the disc-barrows. At Silbury Hill (p. 82) the Roman
road skirts the edge of the mound.

A couple of hundred yards east of the Dyke in a plantation is a good
stretch of the **Dorset Cursus** which here incorporates a neolithic long
barrow 140 ft long in its west bank. The Dorset Cursus, one of the
largest prehistoric monuments in Britain, but largely ploughed out,
runs for about 6 miles with a parallel pair of banks and ditches on
either side, usually 300 ft apart (ST 970123 to SU 040191). It represents
a monument peculiar to Britain – there are other examples in these
islands, but nowhere else. The name 'cursus' was given to a site discovered in 1723 at Stonehenge by the eighteenth-century antiquary
William Stukeley, because he thought it looked like a racecourse, and
it is now used to describe any site of this type. During the course of
its length it either incorporates a number of long barrows within its

structure, as on Oakley Down and Gussage Hill, or is aligned on and associated with such barrows. It does appear in these circumstances to be connected with the cult of the dead in neolithic times *c.* 2000–1800 BC, but its exact function is not known. It ends on Bokerley Down where there is an earthwork of much later date, the Roman **Bokerley Dyke** built in the fourth century AD.

To the east of the Bokerley Dyke and north of Cranborne near Fordingbridge is an extensive Roman villa site at **Rockbourne** (SU 120170). First found in 1942 in the accidental manner by which so many Roman remains have appeared in this country – here a farmer digging out a ferret found quantities of oyster shells and subsequently a mosaic floor – work has continued at the site since 1956. It is a courtyard villa of huge dimensions: more than 70 rooms have been found and there are still more to be excavated. The size of the villa indicates that it might have been the focal point of an imperial estate of which the Bokerley Dyke might have formed a boundary. There was a villa on the site in the first century AD which was replaced by a building in stone in the second. It appears that the villa's main period of importance was in the third and fourth centuries. There is a well-preserved bath suite and several hypocausts. One hypocaust is most unusual in having the *pilae* that supported the floor above it made of curved roofing tiles (*imbrices*) in pairs, instead of the more usual flat tiles or bricks piled up at intervals. Despite the size of the villa it apparently had few mosaic floors, and none of them has figure decoration as in some of the other larger villas in the south, such as Bignor or Brading. At Rockbourne the mosaics all have geometric patterns of fairly average workmanship and quality, where one would have expected more from a villa of this size. The finds from the site are displayed in an adjacent museum. It houses a good selection of pottery and metal artifacts; of particular interest are two much-damaged Roman milestones found re-used in the building fabric of the villa. One is of Trajan Decius (AD 249–51), and the other of Tetricus II (AD 272). The troubled times that struck the villa are indicated by a hoard of coins weighing over

36 Unusual hypocaust in the Roman villa at Rockbourne, which uses curved roofing tiles as *pilae* instead of the more usual flat tiles

50 lb found in 1967 outside the wall of room L. It comprised 7714 antoniniani and three denarii that represented almost every emperor between AD 250 and 290. Similar large hoards are known from elsewhere in the south, notably the immense hoard from Dorchester, now in the Dorchester Museum.

To the north-west of Blandford Forum are two of the most imposing Iron Age hill forts in the area – after Maiden Castle – at Hod Hill and Hambledon Hill and both are probably contemporary in date. **Hod Hill** covers a rectangular area of 50 acres defended on three sides by two ramparts and their attendant ditches, and on the west side, which falls steeply down to the river Stour, there is only one rampart and ditch. Originally there were two entrances, Steepleton Gate at the north-east angle and West Gate at the south-west angle. Both have inturned entrances so that any attackers forcing the gate could be caught by enfilading fire from the defenders. There appear to have been three main building periods, beginning in the third century BC and continuing down to the Roman conquest. Suetonius tells us that the future emperor Vespasian, campaigning in the south-west in the early years of the Conquest, took 'more than twenty towns, besides the entire Isle of Wight'. Hod Hill was certainly one of those towns, or *oppida*, as the evidence from excavations shows. Within the hill fort were literally hundreds of circular huts, which can still be seen as depressions in the south-east corner; one marked off by a rectangular

37 Hod Hill Iron Age hill fort with
a Roman fort in its north-west corner

palisade may have been the chieftain's residence. The Roman attack of *ballistae* fire was concentrated on this area and it seems that the inhabitants soon surrendered and were moved off to a new area in normal Roman fashion. Then, instead of merely slighting the gateways and disabling sections of the defences as usual, they decided to build a Roman fort in the north-west sector of the Iron Age fort. It was of regulation pattern, 1000 × 530 ft, enclosing almost 11 acres, utilizing the original banks and ditches to the north and west and throwing up new ones on the sides facing the interior of the old fort. There were two main gates in the defences, on the south and west sides, and an additional small gate was cut through the native rampart to give access to the river and provide water for the cavalry detachment that the remains of stables indicate was stationed here. The fort only seems to have been occupied during the first ten years or so after AD 43.

Hambledon Hill fort (SI 845126), which faces Hod Hill fort, is a large multi-vallate fort that sprawls along the top of the hill and covers 30 acres in all. It was built in two phases, the first one probably in the third century BC and a later extension that incorporated the southern end of the hill some time between about 50 BC and the Roman invasion. There were three original entrances on the north-east, south-east and south-west, all of which had defensively inturned gateways. Within the fort there are several hundred hollows which must be the remains of huts, as at Hod Hill. A neolithic long

38 Hambledon Hill's multi-vallate defences enclose an earlier neolithic long barrow where the banks and ditches narrow towards each other

39 Maiden Castle hill fort from the air. The small Romano–Celtic temple foundations can be picked out on the right

barrow 208 ft in length and 11 ft high lies inside the defences on the highest point of the hill, and outside the south-east entrance to the Iron Age fort are the faint remains of a neolithic causewayed camp.

Just under 2 miles south of **Dorchester** (*Durnovaria*, SY 694900, where only one Roman mosaic remains to be seen *in situ* in Colliton Park) lies the great hill fort of **Maiden Castle** (SY 669884). Here, in this huge fort of 45 acres surmounting two low hills linked by linear ramparts and deep ditches, lies the evidence of Suetonius' words (p. 56). As Vespasian and his legions bulldozed their way towards the south-west the Roman military machine was brought, for a short while, to a halt here in about AD 44. The fort's earlier history goes back to *c.* 3000 BC when it was a neolithic causewayed camp, and a neolithic long barrow over 1500 ft in length was built 1000 years later. Its later history is the telling part, starting about 300 BC. In 150 BC the great ditches were dug and the ramparts thrown up, and then some time around 75 BC the defences of the last phase were strengthened and the major entrances at the west and east ends were remodelled. At the west end, walking through the ramparts looming above and guarding the entrances, the great strength of the place is very apparent. Standing on the high ramparts and looking down into the deep ditches the reason for their vast scale is suddenly more apparent here than in many other Iron Age hill forts – they were necessary to combat the new weapon of war that could outdistance the hurled spear with greater accuracy – the sling.

Vespasian must have realized the strength of the western defences, so he turned his troops against the less well defended eastern gateway.

The defenders had prepared for the Roman onslaught with ample ammunition for their deadly slings in the shape of over 50,000 seaworn pebbles gathered from the nearby Chesil Beach; but they were no match for Roman artillery such as *ballistae*. Standing on the ramparts it is so easy to envisage the attack, the legionaries steadily advancing under cover of their linked shields (a *testudo*), after a heavy bombardment to soften up the defences, and then the final clash of arms as disciplined, armour-clad legionaries met the British. Many of the defenders had fallen under the rain of death from the bombardment; in the Dorchester Museum is the vertebra of a British warrior pierced by a Roman iron bolt. It was excavated from the pathetic war cemetery found at the eastern gateway in the mid-1930s by Dr R. E. M. (now Sir Mortimer) Wheeler. Even at this terrible time the survivors did not forget the slain and their needs on the long road into the next world. Beside each body buried in the cemetery was laid a mug of beer, a shoulder of lamb or other sustenance for the dark journey ahead.

The hill fort was then slighted and the remaining inhabitants probably moved to the nearby Roman town of *Durnovaria* when it was built around AD 60–70. Then, about AD 367, a small Romano–Celtic temple was built in the northern section of the fort. Its foundations, together with those of a small two-roomed house nearby (probably for the officiating priest), have been consolidated and protected within a fence from grazing sheep. The plan is typical of such temple-shrines known from the late fourth century AD – it has a central square *cella* (sanctuary) surrounded by a verandah. The sanctuary walls were covered in painted plaster and its floor was of black and white mosaic tesserae while the verandah floor was made up of red tesserae. The excavations produced a curious bronze statuette representing the

40 The Romano–Celtic temple at Maiden Castle. On the right is the entrance to the *cella*, or sanctuary, and the foundations of the small priest's house are on the far side

Celtic three-horned bull-god Tauros Trigaranus and figures of the Roman goddesses Minerva and Diana. Over 80 coins of the fourth century were found as well as a small hoard of four gold coins (*solidi*) of the emperors Honorius and Arcadius, together with a gold ring. All are to be seen in the museum in Dorchester. From the ramparts can be seen several Bronze Age barrows, from which gold ornaments and a small amber cup have been excavated.

To the south of Maiden Castle the territory above Weymouth Bay is commanded by another Iron Age hill fort, **Chalbury** (SY 695838), a simple fort with only a single rampart and ditch enclosing 10 acres. The hill was so steep that it did not need to be more heavily fortified. The excavations found a scatter of disarticulated human remains, originally thought to indicate cannibalism but now interpreted as evidence of exposure of the dead whose remains were subsequently scattered.

Not very far away is a Romano–Celtic temple on **Jordan Hill** (SY 698821). The building is 247 ft square, and a rather strange pit 12 ft deep was found in the south-east corner. In a stone cist at its bottom were a sword, a spearhead and two urns. However, the curious part of the find was the filling of the actual pit – in each of 16 distinct and separate layers of ash and charcoal, each sealed from the next by roofing slabs, were found the remains of a bird and a Roman coin. Buzzards', crows', ravens' and starlings' bones were identified, and the coin evidence suggested that the temple was mainly in use in the fourth and early fifth centuries. The strange contents of the pit obviously had some religious significance and recall the ritual shafts found in Celtic sanctuaries in Europe which have been interpreted by Professor Stuart Piggott as 'a *favissa*, the pit in which objects rendered holy by sacral use, and the bones or ashes of sacrifices, were buried in the consecrated area'. Outside the area of the temple nearly 100 burials were dug up in the middle of the last century, and between the temple and the cliff edge in recent years parts of the walls of another small building were found. They could represent another small shrine or, more likely from the situation, a Roman signal station.

The rather romantic name of the **Grey Mare and her Colts** (SY 584870) conceals a sadly overgrown neolithic long barrow of *c.* 2000 BC. The site takes its name from the damaged remains of the burial chamber, three upright stones and a capstone which has slipped from place. Close by is **Kingston Russell** stone circle (SY 577878), consisting of 18 fallen sarsen stones; originally about 80 ft in diameter, it was in use in the Bronze Age, *c.* 1600–1000 BC.

The **Nine Stones** stone circle is strangely situated on the main A35 road west of Winterborne Abbas (SY 610903). Traffic thunders by and the Ancient Monuments sign is barely glimpsed before your car has passed it. The circle is formed of nine standing sarsen stones in an irregular grouping about 27 ft in diameter. It dates from about 1500 BC. The setting – in a leafy glade across a small stream – is idyllic if noisy. On the hillsides round about are a number of clearly defined Bronze Age barrows.

41 The small Romano–Celtic temple at Jordan Hill, Weymouth

42 The tumbled facade of the Grey Mare and her Colts, a neolithic long barrow

43 Nine Stones Circle, Winterborne Abbas

44 The Cerne Abbas Giant wielding his huge club. Note the hill fort above him higher up the hill

Eight miles north of Dorchester the little village of Cerne Abbas is dominated by the great figure of the **Cerne Abbas Giant** (ST 666016), a hill figure unique in Britain. The Giant stands with a Herculean club uplifted in his right hand, while his left hand is outstretched. He is 180 ft high, his shoulders are 44 ft across and his club 120 ft long. The figure is outlined in the chalk by trenches and, unlike the Long Man of Wilmington (p. 40), has the internal features of his face, ribs and thorax picked out together with an enormous phallus and testicles – obviously a fertility figure. The last-mentioned features have caused great controversy over the years since the first illustration of him appeared in the *Gentleman's Magazine* in 1764. Legend associates him with St Augustine's visit to the area in the sixth century AD, but he seems to be even earlier, possibly connected with the emperor Commodus (AD 180–93) who suffered delusions of himself as Hercules and promoted the cult. The stance of the figure is certainly Herculean and known from representations on altars and pottery in Roman Britain. Higher up the hill, above the Giant's left hand, is a small enclosure, 100 × 78 ft, known as 'The Trendle' or the 'Frying Pan'. It is possibly of Iron Age date. For centuries it has been the location of the May Day ceremonies around the maypole, whose openly pagan fertility element, so in keeping with the Giant, has been much inveighed against by the Church over the centuries.

Further towards the north-west area of southern England is the site of **South Cadbury** hill fort (ST 628252). Although the predominant remains on the site are Iron Age, romantic links with King Arthur's

Camelot have been asserted by chroniclers since the Middle Ages. It is one of the few hill forts that have been properly and competently investigated, in a series of excavations brilliantly carried out by Professor Leslie Alcock in 1966–70. To excavate a hill fort with four encircling banks and ditches, the most elaborate defences in Somerset, and covering an area of 18 acres, is a formidable and practically impossible task. The way to do it is to pose all the questions that need to be answered, seek those areas that seem most likely to be able to provide the answers, and to proceed in a properly controlled manner because all excavation is, and must be by its very nature, destruction, and only the written record will remain. Alcock and his team were able to show that occupation of the site went back to before 3300 BC. The great Iron Age ramparts were modified and/or rebuilt at least five, possibly six, times. There was evidence inside the fort of a Celtic ironworker's smithy and also of a Romano–Celtic temple. The south-west gate produced evidence of a massacre at the time of the Roman assault – the dismembered skeletal remains of about 30 men, women and children were found strewn through the gateway area. The corpses were probably left after the battle to be the prey of wild beasts. Some time later the Roman troops returned to slight the defences and burn down the gateway over the remains of the last defenders.

45 South Cadbury hill fort from the air

Around AD 500 South Cadbury was once again fortified and had a large timber hall; pottery of the late fifth and early sixth centuries imported from the eastern Mediterranean and western France was found – evidence of a flourishing town in the period often called Arthurian. South Cadbury at this time was one of the outstanding defended sites and John Leland's identification of it in the early sixteenth century as Arthur's Camelot produced an association for this Somerset hill fort that is not easily dispelled. The fort saw one last resurgence during the reign of Aethelred when it became a Saxon *burgh* and mint striking the typical Anglo-Saxon silver pennies in AD 1010–20. Its eventual destruction was probably carried out on the orders of King Cnut.

The other Somerset site with which Arthur's name is forever linked is **Glastonbury** (ST 493408). The great medieval shrine boasted the grave of Arthur in the nave, and a plaque still marks the plot today – but the medieval monastery lies beyond our bounds. Nearby in the water meadows was found the famous ancient British lake village and there is an associated site close by at **Meare** (ST 446423). The visitor must go to the museums in Glastonbury or at Taunton Castle to see the finds from these classic sites of their type together with reconstructed models, as nothing worth visiting remains on the site today.

Beyond Glastonbury the Mendips rise, their limestone crags majestic and yet eerie with their many underground streams, caves and grottoes.

46 One of the several caverns of Wookey Hole, with the river Axe flowing through

The Romans were interested in the Mendips for the valuable ores they produced, especially lead, and several settlements have been excavated in the area around **Charterhouse** (ST 500565). The great cave at **Wookey Hole** (ST 532480) is easily one of the most awe-inspiring sites even if one is not interested in its archaeological content. The river Axe flows through it to emerge into the sunlight from a cave lower down. In the caves, several of which can now only be reached via underwater entrances, evidence of occupation has been found going back to palaeolithic times when woolly rhinoceros, bears and hyenas used them as dens. Early man left his flint implements there and they were used at intervals for human occupation down to the Roman period. Medieval legend connected the great cave with the Witch of Wookey Hole, still pointed out as a figure turned to stone.

To the north of Wookey Hole are a number of other cave sites in the Cheddar Gorge, notably **Gough's Cave** (ST 466538) inhabited *c*. 25,000 – 10,000 BC. A small museum on the site at the entrance to the cave mouth displays many finds of flint and bone implements and also the burial of an adult male, which seems to have been deliberately made in the cave accompanied by part of an antler baton. Another cave that can be visited outside the Cheddar group is **Aveline's Hole** (ST 476586), which has an inner cave reached through an outer one.

The most important neolithic site in this area is at **Stanton Drew** (ST 601634), 6 miles south of Bristol, where there is a complex of three stone circles, avenues, standing stones and a group of stones in a U-shaped setting (a 'cove'). Such a grouping of monuments must obviously indicate an area comparable in its sanctity to Avebury and Stonehenge in Wiltshire. Not so many of the stones remain standing as at the two latter, better known sites, and the date of Stanton Drew appears to be about 2000–1600 BC, not quite so long a span of time as indicated for its Wiltshire counterparts. Essentially the monument consists of the Great Circle, about 365 ft in diameter, which is slightly oval-shaped, its longest diameter being its north/south axis. Originally there were probably 30 stones of which only 27 are still visible and three alone remain standing. An avenue of stones went from its north-east side towards the river Chew and eight of its stones are visible. Close by is the north-eastern circle, only about 100 ft in diameter with eight stones, half of them still standing. This circle also has an avenue with seven visible stones leading from it heading for the river Chew and joining up with the avenue from the great circle. The third circle, the south-west circle, has a diameter of 140 ft with eleven recumbent stones still visible. West of this circle (behind the Druid's Arms Inn) lies the 'cove'. It consists of two large upright stones with a fallen, broken stone lying between them. One last stone remains to be mentioned – Hautville's Quoit. This standing stone on the other side of the river Chew is actually on a line taken from the south-west circle through the Great Circle some 500 yards away. It is a sarsen stone while most of the others seem to be of a local conglomerate. Like so many similar monuments involving stone circles or alignments throughout Britain there is a local legend to account for them – at

47 Entrance to the Stoney Littleton neolithic long barrow

Stanton Drew the stones are a wedding party whose celebrations strayed past Saturday midnight into Sunday morning, and thus was their disregard of the Lord's Day rewarded.

A very fine example of a neolithic long barrow of the 'true entrance' type can be seen at **Stoney Littleton** (ST 735572), 5 miles south of Bath. Later long barrows have a false entrance, presumably as a precaution against tomb robbers. The Stoney Littleton barrow is 100 ft long and its entrance lies between two 'horns' at its widest end at the south-east. A huge lintel hangs over the doorway and in its western jamb is the impression of a large ammonite fossil. Beyond the doorway is a 48-ft-long gallery with three pairs of opposing side chambers and a terminal chamber. All the gallery and side chamber walls are built of dry stone walling and covered by a corbelled roof. A plaque erected in 1858, when the barrow was restored for the sum of 16 shillings, says of it 'declared by competent judges to be the most perfect specimen of Celtic antiquity still existing in Great Britain'.

It is appropriate here to mention the **Wansdyke**, a linear earthwork consisting of a single bank and ditch which is on the north of Stoney Littleton running east to west for about 50 miles. It falls into two sections, from **Maes Knoll** (ST 600660), a ploughed-out Iron Age hill fort, part of which the Wansdyke incorporates on the west, to Bathampton Down (ST 780660), and from Morgan's Down (SU 625676) to Savernake Forest (SU 197666). Its western end passes to the north and close to the Stanton Drew circles. Near Bath it actually runs on the Roman road indicating that it must therefore be of Roman or post-Roman date. Generally it is thought to be a defensive earthwork of the sixth to seventh centuries AD and it has been associated with the

British leader Ambrosius who checked the first phases of the advances of the Anglo-Saxons. Such a vast building undertaking certainly indicates forceful leadership and cohesion to produce a rampart of this great length. From this base Arthur was able to move with his British troops against the Teutonic masses and delay their invasions for 50 years by his great victory at *Mons Badonicus* (Mount Badon), about AD 499 and probably somewhere in the area of Bath.

The Roman bath at **Bath**, *Aquae Sulis* (ST 751647), is probably the best known of the Roman remains in Britain after Hadrian's Wall. Roman Bath was quite a small town, only 22 acres in area (St Albans was 218 acres). It grew up around its hot thermal springs centred on the Great Bath built late in the first century. This is still most impressive, overshadowed by the tower of Bath Abbey. Around it were the other smaller baths, their water at varying temperatures. Associated with the baths was the cult of Sul Minerva whose temple was nearby although nothing is to be seen of it today except for some of its sculptures displayed in the museum within the baths. The most famous piece is the fragment from the temple pediment with its facing Gorgon head. Many personal relics of bathers are exhibited in the museum: dedications to various deities, gemstones from rings, earrings, etc., and a notable small lead plaque, the Bath curse, one of several examples known from Roman Britain (others from Caerleon, Kelvedon, London (two), Lydney and Red Hill). The invoker of the curse appears to be a jilted lover as it begins, 'May he who carried off Vilbia from me become as liquid as water', and goes on to list the names of nine possible miscreants! In recent years extensive excavation carried out by Professor Barry Cunliffe, often in most difficult and cramped conditions in cellars and narrow spaces between basement floors, has added much to our knowledge of the Roman city. The hot springs were a mixed blessing: while the water was controlled by Roman efficiency and engineering the town flourished as a spa, but the gradual breakdown of the drainage system in the face of the rising water-table led to more and more serious flooding until the site had to be abandoned. Fragments of fourth- and fifth-century pottery thrown into the marsh that then covered the site of the baths and temple show that there was still some Roman occupation in the area even at this late period. Today you can walk round the Great Bath which is open to the sky and flanked by a colonnade. At one end is the stone that served as a diving board. The first modern view of the Great Bath was in 1871 when Major Davis found its steps and part of the lead-lined bottom. In 1727 the first remains of the bathing establishment had been found, but it was to take 150 years before public interest was sufficiently aroused by Davis's finds to set up the excavations of the 1880s when the Great Bath was cleared, and the Circular Bath and its associated hypocaust uncovered. Photogenic as the whole site is, there are still parts of the baths where the water gets hot enough to make steam a dangerous enemy of the camera.

North of Bath are several sites of neolithic and Iron Age date. There are fine Iron Age hill forts, both unexcavated, at **Old Sodbury Camp**

48 The Great Bath at Bath in the shadow of the Abbey

(ST 760826) and **Uleybury** (ST 785990). At Uley is probably the best-known of the chambered neolithic long barrows in the Cotswolds, **Hetty Pegler's Tump** (SO 790001). Its name derives from one of the seventeenth-century owners of the field, Hester and Henry Pegler, who died in 1694 and 1695 respectively. The mound is 120 ft long, 85 ft wide and rises to 10 ft high. An entrance at the east end beneath a massive lintel slab supported by two uprights gives access to a gallery 22 ft long and varying in width from 3 to 5 ft. Originally there were two pairs of facing side chambers on the north and south sides, but those on the north have been blocked off since 1821. The gallery con-

49 Entrance to Hetty Pegler's Tump with its huge lintel above the doorway

tinues past the side chambers to form an end chamber at the west
end. During the 1821 excavations the remains of 15 skeletons were
found, and a later, intrusive Roman burial of the Constantinian period
was found above the north-east chamber. This barrow is part of a
series known as the Severn–Cotswold group, which were used for
communal burial of bodies during the neolithic period from about
3000 BC to about 1800 BC. Others of this type are Wayland's Smithy
(p. 77), West Kennet (p. 82), and Stoney Littleton (p. 66). Three other
chambered long barrows in the area, but not so well preserved –
Nympsfield (SO 794013), **Gatcombe Lodge** (ST 884997) and **Windmill Tump** (ST 932978) – lead the way across country to Cirencester.

   Roman **Cirencester** was founded in the late first century as the
civitas, the local tribal capital, of the Dobunni tribe and was named
Corinium Dobunnorum (SU 016955). It acted as a market town for the
surrounding area which was rich in farms, and consequently
flourished as the evidence of town houses found during recent excavations shows. Unfortunately nearly all the excavated areas have been
built on so that there is little to see. A short section of the town wall
remains north of London Road, in the modern roadway of Tower
Street the outline of the walls of the basilica can be seen, and south-
west of the town is the grass-covered form of the amphitheatre. Recently
a magnificent new museum has been opened which shows to the best
advantage the finds from the town and surrounding area, and especially the coloured wall plaster and mosaics. It is for its mosaics and
the influence of its 'school' of mosaicists that Cirencester is famous
in the world of fourth-century Roman archaeology. There seems to
have been a group of mosaicists established in *Corinium* who not only
produced mosaics for houses within the town but who were also prepared to travel with their pattern books to the villas of wealthy local
landowners and lay mosaics to order. Certain of their favourite designs
are very easily recognizable, such as the grand conception of Orpheus

69

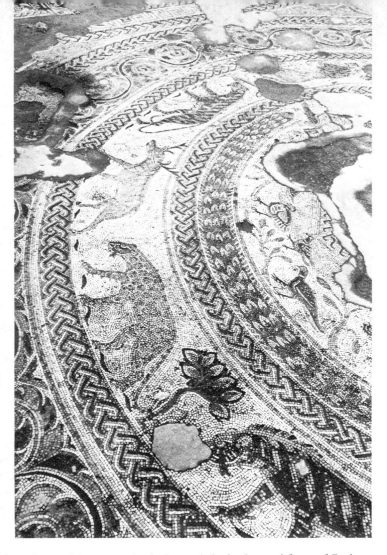

50 Some of the many animals that encircle the damaged figure of Orpheus in the centre of the mosaic pavement in the Woodchester villa

charming the wild beasts where he is shown in the central medallion with the animals circling him in the border – examples came from the town itself in Dyer Street and Ashcroft House, and outside from Barton Farm (now in the museum) and Woodchester (below). Some 40 pavements produced by the *Corinium* 'school' are known and include work at famous villas such as Chedworth (p. 71) and North Leigh (p. 74).

The Roman mosaic pavement at **Woodchester** (SO 840030) near Stroud is the largest ever found in a villa in Britain. It measures 45 ft 10 ins square in a room that was almost 50 ft square. The mosaic is located in the old churchyard and was known as early as 1695 but it was not properly inspected until 1794–6 when the antiquary Samuel Lysons was able to ascertain its form and decoration which he published in 1797. The pavement was covered over and is only cleared

51 Part of the north wing
of the villa at Chedworth

and open to view at long intervals (1880, 1890, 1926, 1935, 1951, 1963
and 1973). The design centres on an octagon with Orpheus and his
lyre breaking the lower side on the south and merging with a circle
round which marches a procession of birds; outside this, beyond two
bands of cable ornament, is another circular procession of splendid
animals which include a lion, wild boar, horse, gryphon, bear, leopard,
stag, tigress and an elephant. This circular design is enclosed in a detailed parallel frame and in the spandrels between the circle and the
angles of the frame are four pairs of draped, semi-nude nymphs. The
mosaic formed the floor of the great dining-room of the villa and,
although about 65 rooms are known so far, there must still be many
more to be found, including the bath suite.

The best villa in the Gloucestershire area, and certainly one of the
finest in Britain, is **Chedworth** (SP 053135). Sited on the lower slopes

52 The Great Witcombe villa; its mosaics are preserved in the small houses over the site of part of the bath suite

of a hill, it was discovered by accident in 1864 and has been extensively excavated since then. Its major rooms and their mosaics have been covered by houses to preserve them. It was built round a courtyard and the principal remains are on the west and north sides (most of the south wing is still buried). The main rooms were in the west wing; the dining-room floor is covered with a mosaic pavement which probably featured Bacchus in its damaged central roundel. Charming figures of the four seasons decorate the corner angles (Autumn is largely destroyed) and the whole is bordered by a Greek key pattern in black and white tesserae. The adjoining rooms on the north were private rooms which led to the bath suite of five rooms with a hypocaust under the hot room (the *caldarium*) to produce the highest temperature in the series of rooms.

In the north-west corner of the villa is a *nymphaeum*, the shrine of a water goddess, which supplied the villa (and the present house) with fresh water. Several of the stones from the rim of the pool, now in the museum on the site, have the *Chi Rho* monogram incised on them, showing that at a later date the pool and shrine were christianized. A large part of the north wing was given over to a bath suite which in its early form was similar to a Turkish bath, relying on damp heat; it was then remodelled on the lines of a Swedish sauna bath, based on dry heat and cold plunge baths. A series of private rooms, possibly bedrooms, a kitchen and a large dining-room completed the wing. The east side of the villa's courtyard was closed off by the continuation across of the corridor which fronted the other three wings.

Another villa in a charming situation is the one at **Great Witcombe** (SO 899142). It is approached up a long, narrow farm road off the A46. Like Chedworth it was built round a courtyard and its bath suite was located in the west wing. Samuel Lysons excavated it in 1818 and three of the rooms of the bath suite are now protected by roofing. The outline foundations of parts of the villa can be seen and conservation work is in progress on them. The mosaics in the bath suite have geometric

53 Belas Knap long barrow. The false entrance is
at the north end, on the left

patterns and an unusual decoration of marine life that includes dolphins, various fish, eels, a sea cow and a sea goat.

The **Belas Knap** neolithic long barrow (SP 021254) is the finest
of its kind in north Gloucestershire. It stands 950 ft above sea level
on the western edge of the Cotswolds at the end of a long walk from
the nearest road. It has been explored many times over the years –
from Roman times, to judge from Romano–British potsherds found
at its north end – but was finally restored to its present shape in 1930–
31. It is now about 178 ft long where once it must have been in the
region of 200 ft, 60 ft wide as against 80 ft, and nearly 14 ft in height.
It is orientated north–south instead of the more usual east–west. Built
about 3000 BC, it belongs to the false entrance category of long barrow;
unlike, for instance, Hetty Pegler's Tump where the entrance opens
on to a gallery, it has a false entrance at its northern end set between
two forward projecting hornworks which create a U-shaped forecourt.
When explored in 1863–5 an adult male skull and skeletal remains
of five children were found in the blocking of the false entrance. The
actual burial chambers are located in the long sides of the mound.
One to the north-west and another to the north-east, although on
opposite sides of the mound, seem to be intended as a pair, as found
along the galleries of 'true entrance' barrows (e.g. Hetty Pegler's
Tump, p. 68, Stoney Littleton, p. 66). There is another chamber in
the south-east sector of the mound and in its tail, the south end,
another chamber that may well have been a concealed cist and not
an accessible chamber like the other three. Most of the dry stone
walling seen in the false entrance and the side chambers is original
in the lower courses, but the roofs of the chambers are modern reconstructions. The remains of multiple burials were found in these
chambers in 1963–5; 14 people in the north-west one, 12 in the north-
east, four in the south-east, and parts of a skull in the south chamber.

Nearly 20 miles away across the border into north Oxfordshire are
the **Rollright Stones** (SP 296309). There are actually three monu-

73

ments involved here but all are bound tightly together in local legend. A stone circle of about 70 stones and some 100 ft in diameter is the major monument. It is known as the King's Men. On the other side of the A436, separating it from the circle and also placing it in Warwickshire, is a solitary tall stone, imprisoned within iron railings, known as the King Stone. A couple of hundred yards to the east of the stone circle across a field is a group of four stones, the walls of a burial chamber, with a fifth stone, the capstone, slewed between them. They are known as the Whispering Knights and are similarly imprisoned within iron railings. All three sites are probably contemporary, around 2000–1800 BC. The King Stone may once have formed part of a burial chamber, the Whispering Knights certainly were and would have been concealed beneath a now vanished mound. Local legend associates the sites with a boastful king who, marching with his army, crossed a local witch – he was turned into the King Stone, his men into the stone circle and his knights into the Whispering Knights. In the rhyme, the witch then changed herself into an 'eldern tree'.

At **North Leigh** (SP 397155) is a Roman villa that can be linked via its mosaics with the mosaicist who worked at the Chedworth villa, which in its turn links with the Cirencester school (p. 69). Others of the mosaics found show similarities with those found at Cirencester, Bignor and St Albans. The North Leigh villa is of the large courtyard type and although it was first excavated in 1813–17 it has been an

54 The Rollright Stones; they
are also called the King's Men
55 *Above* The Whispering
Knights, to the east of
the Rollright Stones
56 Mosaic pavement in the
dining-room of the villa at
North Leigh

unfortunate site, left open to damage and never properly examined. Work is now being carried out by the Department of the Environment to conserve those parts extant and to re-excavate the site. It lay within a complex of outbuildings easily identifiable from aerial photographs; also discernible at ground level in the adjacent fields are the outlines of the north-east and south-west wings. The foundations of the north-west and south-west wings are laid out on the site, and the dining-room, which was in the western corner with a fine three-colour geometric mosaic, is protected under roofing. Originally it had good coloured wall plaster but this has now all disappeared.

Striking south from North Leigh and past Oxford there are three relatively minor Iron Age hill forts at **Cherbury Camp** (SU 374963), **Dyke Hills** (SU 574937), and **Sinodun Camp** (SU 570924). The first two were defended on three sides by water and marshes. Then we come to Uffington in Berkshire. Here, in the Vale of the White Horse on the northern escarpment of the Berkshire Downs, is the best-known and strangest of all the prehistoric monuments in Britain. The **White Horse of Uffington** is cut into the turf on a 30 degree angled slope and is some 365 ft long, from its front ear to its tail tip, and 130 ft high. In a twelfth-century cartulary of Abingdon Abbey the Horse is mentioned in a context that shows it was already known and had given the area its name in the reign of William I. But it goes back

even earlier. It is certainly as early as the late Iron Age, when representations of horses in this peculiar linear fashion are well known. Such horses are shown on the metal bands from the rim of the Marlborough Bucket (Devizes Museum) and the Aylesford Bucket (British Museum) as well as on the reverses of gold coins of the Atrebates, an ancient British tribe that inhabited the area of Berkshire, Sussex and parts of north and east Hampshire. Their capital was at *Calleva Atrebatum* (Silchester, p. 84).

The Horse is famous in folklore and literature and has been the centre of an ancient festival at its scouring, which has taken place generally every seven years since its first mention in 1677, if not earlier. Like so many local festivals it had run into opposition by the eighteenth century and now relies on the Department of the Environment for its maintenance.

Close by is an Iron Age hill fort, **Uffington Castle,** which may be contemporary with the Horse. The hill fort covers 8 acres, has a strong bank and ditch with a counterscarp bank to defend it, and an entrance through the defences on the north-west. A silver coin of the Dobunni has been found inside the fort.

The White Horse is also linked in legend with the neolithic long barrow, **Wayland's Smithy** (also known as Wayland Smith's Cave), only half a mile away across the Downs. Wayland the Smith is said

57 The White Horse of Uffington with the nearby Iron Age hill fort

58 Reverse of an uninscribed gold stater of the Atrebates tribe, showing a disjointed horse

59 The entrance to Wayland's Smithy long barrow with its facade of huge sarsen blocks

to have made the White Horse's shoes here, and any traveller whose horse cast a shoe in the area had only to leave a silver groat on the capstone of the Smithy to find the animal mysteriously shod again. Wayland's Smithy (SU 281854) is but one of many prehistoric sites associated with the northern metalworker god and his cult which, judging by the evidence of place names, was very strong in the Berkshire and South Downs area. The barrow is an outlying member of the Cotswold group, and excavations by Professor Richard Atkinson have shown that it was constructed at two periods. In the first period it consisted of a ridged wooden mortuary hut with a stone floor. Fourteen bodies were eventually piled into it, whereupon it was surrounded by sarsen boulders and heaped over with chalk. This structure disappeared into the interior of the mound seen today – the mound of the second period – which is 185 ft long, 43 ft wide and has 10-ft-high sarsen stones at the entrance at the south end. These sarsens give on to a cruciform plan – a passage 20 ft long with an opposing pair of chambers, and its continuation beyond them forming another chamber. Both of the barrows seem to have been built between 3700 and 3400 BC.

South of Uffington is the late neolithic and Bronze Age barrow cemetery known as **Lambourn Seven Barrows** (SU 328828). The title is a misnomer as in all there are over 40 barrows in this cemetery, one of the finest in England. It lies to the west of the B4001, mainly on either side of a minor road from Lambourn to Kingston Lisle. It is a typical cemetery of the kind associated with the Wessex Bronze Age (p. 13) and has many different types of barrow in it. The oldest is the neolithic long barrow which lies north-east of the main Seven Barrows group beyond Seven Barrow Farm. The main cluster of the group lies east of the road where it makes a wide curve and is joined by a cart-track. Here there are bowl-, bell-, and saucer-barrows, one disc-barrow and two double-bowl-barrows. The date of this part of the cemetery, judging by the finds of beaker pottery and flint implements, covers some 400 years and is contemporary with the main phases of Stonehenge, *c.* 1750–1350 BC. Elsewhere in the cemetery

60 Lambourn Seven Barrows, a barrow cemetery of over 40 barrows of
neolithic and Bronze Age date
61 Windmill Hill causewayed camp. The breaks in the ditches which give this
type of camp its name are clearly visible

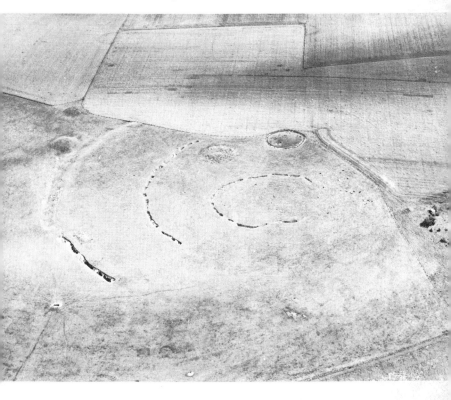

62 Part of the Great Circle and its ditch
within an outer bank at Avebury

some of the barrows appear to be of later date, up to the beginning of the first millennium BC.

On the northern edge of the Marlborough Downs begins the series of famous Wiltshire sites that stretch away south to Salisbury Plain and Stonehenge. The earliest site is the neolithic causewayed camp of **Windmill Hill** (SU 087714) up above Avebury. It is quite a long walk to the top of the hill, where there is now little to be seen of the original ditches and causeways excavated in the 1920s. This camp has given its name to the earliest phase of the neolithic in England – the Windmill Hill culture. It is characterized by its pottery which is round-based and rather sagging in appearance. There are three irregular, broken ditches surrounding approximately 20 acres; the area was used as a centre for religious gatherings, or as a cattle pound and market, rather than for defence which would have been completely impracticable. The camp was in use about 3350 BC and some 1500–2000 years later a Bronze Age bell-barrow was built between the inner and centre ditches of the site, with several other barrows running away towards the east to form a small cemetery.

The great henge monument at **Avebury** (SU 103700) is the largest of its kind in Europe, covering an area of $28\frac{1}{2}$ acres and enclosing a large portion of the present village, with a Saxon church just outside its bank and ditch. The site is surrounded by a huge earthwork with a deep ditch on its inside face and there were entrances at each of the four cardinal points of the compass. On the interior plateau formed by the deep excavation of the ditch stands the Great Circle of sarsen stones, the largest one weighing over 40 tons. Unlike the sarsens at Stonehenge but like those of the Rollright Stones they have not been dressed or finished, but merely chosen for their shape as uprights. The diameter of the circle is 1400 ft and within it are the

80

63 The Kennet Avenue
near Avebury

remains of two other circles – the Central Circle and the South Circle,
both about 350 ft in diameter. It has been suggested that there was
also a Northern Circle which would have lain beneath the place where
the Swindon road enters the Great Circle through the ditch and bank.
This circle would have predated the earthwork and was probably
never completed. Only a few of the stones of the Central and South
Circle still remain – four and five respectively – and there appears to
have been a setting of stones known as a 'cove' in the centre of the
North Circle. Similar settings are known at Stanton Drew (p. 65) and
Arbor Low (p. 137). It is amazing how impressive the site of Avebury
still is despite the combined forces, over the centuries, of nature and
stone-robbers (one of whom was crushed under a falling sarsen in
medieval times and whose remains now repose in the local museum
just behind the church). The close association of the village with the
monument and the adjacent church once again recalls Pope Gregory's
advice about pagan shrines (pp. 51–2).

Avebury was in fact part of a larger complex, and from its southern
entrance leads the **Kennet Avenue** (SU 103700). It consisted of 100
pairs of standing stones, approximately 50 ft apart, marching across
the fields and up to the top of Overton Hill a mile away. Here, somewhat incongruously situated beside the very busy A4 and opposite a
large transport café, is **The Sanctuary**. There had been a stone circle
here but it was destroyed in the nineteenth century. Excavations
carried out to trace the circle in 1930 revealed an earlier version which
had been laid out using wooden posts. There seem to have been three
building phases with circular wooden-roofed buildings carried out by
the neolithic people who built Woodhenge (p. 90) and probably dating
to before the stone circles at Avebury. Then the beaker people who
built Avebury arrived and demolished the wooden buildings in favour

of two concentric rings of sarsen stones. All this work would have been contemporary with the laying out of the Kennet Avenue leading up to The Sanctuary from Avebury. Now the locations of the sarsen stones are marked out in the grass by concrete posts and there is an explanatory plan on a pillar near the entrance gate.

To the west of Overton Hill, on either side of the A4, lie two more extremely important prehistoric monuments – the West Kennet long barrow and Silbury Hill. **West Kennet** long barrow (SU 104677) is on the south side of the A4 opposite Silbury Hill. It is one of the largest long barrows in England and Wales, 350 ft in length, and certainly the most impressive. It has long been a happy hunting ground for bones, but when it was properly excavated in 1955–7 by Professors Piggott and Atkinson they were lucky enough to find four intact burial chambers which produced a lot of skeletal material and beaker pottery. The entrance to the mound faces east and is fronted by a huge standing sarsen stone flanked by other smaller ones, which hide the concave forecourt in front of the entrance proper. The edge of the mound was originally provided with a retaining kerbstone of small sarsens which have disappeared. For a very long period, possibly several centuries, the barrow was used for communal burials, and the blocking sarsens were only erected at the final sealing of the mound some time late in the third millennium BC. From the concave forecourt a passage leads to a large chamber at the end past two pairs of chambers opening off on either side. It is uncertain how many people were buried in these chambers: earlier remains would have been swept to one side as a new corpse was brought in and probably a lot of the remains were dumped unceremoniously outside the barrow at the same time. At least 46 individuals were represented by skeletal material found, and about 12 of these were children. The bodies were disarticulated in the side chambers and mixed up with pottery and flint implements. Each chamber is roofed by a single large, heavy capstone balanced on a crude attempt at corbelling the roof. Several of the upright stones at the entrance to the chambers, especially on the stone at the entrance of the south-west chamber (first on the left entering the barrow), show signs of having been used as whetstones for axes. There are large areas polished smooth by the sharpening of axe-heads which dealt with the great quantities of timber used as uprights, rollers, etc., in building the chambers. There is an **East Kennet** long barrow (SU 116699) about a mile to the south-west of its famous neighbour. It is covered by trees and has never been scientifically excavated although it is slightly larger than West Kennet and the presence of sarsen stones showing at its east end may indicate a similar plan of facade and burial chambers.

Clearly visible from West Kennet long barrow is the huge mound of **Silbury Hill** (SU 100685). It is the largest man-made mound in Europe, about 130 ft high and covering just over 5 acres. It is certainly of pre-Roman date as air photographs clearly show the Roman road from *Cunetio* (Mildenhall) to *Aquae Sulis* (Bath) making a detour around its base. Radio-carbon dates from Professor Atkinson's recent

64 West Kennet long barrow, its entrance partly concealed behind the facade of sarsen blocks
65 The Roman road from Mildenhall to Bath skirts the huge mound of Silbury Hill, showing that the road is later in date than the mound

excavations in 1968–70 suggest a date of around 2500 BC. It seems to have been built in four phases, involving a great deal of manpower. Shafts sunk into the mound and tunnels driven through it in 1776, 1849 and 1968–70 produced no evidence of a burial chamber, although much useful information was gleaned in the latest examination. If it has no significance as a burial mound it might have served some other ritual or even astronomical purposes; it seems to be contemporary with Avebury, but its true function remains a mystery.

Just to the south of these sites, across the north end of the Marl-borough Downs, is another fine section of the **Wansdyke** (ST 780660 to SU 625676, p. 66) which runs for some 10 miles. We must now look slightly to the east, to Hampshire, to mention a few interesting sites before returning to the southern parts of Wiltshire and Salisbury Plain to complete our survey of sites in southern England.

Near the Vale of Pewsey at Westbury is another chalk figure of a white horse, almost as well known as the Uffington Horse but not as old. As seen nowadays the **Westbury Horse** dates from 1778 but there seems to be some evidence that it replaced an earlier horse on the site. As with its Uffington counterpart local legend ascribes it to a victory monument of Alfred over the Danes, here commemorating the battle of Ethandun in 878. Nearby is an Iron Age hill fort, **Bratton Castle** (ST 901516), covering 25 acres enclosed by double banks and ditches on three sides, but there is no connection here with the Horse because the fort is earlier.

The Roman town of **Silchester**, *Calleva Atrebatum* (SU 640625) was the cantonal capital of the Atrebates tribe. The site today is one of the few Roman towns in Britain not built over (the others are St Albans, Caistor St Edmunds near Norwich, and Wroxeter). The area of some 107 acres within the hexagon enclosed by the walls was exca-vated between 1890 and 1909 and is now under the plough. Unfortun-ately the excavators at the time did not appreciate fully the significance of stratigraphical evidence, and so while there is a vast collection of material from the site little is known of its chronological relationships, only the place where it was found. Later small-scale excavations in 1938–9, 1954–8 and 1961 have endeavoured to clarify some of the problems of chronology missed by the earlier excavations. It is still possible to look across the site at the right time of year and recognize in the standing crops the lines of walls of the many buildings excavated and now concealed beneath it. This becomes even more clear in aerial photographs, and the combination of the latter and fieldwork has given us the most complete plan of a Romano–British town yet known. The walls are still quite impressive in parts and are almost entire in their circuit, again the only example of such length in Roman Britain. It is possible to follow their course, although at times it is on private property, and also to see the two best preserved of the four main gates, the North and the South Gates, at Rye House and Manor Farm respectively. Of the three temples in the town two lie under the present site of St Mary's Church near the East Gate just inside the wall. In the churchyard is a small column from one of the temples. Curiously the road that runs from the East Gate and the area of the temples is known as the Devil's Highway. One of the most famous buildings excavated in the town was the early Christian church, which was located in the centre in Insula IV on the south side of the forum. Re-excavation of it in 1961 only served to confirm the earlier identification which was based on the fact that this small building (it is only 42 × 33 ft), like other early churches, has an apse at the west end, a nave and faced west. It is probably of fourth-century date.

66 Though the interior of the Roman town of Silchester is under cultivation, its outline plan is still very clear

The vast number of finds from the site are principally housed in the Reading Museum as a special collection on loan from the Duke of Wellington; there is a small museum on the actual site near the rectory just outside the west wall, and a few items, including three mosaics and the famous bronze Silchester Eagle found in the forum, are at Stratfield Saye, the home of the Dukes of Wellington.

To the south-west of Silchester is an interesting Iron Age hill fort, **Ladle Hill** (SU 478568). It is unusual in that it was never completed, and it is therefore possible to see the way in which the defences of such a fort were constructed. The area to be enclosed was just under 7 acres and the work was started by digging a ditch along a line probably marked out by a line of withies. Several gangs of men started to dig at different points following the initial outline. The ditches that they dug were intended to meet up and the spoil cast up from their excavations would form the rampart. For some reason not now apparent to us the work was halted – perhaps the need for fortification was no longer there. Anyway, tools were literally put down by all the gangs scattered around the circumference of the fort, and there it was left. Earlier inhabitants of the area before the fort-building operations had constructed a disc-barrow to the north of the fort's present location, and there is a bell-barrow about 106 ft across to the south-east. In its centre is a depression indicating that it has been robbed at some point by a hole being sunk through the middle of the barrow seeking the burial. These barrows are, of course, about 1200 or 1000 years older than the hill fort which dates to the second or first century BC.

Close by is another Iron Age hill fort on **Beacon Hill** (SU 458573). It covers about 12 acres in an hourglass shape and has a single entrance on the south. Strangely for an English hill fort it is better known for its Near and Middle East connections – in 1927 Sir Leonard Woolley,

67 The unfinished hill fort at Ladle Hill, with a large disc-barrow just
outside the defences
68 Beacon Hill fort sinuously follows the contours of the hill top

who discovered the great Royal Death-pit at Ur, Mesopotamia (now southern Iraq), excavated several of the storage pits indicated by hollows within the fort. In the south-west corner of the fort, which is fenced off, is the grave of Lord Carnarvon, famous for the discovery with Howard Carter of the tomb of Tutankhamen at Thebes, Egypt, in 1922. Carnarvon's family home was at Highclere Castle nearby.

Just to the south of these two Iron Age hill forts, on either side of the A34 at Burghclere, is a barrow cemetery, known as the **Seven Barrows** (SU 462553). There are actually ten barrows, and possibly more as ploughing has damaged them. The main group of seven barrows west of the A34 at the south end of the cemetery includes bell-, bowl- and disc-barrows with diameters ranging from 40 ft to over 180 ft. The three barrows to the north on the other side of the A34 are all bowl-barrows between 60 and 100 ft in diameter. The arrangement of this cemetery in a classic north to south line is familiar from those in the area of Stonehenge, and they are probably all more or less contemporary, around the mid-second millennium BC.

The last sites to be considered in southern England are the great group in south Wiltshire centred on Stonehenge and the area of Salisbury Plain. **Stonehenge** itself (SU 123422) must be the best-known archaeological monument in Britain, if not in Western Europe – it is certainly a unique structure. Why this particular area of Wiltshire should have become so prominent in prehistoric cult and religion we simply do not know. Literally hundreds of books have been written about Stonehenge since 1655 when Inigo Jones published his plan of the monument in *The most notable Antiquity of Great Britain, vulgarly called Stone-heng*, and William Stukeley peopled it with Druids. They all have the vast proportions of the monument as a common denominator and then they go their separate ways ranging from erudite excavation reports to the lunatic fringe.

The history of Stonehenge is a complicated one and what we see today is only the later part of its five building phases. Stonehenge I, as it is called, was built about 2600 BC. At this point it consisted of a simple ditch with its spoil piled up on the outside to form a bank – a feature of most henge monuments – and with a diameter of around 380 ft. On the interior side of the ditch was a ring of 56 holes known as the Aubrey Holes, some of which later held cremations. There was a break in the bank and ditch to the north-east and just outside stood the Heel Stone, a natural sarsen stone 15 ft high. There was possibly a small structure or stones at the entrance and near the centre.

Stonehenge II, about 200 years later, saw a drastic change – a double ring of bluestones, at least 80 of them, was set up with an entrance facing the north-east. The bluestones weigh around 4 tons each and were brought from the Prescelly Mountains in Pembrokeshire by sea, river and finally on rollers across the Downs. Also at this time the Avenue was laid out heading for the river Avon to the west of Amesbury. Probably the bluestones were brought on their rollers up this Avenue, and it appears that a small ditch around the Heel Stone was dug then to preserve the sanctity of the stone as it now formed part of the Avenue. This phase of the work was never completely finished and the third period of Stonehenge, which is itself divided into three, began.

In Stonehenge IIIa the recently erected bluestone double circle was dismantled, the stones were placed on one side, and the area of the site was levelled off. Then about 80 great sarsen blocks weighing between 20 and 30 tons each were brought from the Marlborough Downs near Avebury, a distance of 24 miles. These were set up in the circle and horseshoe formations we see today. The circle is 100 ft in diameter, and a continuous row of lintels links each upright around the horseshoe setting, which was made up of five pairs of uprights with a lintel across, known as trilithons. The huge lintels bridging the gaps from one upright to the next were, like the uprights, carefully finished. Each lintel has a carefully cut and smoothed hole at either end and this slots over a projection at the top of each upright sarsen to form a perfect mortice and tenon joint. There has been much speculation as to how these huge and heavy lintels were raised to the top of the uprights and slotted so perfectly in place. Pulleys and block and tackle were unknown, and the only aids available were the roller and lever. It seems that the lintels were 'rocked' into position – each one was placed on a cradle of timber and was gradually lifted, each end of the cradle being raised alternately by inserting baulks and crosspieces until the required height was reached and the lintel could be either slid or tipped over into place. Considering the difficulties that would arise even nowadays with modern equipment, the beaker folk who were responsible for this simple but brilliant solution must have had a thorough understanding of the problems posed in moving such huge weights. The careful direction of labour needed for such an operation reveals a well organized and socially structured society. The new monument, like its predecessor, was still orientated towards the midsummer sunrise and the midwinter sunset, which again displays remarkable astronomical knowledge. Stonehenge IIIb saw the return of 20 of the bluestones, carefully dressed and finished, and set in an oval within the horseshoe of trilithons. Possibly the remaining 60 bluestones were intended to be placed in two circles outside the sarsen circle. This phase of the project was never completed, although the holes to receive the stones, known as the Y and Z holes, were dug. The final phase, Stonehenge IIIc, came about 1800 BC. The oval setting of bluestones was taken down, a circle of bluestones was set up between the horseshoe and the outer sarsen circle, and a horseshoe of 19 bluestones was erected within the five trilithons. The largest of the bluestones, about 12 ft high, was stood up in front of the central trilithon. It subsequently fell and is now mistakenly known as the Altar Stone.

In 1953 pecked carvings were noticed on several of the sarsens, especially on stone 53 of the southern trilithon on its right-hand upright immediately beneath a deeply cut seventeenth-century inscription. The carvings here represented a long-bladed dagger and an axe-head. It was suggested that, as the dagger had parallels in the Mediterranean world of the Mycenaean empire, especially on a relief

69 William Stukeley's engraving of Stonehenge in 1740, complete with Druid, right

70 Aerial view of Stonehenge

on a grave stele from Grave Circle A at Mycenae itself, an architect with Mycenaean connections and knowledge was involved. Finds from Bronze Age barrows in the area of the Wessex Culture also pointed to Mycenaean connections and the chronological puzzle seemed solved. Since then new evidence in apparently more accurate carbon-14 dates would seem to indicate that Stonehenge predates the Mycenaean empire and its knowledge of megalithic buildings by about 500 years; in this event the final phase of Stonehenge was old when someone – a

Mycenaean tourist (?) – carved the dagger on the trilithon upright. The question is still very much an open one as there is much to be said on both sides of the chronological argument.

Within the bank and ditch on the north and south are two so-called barrows – this is a misnomer as the North and the South Barrows only appear to mark the sites respectively of a pair of standing stones which have long since disappeared. They were probably like the two Station Stones, one now fallen, which are on the east and west sides of the circle on the line of the Aubrey Holes and had some geometrical or surveying function.

The significance of Stonehenge as some kind of astronomical observatory cannot be overlooked. In recent years much new evidence has come to light on this aspect of the monument and also in relation to other henge monuments, standing stones and circles in Britain. While such settings of stones may well have had an astronomical function it must also be remembered that many of those still standing have suffered over the centuries at the hands of despoilers as well as from nature. Many of the extremely precise measurements postulated by some scientists must necessarily contain more than a shadow of doubt when alignments are based on weathered stones or, worse, a trajectory taken from the socket left by a stone long since broken up and carted away.

About half a mile to the north of Stonehenge is a curious monument known as the **Cursus** (SU 115428). It takes its name from the eighteenth-century antiquary William Stukeley's idea that it was a kind of prehistoric race track (p. 54). Almost 2 miles in length, most of it has now been destroyed by ploughing. However the low bank and ditch that form it, running in parallel pairs with about 100 yards between them, can still be seen in parts, and so can the neolithic long barrow at its eastern end upon which the whole structure appears to have been aligned. It seems to have been built at much the same time as the first phase of Stonehenge.

While Stonehenge is the best known monument of its type, 2 miles to the north-east beside the A345 are the remains of another monument equally distinctive in its individual way – **Woodhenge**, (SU 150434). This site was discovered by aerial photography and excavated in 1928. It took the normal henge monument form, having a ditch inside the bank and enclosing an area of about 150 ft in diameter. The excavators found evidence of a series of concentric rings of post holes for wooden uprights, which are now marked by small concrete pillars, and the grave of a three-year-old child who had died from a fractured skull. The grave is now marked by a small cairn. It is intriguing to speculate on the form that the sanctuary at Woodhenge took – it is possible that it was a circular building with a roof supported on the concentric timber posts but with the central area open to the sky, or it could have been just a series of posts with no roof. The posts might even have been carved like North American Indian totem poles. If it was a roofed building it is only the second example known in Britain from this period, the other being the Sanctuary at Avebury (p. 81).

71 Normanton Down barrow cemetery contains barrows of almost every type known in southern England

The area of Stonehenge contains the largest concentration of prehistoric burial mounds in the whole of Britain. The vast numbers of these barrows, generally in cemeteries and of varying types, only serve to underline even more strongly the sacred nature of this whole area from neolithic times onwards. The nearest group to Stonehenge is on Normanton Down, less than half a mile away. There is another group at the crossroads at Winterbourne Stoke, and another at **Snail Down** (SU 218522). The latter are on a military firing range and have been much damaged by tanks, so I shall deal only with the first two cemeteries. **Normanton Down** (SU 115413) has a group of 26 barrows of many different types arranged in an east to west line. They were all opened at some time in the eighteenth and nineteenth centuries by

William Stukeley or Sir Richard Colt Hoare. There are twelve bowl-barrows, seven disc-, four bell-, two saucer- and one, the earliest of the group, neolithic long barrow. The most famous barrow in the group is the seventh from the west end, the Bush Barrow excavated by Colt Hoare in September 1808. It is 11 ft high and 50 ft in diameter, and must have been the grave of an extremely powerful Wessex chieftain. The body was armed with three daggers, an axe and a shield. Sewn on to the clothing over the chest was a lozenge-shaped gold plaque $7\frac{1}{4} \times 6\frac{1}{4}$ ins, and there was a sceptre or mace with a head made of fossil rock. The shaft of the sceptre was decorated with bone mounts ornamented with a cut denticulated pattern. The original finds are in the British Museum, but the Devizes Museum, which has a magnificent collection of material from the Wiltshire barrows, contains copies. The Normanton Down cemetery produced a number of gold objects, five daggers, some of them with their handles ornamented by minute gold pins, pottery, necklaces with beads of shale, amber and gold beads and faience beads of Egyptian origin.

The group of barrows at the junction of the A303 and A360 at **Winterbourne Stoke** (SU 101417) is laid out in two almost parallel rows. They are just a mile and a half to the west of Stonehenge and are lined to the north-east. The earliest barrow is the well-defined neolithic long barrow close to the road junction, and the remaining barrows of the Bronze Age seem to be aligned on it. Moving away from the wide end of the long barrow to the north-east there are a bowl-barrow, a bell-, pond-, another bell-, and six bowl-barrows. The parallel line of barrows on the west starts with a bowl-barrow, followed by two disc-barrows, a bowl- and then two pond-barrows. North-west of this parallel group of barrows, just on the east side of the A360 at SU 100418, is another small group of five bowl- and two saucer-barrows. This cemetery with its two groups of mounds shows examples of every type of barrow in quite a small area, and is one of the best to be seen in Britain. The contents of the barrows were those of normal Wessex-culture barrows – bronze daggers, pottery cups, beakers and urns, and various types of necklace beads.

Two final noteworthy sites remain in this area of southern England, both of them Iron Age hill forts. On the road south from Stonehenge to Salisbury, the A345, is **Old Sarum** (SU 137327). The site is the precursor to Salisbury and is notable for the Norman motte that dominates the huge ditches and ramparts, and for the outlines of the Norman cathedral in the turf within the fortifications. Despite the Norman predominance the site is much earlier: the defences are early Iron Age in origin and traces of a Roman building and pottery were found in excavations in 1909. Old Sarum was probably the site of the Roman posting station of *Sorviodunum*.

The other Iron Age hill fort to be mentioned is over the county border in Hampshire, at **Danebury** (SU 323377) near Stockbridge. This fort is generally accepted as the finest in Hampshire and is certainly one of the most complex in Britain. It is only recently that excavations by Professor Barry Cunliffe have begun to unravel the

72 The various types of Bronze Age round barrows in the Winterbourne Stoke cemetery seem to take their alignment from the earlier neolithic long barrow close to the modern crossroads

73 Entrance to Norman Old Sarum across the Iron Age bank and ditch

story of this at present heavily wooded site. Its shape is roughly oval and it has two banks and ditches around it; the outer defences enclose about 27 acres and the inner defences about 13 acres. In places the inner bank still stands to a height of 16 ft, and it is almost 60 ft wide at its base. The history of the site begins in the early Bronze Age with a series of ritual pits, one of which contained the dismembered remains of a dog. Some time in the fifth century BC work started on the first stage of the hill fort, which was modified c. 400 BC. Then, along with

74 The east entrance of Danebury hill fort, looking
out of the fort, after excavation

so many other hill forts threatened by the Belgic invasions, the main
eastern gateway was refortified about 100 BC and other parts of the
fort were strengthened. Less than 20 years later the gate had been
burnt down and the fort abandoned, and so it remained until the next
invasion threat from the might of Rome. This seems to have passed
the fort by, and it then sank into oblivion. Among the many interesting
finds made during the excavations was a hoard of 21 sword-shaped
iron currency bars that had been hidden in a pit outside one of the
huts. Danebury hill fort is unusual in another archaeological sense,
as it features in a scheme run by Hampshire County Council to attract
people to the site which is open as a public amenity area.

3 The South-West

The south-western counties of Somerset, Devon and Cornwall, push-ing a peninsula out into the Atlantic, have always been a source of legend and romance. They are associated with King Arthur, King Mark of Cornwall, Tristan and Isolde of Dark Age and early medieval folklore, and the later wreckers, smugglers and aristocratic families in the eighteenth and nineteenth centuries. Our interest lies largely in the prehistoric remains that are scattered throughout the counties, and also in some of the early Christian and Dark Age monuments found there.

Little remains of the Roman signal stations at **Martinhoe** (SS 663493) and **Old Burrow Walls** (SS 788493) in North Devon which faced out across the Bristol Channel, keeping a wary eye on the Silures tribe across the water. Inland there are a couple of small Iron Age forts at **Bat's Castle** (SU 988421) and **Shoulobarrow Castle** (SS 705391), a Bronze Age cemetery at **Five Barrows** (SS 733368), and a small stone circle at **Withypool Hill** (SS 836343). On Winsford Hill (SS 890335) is the **Caractacus Stone,** an early Dark Ages memorial stone of a type that is peculiar to the south-west and will be met again on the south coast.

Three and a half miles north-west of Honiton is **Hembury** hill fort (ST 113031), certainly the most important prehistoric site in Devon, if not in the whole of southern England. It started life as a neolithic causewayed camp upon which an Iron Age fort was later super-imposed. This fort is roughly triangular in shape and covered an area of some 7 acres. On the north and west sides are triple banks and ditches, while there are only double ones on the east. The main en-trance was in the middle of the west side and there was a smaller one at the north-east corner. Each was approached by a long passage up to the gateway so that attackers would be subject to enfilading fire from the defenders. There seem to have been two stages in the con-struction of the defences, which were begun in the second century BC and completed by the addition of two banks and ditches in the first century BC. It would have been a stronghold of the local tribe, the

95

Dumnonii. For some reason, possibly a change of occupants, in the early years of the first century AD a double bank and ditches were built across the middle of the fort; the southern half of the divided area was used as a cattle pound and the other half for human occupation. Then, in about AD 70, everyone seems to have left for a new and unknown destination. Such is the evidence of excavation at the site, and the new site where the inhabitants moved to is not known.

Nearer the coast, 3 miles north-west of Seaton, is another, much simpler, Iron Age hill fort, **Blackbury Castle** (SY 187924). This is only 4 acres in area with a single bank and ditch, although it did have an unduly strong, large gate closing an entrance passage 180 ft in length. There was little evidence found of occupation and it is possible that the fort was more of a cattle pound and left unfinished.

The Roman capital of the south-west was at **Exeter,** *Isca Dumnoniorum* (SX 919925), the cantonal town of the Dumnonii. Exeter suffered badly from bombing in the Second World War, and when excavations were later carried out, largely by Lady Fox, much of its Roman history was recovered. It is possible to see some fragments of the Roman walls incorporated at the base of later medieval walling. The stonework is a dark purple colour above a chamfered plinth: it is best seen in the area around Northernhay and Southernhay. Finds from excavations in the city, and from the prehistoric remains on Dartmoor, are displayed in the Rougemount House Museum in Castle Street.

To the west of Exeter rises the bleak granite massif of Dartmoor, famed for its prehistoric antiquities as well as its ponies and prison. The moor is almost littered with Bronze Age sites, hut circles and stone rows, as a glance at the Ordnance Survey maps shows. On **Shovel Down,** Chagford (SX 655506) there are stone circles, rows, cairns and standing stones spread over quite a wide area. At the northern end, near Batworthy, are two double rows of stones which are aligned on a cairn which had a cist at its centre. Another double stone row starts from this cairn and heads off south-east to a cairn 400 ft away and a single upright stone at its southern end. The tallest stone, 10 ft 5 ins high, is called the Longstone; to the south of it another double row of stones leads to a single stone 4 ft 6 ins high. This is the sole survivor of three stones known as the Three Boys. A hundred yards away to the south-east is a stone burial cist. The complexity of this site is typical of many on the moor, where conditions make it difficult in most instances to date them more precisely than to say that they are of the Bronze Age.

To the north of Shovel Down is a neolithic site, **Spinsters' Rock** (SX 700908). Once a covered long barrow, all that now remains are three upright stones of the burial chamber, restored after the chamber's collapse in 1862. A charming local tale ascribes the stones to three spinsters who erected them before breakfast one morning.

Cranbrook Castle (SX 738890) and **Prestonbury Castle** (SX 746900) are two Iron Age forts strategically placed on hill tops facing each other across the valley of the river Teign. Cranbrook is on

the south side, Prestonbury on the north. The latter, although only
a third of the size of Cranbrook, has strong multi-vallate defences with
an entrance on the east. Cranbrook, about 8 acres in area, only has
a simple ditch and rampart but has two entrances, on the south-west
and the south-east. It is possible that these two forts so well placed
to watch each other represented opposing interests in two of the
local tribes.

One of the best known of the many hut groups on Dartmoor is the
Bronze Age settlement site at **Grimspound** (SX 701809). Here, within
a dry stone walled area of about 4 acres, are two dozen huts all about
15 ft in diameter. The enclosing wall is about 9 ft thick and was probably 6 ft high, with an entrance on the east side. Each hut contained
a hearth or cooking hole, and a stone in the centre of the floor acted
as a base for the main piece of timber supporting the roof. Several
huts had raised areas that were probably sleeping benches. The enclosure had its own water supply – a spring at the lower end. The community who occupied Grimspound grazed their animals on the moor
and returned to the safety of their walled encampment at night. Near
the dwelling huts were other stone huts, less substantially built and
lacking hearths, and cattle pens were built up against the inside of
the encircling wall. From the little evidence found in the excavations
it appears that Grimspound was in use towards the end of the Bronze
Age, around 1000 – 800 BC.

75 Grimspound settlement with its huts surrounded by an
enclosure wall and an entrance on the east

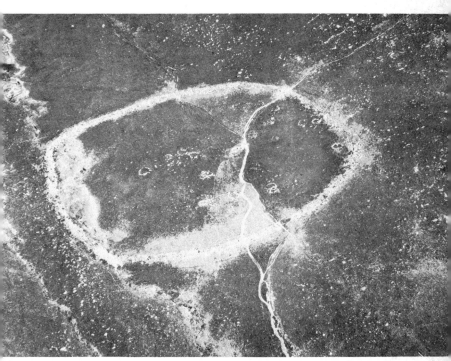

To the south-west of Grimspound at **Merrivale** (sx 553746) is a group of standing stones, circles, a cairn and a cist beside the A384. Two double rows of stones run east-west; the one on the north, almost 600 ft in length, has a single stone blocking its eastern end; another row on the south, over 800 ft in length, is similarly ended with a single stone. Near the centre of the south row is a small cairn within a circle. South-east of this circle, 160 ft away, is a large stone cist and west of this is a cairn with a 140-ft stone row abutting on to it from the south-west. Another stone circle is located some 400 ft to the south. The complexity of such alignments has puzzled archaeologists for years, and as more and more evidence is accumulated their interpretation as astronomical siting points gains more validity.

On the south-west edge of the moor is another group of monuments at **Ditsworthy Warren** (sx 590670), a typical group of Bronze Age Dartmoor antiquities; it consists of **Legis Tor** (sx 573654), a large site of $4\frac{1}{4}$ acres with four enclosures, and **Trowlesworthy Warren** (sx 575645), with three enclosures and two stone rows.

Kent's Cavern (sx 934642), a mile east of Torquay harbour, is one of the most important inhabited caves of the Old Stone Age excavated in Britain. The Cavern is actually two parallel main chambers with a series of galleries leading off them. Finds of prehistoric animal bones here included the remains of mammoths, woolly rhinoceroses, cave bears, hyenas and lions. Man also left evidence of his use of the Cavern in various types of flint tools – three harpoons, a bone sewing needle and an ivory rod which must have had some ritual or ceremonial significance. In all, the timespan during which the Cavern was occupied ran from about 100,000 BC down to 8000 BC. Digging started in the Cavern in the early 1820s at a time when such a timescale would have been thought totally impossible and, indeed, blasphemous in the light of fundamentally accepted biblical narrative.

Crossing the county boundary into Cornwall and going on to Bodmin Moor we come to the spectacular neolithic burial chamber of **Trethevy Quoit** (sx 259688). Nothing now remains of the mound that once covered it and so the seven stones forming the chamber, plus their capstone, stand tall and clear. The capstone is over 11 ft long and the stones on the southern side are almost 15 ft high. The chamber itself is divided into two by a huge cross stone with a portion broken away leaving enough space to admit a body. An antechamber is formed in front of the cross stone by the projection forward of the capstone and two side stones. At St Cleer (sx 236687) is **King Doniert's Stone,** possibly commemorating a post-Roman chieftain of Dumnonia who was drowned in AD 875. A little to the north are three Bronze Age stone circles known as **The Hurlers** (sx 258714). The three circles are set on a line north-east to south-west; the northern circle is 110 ft in diameter and still has 13 stones; the centre circle is 135 ft in diameter with 17 stones, and the southern circle, 105 ft in diameter, has nine stones. Apparently each circle at one time had between 25 and 30 stones. Generally the stones in such circles were merely stood in their places, and they may or may not have been

76 Trethevy Quoit neolithic burial chamber
77 *Right* King Doniert's Stone at St Cleer
78 The Hurlers stone circles

dressed and finished (cf. the Rollright Stones, p. 74). The constructors of The Hurlers took great trouble to sink the stones in their pits at varying depths and to pack them with granite blocks to ensure that the tops were all level. In the middle of the central circle a fallen stone was found, and the area within the northern circle seems to have been paved with granite slabs. The curious name of the site was explained by William Camden, the seventeenth-century antiquary, as coming from some impious local men who persisted in 'hurling the ball' on Sunday, and were duly punished by being transformed into stone.

To the north-west of Bodmin Moor on Hawks Tor Downs is another stone circle called the **Stripple Stones** (sx 144752). Within an area 225 ft in diameter surrounded by a bank and ditch is an irregular circle of 15 stones. Only four still stand, and a fallen stone lies in the centre of the circle. Like most henge monuments the ditch is on the inside of the bank, not the outside, and it is possible that this site represents a continuity from a neolithic to a Bronze Age sanctuary.

99

79 The Rumps promontory fort with its defensive ditches and
ramparts across the headland in the foreground

At **Rough Tor** (SX 145800) is a series of oval enclosures and huts
defended by a small hill fort. Within the fort the outlines of huts can
be seen but, as is so often the case with this type of monument, it
is difficult to date. Probably the area was in use in the first quarter
of the last millennium BC.

A fine example of a Cornish promontory fort is **The Rumps**
(SW 934810) on Pentire Head above Padstow Bay. The fort actually
contains two headlands with a sheltered area between them, and their
defences are a triple rampart and ditch which cut across the peninsula.
The ditches and ramparts are still quite evident, especially the central
one where the ditch is nearly 15 ft deep. According to the pottery evidence, the occupation of the fort seems to be spread over the last century BC and the first AD, and there were also fragments of wine
amphorae from the Mediterranean, indicating a wide orbit of trade.
On the other side of Padstow Bay just west of Padstow at Harlyn Bay
is an unusual site – the **Harlyn Bay** cemetery (SX 877753). Over 100
cist graves were found here, lined with local slate and covered by slabs.
Within them the dead were laid in a crouching position and accompanied by grave goods consisting of bronze rings, pins and other
jewellery of Iron Age type that can be dated to the fourth or third
centuries BC.

In Cornwall it seems there was a strong tendency for maidens to
be turned into stone, as the many local names attached to prehistoric
monuments and featuring maidens testify. At St Columb Major there
is a stone alignment called the **Nine Maidens** (SX 827630). It is the
only alignment in Cornwall and has nine stones spread out, north-
east to south-west, over a distance of 300 yards. The stones seem to
have been about 5–6 ft high and must form a ritual site erected some
time in the second half of the second millennium BC. Moving back
to the coast at **Trevelgue Head**, Newquay (SX 827630), we find a

80 Trevelgue Head promontory fort (a cliff castle), looking
across its defensive ramparts

magnificent promontory fort where man and nature have combined
to present an impregnable-looking fortress. The defences of the fort
consist of no fewer than six ramparts and ditches, and these are aided
by the sea which cuts into the promontory making it into a tidal island.
On the landward side are triple banks and ditches and these are
repeated on the promontory itself, the sea cleft acting as one of the
ditches. Excavations indicated that the site was an important centre
of bronze-smelting in the Bronze Age, and occupation continued
down into the Roman period as shown by fragments of Mediterranean
amphorae found in the huts of Roman and Dark Age date within the
fortifications.

On the other side of the Cornish peninsula at **Castle Dore**
(SX 103548), near Fowey, is a small but interesting hill fort. It is extremely well preserved, and roughly circular with a maximum diameter of just over 400 ft; its two banks still stand between 6 and 7 ft
high, and its ditches 20 ft wide and 4 ft deep. There was an entrance
through both banks on the east side about 25 ft wide; they were well
designed for defence with inturned wooden gateways which would
put any attackers at an immediate disadvantage. The ramparts were
originally thrown up about 200 BC but it was not until about 50 BC
that the elaborate gateways were provided. Judging by the small finds
of imported material the inhabitants must have been quite prosperous,
profiting from the proceeds of mining and trading in tin and iron ores.
The fort seems to have been abandoned towards the end of the second
century AD and then reoccupied during the fifth century. Two rectangular timber halls, typical of those known from the Dark Ages, were
built, together with their necessary attendant kitchens. It is during
this period that legend ascribes the fort to King Mark of Cornwall
and associates it with the story of the lovers Tristan and Isolde. By
a curious coincidence (?) at the crossroads 2 miles south of Castle

81 The Tristan Stone near
Castle Dore. Its ancient
inscription is marred by
a modern ordnance bench
mark, the line above an arrow

82 Carn Brea hill fort
dominates the Cornish
countryside

Dore there stands a 6-ft-high memorial stone to a mid-sixth-century
chieftain. Its inscription reads: DRUSTANUS HIC IACIT CUNOMORI
FILIUS – here lies Tristan, son of Cunomorus – and it is known as the
Tristan Stone. The ninth-century biography of St Paul Aurelian
speaks of *Marcus dictus Quonomorus*, who is identified with King
Mark, and perhaps the pieces of the legend and jigsaw puzzle fit too
conveniently together, but who knows?

Moving south-westwards along the coast we find another of the
many Cornish promontory forts of the Iron Age on **Dodman Point**
(SX 060395), and a little further on, commanding a magnificent view
of Gerrans Bay, is the large Bronze Age round-barrow at **Veryan**
(SX 913387). This barrow is one of the largest in England, being over
15 ft high and almost 350 ft in diameter, and it gives a fine idea of
what some of the now sadly denuded Cornish barrows were once like.
Nothing is known of the burial beneath the mound but its style and
size, coupled with finds from barrows of similar type, all show affini-
ties with the great series of barrows from the Wiltshire-based Wessex
Culture.

As we move closer to the tip of the Cornish peninsula so monuments
become more and more prolific, a sure indication of the importance
of the area in prehistoric times as a source of mineral wealth and trade.
At **Carn Brea** (SW 685407) between Camborne and Redruth is a large
hill fort of 36 acres dating from early in the first century AD. Within
the fort the outlines of several of the circular huts of this period can
still be seen. Excavations carried out in the nineteenth century produced pottery, stratified beneath the huts, of much earlier neolithic

date; it was very similar to pottery from the causewayed camp at Hembury, and characteristic enough to be called western neolithic pottery. These earlier occupants of the later hill fort area were apparently involved in the Cornish greenstone hand-axe trade. Their successors in the Iron Age fort 2000 years later were still involved in 'armaments', dealing in tin and copper ores which were the basic raw materials used in the production of the typical long Bronze Age swords and socketed axes. A small hoard of these axes found there were of a type known from Brittany, another indication of the close links that have existed over the centuries between Cornwall and Brittany. The defences of the fort itself consisted of strong ramparts, still well preserved in places, lined with large stone slabs. A simple entrance through the inner of the two ramparts was flanked by guard chambers, and long after the Iron Age fort had fallen into disuse the strength of its position continued to be recognized when a castle was built within its ramparts in the twelfth century AD, and added to up until the eighteenth.

A prehistoric monument peculiar to Cornwall is a *fogou*, or underground chamber. They are curious passageways associated with fortified areas or small villages of courtyard houses, and were at one time thought to have been places of refuge in times of danger. They were built by a trench being dug out on a curving line which was lined with stone slabs converging to form a corbelled roof. The excavated earth was either heaped back on top – which made the *fogou*'s location rather obvious – or merely scattered over the roof to conceal it, and the rest of the spoil was disposed of elsewhere. There were at least two entrances to the *fogou*, but if it was used as a hiding-place in time of attack it would have been easily found and turned into a death trap for its occupants. A far better explanation is that they were merely large scale food stores.

The *fogou* at **Halligye** (SW 712238) is considered to be the finest example in Cornwall. It was associated with a small fortified homestead and ran for part of its length under the inner of the two ramparts that defended the fort. The homestead has now gone and only the *fogou* remains. Basically this *fogou* has a T-shaped plan; the upright

83 Zennor Quoit. Note the deliberately narrowed entrance
between the two front stones

of the T is 54 ft long, and walled and roofed with stone slabs. Just
inside one of the entrance passages a low block of stone has been set
in the floor just high enough to cause any stranger entering to
stumble – if this was done deliberately to act as a warning to anyone
hiding in the *fogou* it does underline the defensive nature, as against
the storage argument, of the site. Like most of the examples of *fogous*
known in the Land's End area Halligye appears to date from some
time in the first century BC and was in use down to the third century
AD.

The next site is on the other side of the peninsula and much earlier
in date – it is the neolithic burial chamber at **Zennor Quoit**
(SW 469380). This is an example of a group of burial chambers known
as Penwith tombs, whose basic characteristics are a squarish chamber
with either a closed or severely restricted entry beneath a round cairn.
At Zennor Quoit, the covering cairn of stones has completely disappeared, leaving the chamber exposed. It consists of five upright
slabs which form a completely enclosed burial chamber and in front
of it are two other slabs that form a kind of antechamber with just
a narrow gap between them (they are very reminiscent of the huge
frontal stones found before the West Kennet long barrow and Wayland's Smithy). An immense capstone over 15 ft across leans backwards
at a drunken angle over the burial chamber. This is the result of blast-
ing in the nineteenth century to find the mythical buried treasure so
often associated in folk legend with such monuments. Farmer Gren-
fell, who perpetrated this outrage in 1881, found a 3-in. whetstone
and a fragment of a cord-ornamented pot for his pains.

Inland from Zennor Quoit at **Chysauster** (SW 473350) is the best
example of the 20 or so known villages of courtyard houses in Devon
and Cornwall. It is a group of eight houses in two rows of four with

a couple of outlying houses and a *fogou* and no traces of any surrounding defensive wall, although there is a hill fort, **Castle-an-Dinas**, only a mile away. Some of the known villages of this type are fortified, but the need does not seem to have arisen at Chysauster. Five of the houses have been completely excavated: they are oval in shape, set around a courtyard with a series of rooms opening off it in the thickness of the surrounding wall. The rooms could have been roofed with a rough corbel vault, and there is some evidence of this, but thatch is also a possibility as many of the houses had a stone with a socket in it in the circular rooms opposite the entrances. Such a socket would act as a base for a length of timber supporting the roof. The houses have well-paved floors, some with open hearths and covered drains. Finds from the houses consisted mainly of hand mills for grinding grain, pottery and the usual kind of domestic rubbish. The site seems to have been occupied for some 400 years from the late second century BC, but there is little evidence during that period to show how the occupants supported themselves. They had little garden plots marked off behind the houses and the nearby hillsides were terraced. Possibly they relied on extracting tin from the nearby stream and exporting through the *entrepôt* at St Michael's Mount, which is only 4 miles away.

The Iron Age hill fort of **Chun Castle** (SW 405339) just outside St Just is quite small, only 280 ft in diameter with an entrance to the south-west, but it must have been virtually impregnable. Perched on its hill top, its walls at least 12 ft high and faced with granite, it presented a daunting aspect. Any attackers, once having reached the south-

84 Chysauster, an Iron Age village of courtyard houses

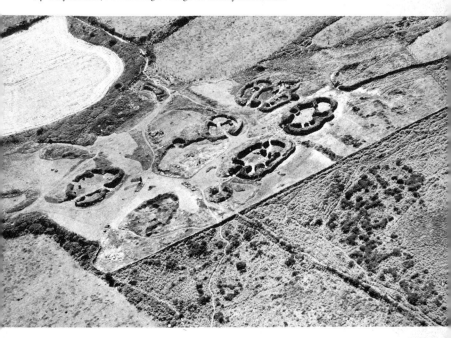

west gate and forced it, would have to turn their right, undefended side to the defenders in order to achieve the second entrance through the inner wall which was offset about 40 ft to the main gate. The walls still stand 8 ft high in places. Within the fort are several circular huts of the Iron Age and the rectangular huts seen overlying them in places belong to the Dark Ages, to the sixth century AD when the fort was once again in use in the iron and tin smelting trade that is so much a feature of Cornish antiquity. A hundred yards west away from Chun Castle is **Chun Quoit** (SW 402339), a neolithic chambered tomb. This, like Zennor Quoit, is a Penwith tomb and has a square chamber composed of four great slabs with a capstone at the centre of a round barrow originally some 35 ft in diameter. There is a scatter of stones on the south side which may indicate that there was once an entrance passage here.

There are other interesting sites in the area of St Just. A mile and a quarter east of the town are the two **Tregaseal** stone circles (SW 387324). Only two stones of the western circle survive, but the eastern circle is much more complete. From an original setting of 20, 16 stones still stand all between 4 and 6 ft high. Their situation is typical of many of the Cornish circles, on flat moorland where everyone participating in the ceremonies would have a good view.

A mile to the west of St Just is the Bronze Age barrow of **Carn Gluze** (SW 355313) on Cape Cornwall. This is a strange and complex monument. It was excavated by William C. Borlase and W. C. Lukis in 1874 with the help of a gang of local miners. While the monument is of Bronze Age date (it belongs to the same period as Stonehenge IIIc) its cult aspect as revealed by the excavations is more in keeping with the neolithic. The initial phase of the monument was a huge T-shaped pit cut 7 ft deep into the rock and approached by steps cut into the slope of its entrance. There were no burials found in it, only a stone bead. Around the top of the pit were four cists (no longer to be seen) which held miniature pots of Middle Bronze Age type. Over these structures a dome, which still stands 10 ft high, was built. It was double walled with a gap of 5 ft between the walls, and just before it was finally sealed another cist was inserted containing lamb bones and pottery. There was then no means of access at all to the deposits beneath the dome. Outside it, at the base of the wall, were found two more cists (one still visible) and the whole monument was then surrounded by an oval stone wall, 65 × 70 ft, and nearly 5 ft high. Between the wall of the dome and the outer ring of the surrounding wall on the south-west a rectangular burial chamber of the type known as an entrance grave was built. Here quantities of burnt human bones and fragments of pottery were found beneath the stone flagged floor. It appears as if we have here a burial made in close association with what can only be interpreted as some kind of underworld cult. Similar ritual pits are known in Britain, but the double wall of the dome also has parallels in Brittany.

Five miles north-east of Land's End, north of the A30, is the Iron Age village of **Carn Euny** (SW 403288). It was occupied before 500 BC

85 The eastern of the two stone circles at Tregaseal
86 The central cairn area of Carn Gluze

and lasted at least into the first century AD. Its houses are of the court-yard type such as those seen at Chysauster, but of slightly earlier date. The floors of the huts were made of beaten rab – the local bedrock – and clay, and several of them had covered drains – they can still be seen today with their stone covers in many a Cornish farmyard. The village is noted for its exceptionally fine *fogou* which is unique in plan and also unusual in being located in the middle of the village. The east entrance to the *fogou* leads from one of the huts into a passage 66 ft long. At its far end is a much narrower 'creep' passage going off to the north-west. A passage at its eastern end leads to a circular chamber with a corbelled roof, unique among *fogous* known at present. Only in the middle of the passageway are the roofing stones original; at the west end two niches, one on either side of the passage, seem to be slots for holding a door. The *fogou* was built in the normal way by excavating a wide and deep trench, lining it with slabs and bringing the roof in by corbelling until a single slab would bridge the gap. Earth was then back-filled over the stones, leaving a low mound showing on the surface.

87 Carn Euny *fogou*

88 Chapel Euny (Brane)
entrance grave

At Brane, about 3 miles south-west of St Just, is the **Chapel Euny**
entrance grave (SW 402282), not to be confused with Carn Euny village. This is typical of such graves found hereabouts and in the Scilly
Isles; they have a short passage lined with stone and open at one end.
The eastern barrow covering the 7 ft 6 ins × 4 ft burial chamber is still
just over 6 ft high and 20 ft in diameter. The burial chamber has
two large capstones and there may have been a third at one time. A
series of upright stones around the edge of the barrow form a retaining
kerb.

Two stone circles remain to be mentioned among the many sites
in the Land's End area of the Cornish peninsula. Both feature the
stony maidens so popular in Cornish folklore. The **Nine Maidens**
at **Boscawen-Un**, St Buryan, is rather a misnomer and not be confused with other ladies of this magic number at **Boskednan**
(SW 435352) or at **St Columb Major** (SW 937675) – the latter a stone
avenue and not a circle. The Boscawen-Un circle is about 70 ft in
diameter and has 19 stones regularly placed in a flattened circle,
which indicates a knowledge of simple geometry on the part of the
builders as more than one centre point would be needed to achieve
the effect. A single standing stone, the largest of the group, forms the
centre of the circle, and there is a small group of four additional stones
on the north-east of the circumference. Close by at SW 416276 are two
more standing stones and two barrows which appear to be connected
in some way with the circle, possibly as sighting marks for astronomical calculations.

The other group of 'stony maidens' lies a mile and a half to the south-
east of St Buryan on the B 3283. The **Merry Maidens** circle and standing stones (SW 433245) consists of 19 regularly placed stones each
about 4 ft high in a circle with a diameter of 80 ft. This is a true
circle, unlike Boscawen-Un or The Hurlers, and must have been laid
out accurately from the central point using a leather thong. A gap at
the north-east point was probably the original entrance into the circle.
Four hundred yards away to the north-east are two large standing
stones, 15 ft and 13 ft 6 ins tall respectively, known as The Pipers.
They are aligned with the centre of the Merry Maidens but cannot
be seen from it. The local legend has it that the Pipers played for the

89 Nine Maidens stone circle, Boscawen-Un
90 Merry Maidens stone circle, St Buryan

Merry Maidens to dance on a Sunday – someone else called the tune and they were turned to stone! Professor Alexander Thom has suggested, backed by most telling arguments and calculations, that many of the free-standing circles such as this were a means of calculating astronomical movements, phases and calendrical facts. The evidence does indeed seem to bear him out on sites laid out such as these – if only the stony maidens could comment!

The Isles of Scilly, 25 miles off the Cornish coast out into the Atlantic, are noted for the large number of Bronze Age burial mounds within their area, notably on St Mary's, and there is evidence that the islands were a good source of flint and chert for Stone Age man. The islands can be seen from Cornwall on a clear day and have for long been associated with legends that identify them variously as the Fortunate Isles or the Isles of the Dead or the Blessed. Geological arguments prove that the Scillies were never joined to the Cornish mainland but poetic licence, especially in Tennyson's *Idylls of the King* with its story of Arthur, identifies the intervening area as the legendary drowned land of Lyonnesse. The most extensive site is on the west side

91 Bant's Carn burial chamber, St Mary's, Scilly Isles
92 The upper and better preserved of the two burial chambers at Innisidgen, St Mary's, Scilly Isles

of St Mary's, **Bant's Carn** burial chamber (sv 911123). It is an entrance grave set within a mound about 40 ft in diameter. There are an inner and an outer retaining wall and an entrance on the east side. Originally there were four capstones over the burial chamber but only three now remain in place. Pottery found in excavations was of neolithic and Bronze Age type and indicated that the tomb had been used for communal burials over a period of at least 500 years. Nearby are the remains of a village of about a dozen round or oval huts. Originating in the late Iron Age, it seems to have been occupied throughout the Roman period and possibly even later. The huts are about 25 ft in diameter and have walls of large, well-laid granite blocks and small gardens rather like those at Chysauster in Cornwall. This is the only group of huts to be seen in the islands, although isolated examples

93 Porth Hellick Down burial chamber

are known and there may have been other villages on land now below the high water mark.

At the northern end of St Mary's are the two **Innisidgen** burial chambers (SV 921127). Both are entrance graves set within a mound, the upper one being 26 ft in diameter with an entrance on the south-east which is covered by five large capstones. The Lower Innisidgen chamber is not located in a prominent position as is its companion, but lies at the bottom of the hill partially covered by blown sand.

The last of the major Bronze Age monuments in the Scillies is the group of five chambered tombs on **Porth Hellick Down** (SV 928108). Four are rather ruined but the fifth in the group is the best preserved example of its type in the islands. It is located within a circular mound 40 ft in diameter and still 5 ft high. There is a dry stone retaining wall with an entrance on the north-west. The entrance passage is unroofed and curves left into the burial chamber which is covered by four capstone slabs. At the junction of the entrance passage with the burial chamber a slab is set at right angles to the wall, which restricts the passage to only 2 ft in width. This is a feature found in tombs in the Iberian Peninsula and there can be no doubting the seaborne influences on the cultures of the Scillies from both Spain and Cornwall, as the architectural and pottery evidence suggests.

There is little to be seen of the Iron Age; most of the evidence available comes from scattered excavations, although several of the earthworks are similar to the cliff castles found in Cornwall. There are banks across the hillside below the **Old Blockhouse** on Tresco (SV 897155) and three curved lines of rampart and ditch on the south-eastern tip of St Mary's at **Giant's Castle**. Pottery from sites such as these suggests occupation around 300 BC.

4 East Anglia

To many people the counties of Cambridgeshire, Essex, Norfolk and
Suffolk form a flat area relatively devoid of visible antiquities and
blown by cold winds sweeping in across the North Sea. But not so
long ago there was a land bridge here and mesolithic hunters stalked
game on land beneath those waves. The effect of erosion here has been
rather more destructive than on the Kentish coast. The East Anglian
coastline has produced many a tale of drowned medieval villages and
the sea has also claimed its Roman forts in Walton Castle, north of
Felixstowe, now completely gone, and Bradwell, which is only partially
eaten away.

At **Bradwell** (TM031082) about half of the Roman Saxon Shore
fort of *Othona* built under Carausius at the end of the third century
AD now remains. There is a circular bastion from the north-west
angle of the fort and an internal tower 120 ft south of it. The best
portion of the walls is on the south side of the little barn-like chapel
of St Peter-on-the-Wall. It is built literally on the walls, bestriding
them, and they can be seen in section inside the chapel. The chapel
was built by St Cedd in AD654 and until quite recently stood gaunt
against the sky looking out over the marshy flats populated only by
sea birds – now it has the Bradwell Power Station for company.

Bradwell sits on a silted up creek on the south side of the estuary
of the river Blackwater and opposite, on the north side, is Mersea
Island. At **West Mersea** is a large Romano–British burial mound (TM
023143), excavated in 1912. It lies near the remains of a large and
rich Roman house and is rather similar in its type and location to the
Roman tomb at Keston, Kent (p. 28). The basic construction of the
tomb was like a cartwheel with cremated remains placed in a brick
vault at its centre and six radiating 'spoke' walls going out from it
to join a 3-ft-thick ring wall, 65 ft in diameter. There are parallel type
tombs on the Via Appia outside Rome and in the Mausoleum of
Augustus in Rome itself, all of which, together with the lead casket
and glass bowl found in the vault, suggest a date in the first century
AD. A local story has it that the occupant of the tomb was a Roman

94 The Romano–British burial mound at West Mersea

centurion, and the barrow is said to be still haunted by his ghost.

Camulodunum, modern **Colchester** (TL 995253), was the capital of King Addedomaros of the Trinovantes tribe of Essex. Around 10 BC the Catuvellauni of Hertfordshire under their king Tasciovanus appear to have mounted a successful attack and Addedomaros was driven out. Tasciovanus was the first person to put the name of the town on his coins – gold staters and quarter-staters with a cruciform ornament on the obverse and a horse galloping to the right on the reverse – which are now very rare. His name appears above the horse: TASCIOVAN, and a monogram of CAMV can be seen below the horse's legs. Tasciovanus' triumph seems to have been short-lived and Adde-domaros regained his throne. Twenty years later a son of Tascio-vanus, Cunobelin, appears as king of the whole of the south-eastern region with his capital at Colchester. He struck gold staters with a galloping horse and his name shortened to CVNO on the obverse, and an ear of wheat with the town's name as CAMV on the reverse.

It was against Colchester that the Roman emperor Claudius marched in person at the conquest in AD 43. The various earthwork defences around the town were overrun and some of the dykes and ditches are still a feature of the landscape (notably at **Gosbeck's Farm**, TL 965225, **Bluebottle Grove**, TL 965245, and **Gryme's Dyke** at TL 956267 to TL 965200). Claudius made a new foundation for retired veterans called *Colonia Claudia Victricensis* and it was provided with the usual government offices and a huge temple dedicated to Claudius himself, the living god. His veterans were to rue this. Tacitus tells us in his *Annals*, xiv, 31, how the frightened settlers took refuge in the temple of Claudius seeking to escape the wild vengeance of Boudicca, queen of the Iceni, when she sacked the town in the revolt of AD 60. 'Reliance was placed on the temple's protection. . . . Then a native horde surrounded them. When all else had been ravaged or burnt, the garrison concentrated itself in the temple. After two days' siege, it fell by storm.' The defenders were massacred, as was the in-fantry of the Ninth Legion that attempted a rescue bid. So much for

literary record. In 1919 Dr R. E. M. (later Sir Mortimer) Wheeler
pointed out that the Norman castle at Colchester, the largest Norman
keep in England, was actually built on and around the podium of the
Roman temple of Claudius. Vaults had been found beneath the floor
of the Norman castle in 1683, but not recognized for what they were –
the two great parallel vaults with an off-centre cross wall that formed
the solid base upon which the temple was erected. This podium was
11 ft high and measured 105 × 80 ft with a long flight of steps on the
south side rising up to the entrance colonnade of the temple. Today
the Norman castle houses one of the finest collections of Roman antiquities in the country and it is possible to descend beneath it and walk
through its Roman 'basement'.

Fifty years after the Boudiccan catastrophe walls 2 miles in circumference and with six gates and two posterns were built round the
town, enclosing an area of 102 acres. The main gate on the west, the
Balkerne Gate, survives as one of the most imposing gateways in
Roman Britain. It can be seen partly concealed under the Hole in the
Wall Inn on Balkerne Hill. Good sections of the wall run north from
the inn and beneath it, behind iron railings, the remains of two
arches can be seen from the roadway. On the other side of the narrow
lane is part of the pedestrian footway through the gate with its walls
still standing to about 12 ft. The gate had two main arched carriage-
ways 17 ft wide and a narrower and lower arched passage for pedestrians on either side. It was a truly massive affair with the floor of
its first storey at least 27 ft above the roadway. Much of the circuit
of the walls can still be walked and the tell-tale Roman red bricks are
clearly in evidence in the walls and towers of the city's early churches.

95 The Balkerne Gateway, Colchester, beneath the Hole in the Wall Inn,
with the Roman city wall beyond it

96 The Bartlow Hills Roman barrows with the railway that hacked its way between them before its recent removal

On the other side of the river Deben at **Woodbridge** in Suffolk, on the heathland 100 ft above the river is a group of Anglo-Saxon burial mounds (TM 288487). Here in 1939, when the tallest of the barrows was opened, there was found the greatest and richest archaeological discovery ever made in Britain – the **Sutton Hoo** ship burial. Several of the adjacent mounds had been excavated in the previous year with no great results, but the importance of the ship mound was fortunately realized immediately. Its excavation was a race against time and the excavators left the site only ten days before the outbreak of the Second World War. The site was reopened in 1966–70 and the outline of the long ship revealed again. Much valuable information was gained from the new work, including small elements of jewellery originally found in 1939. Much research has gone into the finds from this site, and it appears that the ship burial was the grave or possibly only the cenotaph of Raedwald, king of East Anglia, who died in AD 624 or 625. The whole of this vast treasure was given to the nation by Mrs E. M. Pretty, the owner of the land upon which the barrows stand. Today it dominates the Early Medieval Room in the British Museum but the barrows still stand on their heath, some no doubt still hiding secrets to be found when they are excavated.

A little to the south of the A604 near Linton in Essex is the village of **Bartlow**. Here is a group of Roman barrows that are still the finest extant in the country despite the depradations they have suffered at the hands of railway engineers and from tunnels being driven into them seeking their contents. Originally there were eight mounds, all with the steep sides typical of Roman barrows; now there are only four left but they are still tall and imposing monuments standing between 20 and 40 ft high. They were tunnelled into in the first

115

half of the nineteenth century and, sadly, most of the burial equipment found in them was destroyed in a fire in 1847. When the railway came it took no note of the barrows' antiquity but went straight through them, destroying as it went and separating the northern one from its three remaining fellows. But the barrows have had the last laugh – they still stand, while the upstart railway was first closed and then the track removed, leaving them in peace once more.

There are few Iron Age hill forts in East Anglia and those that are known are nowhere near as imposing as their contemporaries in the southern counties. They do not command vast areas from imposing heights, but tend to be lowland forts with banks and ditches such as **Ambersbury Banks** (TL 438004) and **Loughton Camp** (TQ 418975), both in Epping Forest. **Wandlebury** hill fort (TL 493534), 5 miles south-east of Cambridge, similarly lies in a wooded area. It is circular, covering about 15 acres, and has two banks and ditches. During the eighteenth century landscaping carried out by Lord Godolphin ruined many of its features, but sections of the banks and the circular outer ditch, quite deep in places, still remain. The fort was originally occupied in the fourth century BC and then was quite extensively refortified late in the first century BC or early in the first century AD, possibly as a reaction on the part of the Iceni tribe of this area against the expansionist plans of the Belgae in Essex.

To the north-east of Cambridge is an extensive series of dykes, the largest of which are **Fleam Dyke** (TL 548540), **Car Dyke** (TL 461713), and the **Devil's Dyke** (TL 567660). They vary in their lengths and all appear to be of Anglo-Saxon date, probably being thrown up as a protective measure by the Saxons who were driven back into East Anglia by the Britons after Arthur's great victory at Mons Badonicus in 499.

Right in the centre of East Anglia at Weeting, Norfolk, is the largest and most famous group of neolithic flint mines in Britain, called **Grimes Graves** (TL 817898). The shafts of many filled-in flint mines show as shallow depressions across an area of about 20 acres of heathland. Flint was an essential part of the Stone Age economy, and a large industry grew up here. Fine quality flint was hewn out of the seams in the chalk with red deer antler picks, many of which have been found in the galleries at the bottom of the deep shafts. Some of the shafts are 30 ft deep and tunnels then radiate out from their base following the rich seams of flint. At the bottom of shaft no. 15, in front of the entrance to one of the tunnels, was found a small chalk 'mother goddess' figurine, $4\frac{1}{4}$ ins high, obviously heavily pregnant and placed on a chalk pedestal. Before her was a heap of blocks of mined flint with seven antlers on top. Her assistance was obviously needed to secure a new shaft with a more plentiful supply of flint. Radio-carbon dates indicate that most of the shafts were being heavily worked during the first half of the fourth millennium BC. The craft of flint knapping did not die out in the area but continued into the present century, supplying flints for flintlock pistols and guns used in Africa and America. Behind the aptly named Flint Knappers Arms in nearby

97 Mining galleries running off from the base of a main shaft
at Grimes Graves
98 A diorama in Norwich Castle Museum showing how the neolithic flint
miners mined the flint with picks made of antler. The dark patches in the
walls are the nodules of flint

Brandon is a huge pile of waster flints giving a good idea of what the
workshop on the surface at Grimes Graves must have looked like as
the mined flint was roughed-out before being transported away.

A mile and a half south of Norwich is one of the most important
neolithic sacred sites in East Anglia at **Arminghall** (TG 240060). Only
a faint depression in the ground and a slight bank remain today, but
this was in its time a most important henge monument of a type similar
to Woodhenge in Wiltshire (p. 90). Within an area 120 ft in diameter
and surrounded by two ditches with a bank between them were eight

99 Despite frequent ploughing the plan of the Roman city within the walls at Caistor St Edmund near Norwich shows clearly in this aerial photograph. The little church in the background stands just inside the east wall, and there are remains of the south gate on the right

oak logs standing upright in a circle 50 ft across. The sanctity of the site is evidenced by the large number of round barrows surrounding it that show up on aerial photographs of the area.

At **Caistor St Edmund** (Caistor-by-Norwich, TG 230035) is the small Roman town of *Venta Icenorum*, covering about 45 acres. It was deliberately founded as a direct result of the revolt of the Iceni under Boudicca in AD 60 and, although the familiar gridiron pattern of streets had been laid out by AD 70, it was another 80 years before stone buildings began taking the place of huts and timber houses within the town. This is almost certainly due to the harsh punitive measures taken against the Iceni to bring them to heel. The interior of the town is farmland and the pattern of the Roman streets and buildings is remarkably clear in aerial photographs. On the ground some sections of the wall can still be seen, especially on the south side. The ever present pieces of red Roman tile and pottery abound in the newly turned furrows, and quite an extensive section of the deep ditch can be seen outside the walls near the little church that stands just within them.

Overlooking the river Waveney inland from Great Yarmouth is another of the four Saxon Shore forts located in East Anglia, **Burgh Castle** (TG 475046). Its Roman name was *Gariannonum* and it is known that a cavalry detachment, the *Equites Stablesiani Garrianonenses* (from what is now Yugoslavia) was stationed there in the late Roman period, about AD 400. The fort was 640 ft long east to west and 300 ft north to south. On the west side, which overlooked the river, the wall has disappeared, but at the foot of the low cliff upon which it stood the stone foundations of a riverside quay have recently been found. The walls on the remaining three sides are quite imposing, rising to 14 or 15 ft, almost their original height. It is still possible to see the junctions where different gangs working on individual sections of the wall met and the bonding courses of red brick running through the sections had to be adjusted.

After the building of the fort walls had begun there was a change in plan: the builders decided to add strong, solid, semicircular bastions. The bastions only begin to be bonded into the walls at about the 8-ft level, indicating that they were an afterthought. They have flat tops and in their centres are circular depressions connected with the mounting of *ballistae*, the Roman catapults that could hurl a stone ball a quarter of a mile. There was a gate in the middle of the east wall, quite narrow and under 12 ft wide, and there must presumably have been some kind of watergate in the now vanished west wall on the river side. A small postern gate beside a bastion on the north wall formed an additional exit. The interior of the fort is under crop and, once more, faint outlines of the interior arrangements can be seen in aerial photographs and also in the crop itself, given the right crop and favourable conditions. After the Roman abandonment of the fort in the early fifth century it lay empty for 200 years until about AD 630 when St Fursa built a monastery within the walls. This survived into the ninth century and then a typical motte and bailey castle was erected in the south-west corner shortly after the Norman Conquest in 1066. This mound was partly removed in the eighteenth century and finally cleared away in 1839.

Rather confusingly there is another Roman site in East Anglia that bears the name of Caister, but with a slight variation in the spelling. This is **Caister-on-Sea**, near Yarmouth (TG 517124), a little town only 1300 × 900 ft beside a small sheltered harbour, founded about AD 125. Its early defences were only a rampart and palisade, but as trade increased and the town prospered it was able to replace this with a substantial flint wall in the middle of the second century. The trade that brought wealth to Caister-on-Sea must have been with the Rhineland, as the town is situated at the shortest crossing point to the mouth of the Rhine. The bulk of the trade was probably in importing glassware, fine pottery and lava millstones. Towards the end of the second century a large house, of a type known as a *mansio*, was built just inside the south gate. Normally such an establishment was provided on a

100 Part of the south wall of
Burgh Castle, looking out
across the river Waveney

101 The late Saxon cathedral at North Elmham. The additions
on the right were made in the fourteenth century when
it was converted into a manor house

main highway for the accommodation of imperial messengers, but
here it seems to have been a seamen's boarding-house. The little town
acquired the other trappings of a self-important municipality and a
forum (market-place) and basilica (town-hall) were built in the centre.
It seems to have been occupied into the fifth century and then reoccupied for some 200 years between the middle of the seventh and ninth
centuries. Rather curiously, amongst the 150-odd burials from the
cemetery outside the south gate there were about a dozen graves that
had been roofed with ship's timbers still with iron nails in them. They
date from the late seventh century and seem almost to be a poor man's
version of the ship burial at Sutton Hoo some 50 years earlier. Today
on the site the foundations of the *mansio* and parts of the town wall
and south gate can be seen.

At **North Elmham** (TF 988216) are the ruins of an early eleventh-
century cathedral, one of the most important buildings of that period
in Britain. The building became 'lost' in later work, notably when
the bishop of Norwich, Henry le Despenser, turned the cathedral into
a fortified house. The site became buried and mistakenly known as
the Castle Hills, and it was not until 1903 that the remains were recognized for what they were – a Saxon cathedral. They became overgrown
again and left for 45 years before they were taken over by the then
Ministry of Works and work began to restore and conserve the site.
Excavations are still in progress. The cathedral is only 130 ft overall
in length; it had a tower at the west end of a long nave, two towers
in front of the transept at the east end (one on either side) and an
apse off the transept. Re-used Roman brick appears amongst the flint
walls, which stand 10 ft high in places. Surrounded by the remains
of a deep moat and bank, it lies mid-way between the vicarage and

102 Warham Camp, a very
symmetrical plateau fort
near the river Stiffkey

St Mary's Church, immediately behind the George and Dragon public
house.

It is in this part of Norfolk that we meet again the old prehistoric
trackway, the **Icknield Way**, which has been steadily making its way
across the countryside past many a hill fort since we last mentioned
it on Therfield Heath (p. 27). When it reaches Castle Acre it bears
off to the north-west to finish at Castle Rising. From Castle Acre there
is a continuation of it as a Roman road called the **Peddars' Way**. It
makes its way towards the Wash and a pleasant stretch for walking
from Fring (TF 727356) to near Castle Acre (TF 817154) gives a good
impression of the Roman road with a well-preserved *agger* (a bank
at the side of the road) heading purposefully on its way. Evidence of
its earlier ancestry can be seen from time to time in the Bronze Age
round-barrows that lie close by in situations more familiar from Dorset and Wiltshire.

Right in the north of Norfolk are two Iron Age hill forts probably
built by the Iceni in face of the threat from the south by the expansionist Belgae. **Holkham Camp** (TF 875447) is a rather poor fort with
a single rampart and ditch, but **Warham Camp** (TF 944409) is a
much stronger affair. It is a plateau fort, not commanding any outstanding area such as its Sussex colleagues, but quite strong for all that.
Almost circular, its double banks and ditches enclose $3\frac{1}{2}$ acres in a
very symmetrical fashion. The entrance was probably on the south-
west by the river Stiffkey beside which it stands. Numerous other
breaks in the defences are not original entrances but the result of landscaping in the eighteenth century and tree removal in the nineteenth.

5 The Midlands

In defining geographical areas problems always arise as to what are their exact delineations. So often modern boundaries, be they internal or external, impose a false division merely to accommodate bureaucratic whims. When dealing with an area which knew no boundaries as such, and which changed its emphasis of settlement pattern over long periods, the problem is multiplied many times over. It is therefore difficult to decide what should be included in a survey of sites in the Midlands. This area in the middle of England saw many different kinds of occupation and people throughout its long history – their personal advancement in knowledge and the land itself often dictated the pattern of their settlement. Thus we find heavy neolithic concentration in the Lincolnshire Wolds, Bronze Age remains in the higher lands of Derbyshire, and Iron Age ones in the lower land to the west in Lancashire and Cheshire. Under the Romans this area was the boundary between the lowland settled zone in the south and the highland military zone. Therefore in this chapter the Midlands are interpreted in their literal sense of 'the middle lands', in other words the region from north Oxfordshire to the area of Hadrian's Wall, a manmade but convenient line of demarcation, and from East Anglia on the east across to Offa's Dyke on the west.

The chalk lands of the Lincolnshire Wolds looking out across the North Sea north of the Wash appear to have been an area favoured by neolithic man. He was able to support himself on the flora and fauna of the area without too much trouble, and the characteristic monument that is found in this area is the neolithic long barrow. Little is known about their contents in this part of Britain as few examples have been excavated.

Two miles north-east of Partney and close to Skendleby are the **Giants Hills** (TF 429712). One of the two barrows here has been scientifically excavated. It is 200 ft long and has a 'saddle' in the middle with each end rising to about 5 ft in height; side ditches remain at either end. Evidence from the excavation indicated that a long wooden enclosure, 189 × 37 ft, had first been erected and some 70 ft inside from the eastern end a platform of chalk blocks had been put up. On this platform had been placed the corpses of at least eight people and the long barrow was subsequently built over it. The finds, including pottery, indicated that the barrow had been built around 2000 BC, and probably much the same date applies to the other Lincolnshire long barrows. A second barrow, ploughed almost flat, lies 250 yards away to the south of the main barrow.

At the aptly named **Deadmen's Graves** (TF 444720), 3 miles north-east of Partney between Horncastle and Skegness, are two long barrows. They lie about 400 yards apart but are very similar in their dimensions: one is 160 ft long, 54 ft wide and 6 ft high, the other is 173 ft long, 60 ft wide and 6 ft high. In both cases the mounds are higher at their eastern ends where the chamber to take the multiple burials normal in such a barrow would be located. Both barrows have been damaged over the years, and there are no signs now of the side ditches that once surrounded them. Another similar long barrow not far away is the **Spellow Hills** barrow (TF 402723), nearly 3 miles north-west of Partney. It is still quite substantial – 182 ft long, 40 ft wide and 7 ft high – but, like its contemporaries at Deadmen's Graves, it has suffered much damage. Its length is twice cut through so that it gives a misleading impression of being three round barrows. Not far north of the Spellow Hills is the **Beacon Plantation** long barrow (TF 373777), to the west of Alford. This barrow, again much damaged, is still very impressive: 257 ft long, 64 ft wide and 7 ft high at its north-east end which covers the burial chamber. The **Bully Hill** barrows (TF 330827) to the north of this neolithic grouping, and 3 miles south of Louth, are a cemetery of Bronze Age bowl-barrows which stand out in the flat Lincolnshire landscape. They stand in a line, six close together and the seventh at a slight distance, ranging in height from 4 to 10 ft, impressive sentinels against the skyline.

The Romans were here at **Horncastle** (TF 258696) where a part of the town wall remains, but the main presence was at **Lincoln,** the legionary fortress of *Colonia Lindum* (SK 977718). Like so many other major Roman towns in Britain the original surveyors chose the site well and it has continued in use right up to the present day. Its Roman history has to be pieced together, jigsaw fashion, from tantalizing and sporadic finds over the years. Evidence shows that the original *colonia* was about 43 acres, and so similar in plan and size to the *colonia* at Gloucester (*Glevum*) that they were both probably laid out by the same Roman public works contractor. In the second century Lincoln expanded to 97 acres. The town had a good water supply brought from a distance by an aqueduct, as it stood on a hilltop and wells would have needed to be very deep indeed to reach the water table. The Lincoln aqueduct is the best example found in Roman Britain: it was a triumph of mechanical skill which carried the water on piers 8 ft above the ground, then underground and then up to 10 ft again to build up the pressure needed to force it into the reservoir at the *colonia*. Pieces of the piping are still found when excavating the foundations for new buildings, and part of the aqueduct's

103 The Newport Arch, Lincoln, the only Roman gateway
in Britain still in use

embankment can be seen outside the town running from the nearby
hills and the water source, a stream called Roaring Meg 1¼ miles away.

Several long stretches of Lincoln's Roman walls remain; in front
of the Eastgate Hotel by the cathedral is a semicircular bastion from
the north side of the east gate. The most substantial portion of Roman
Lincoln to be seen is one of its gates, known as the Newport Arch.
It is a single-span arch, quite simple, with a smaller passageway for
pedestrians beside it. It has the doubtful distinction of having modern
traffic passing beneath it; in 1964 a lorry got itself jammed beneath
it and caused a certain amount of damage. Fortunately it was possible
to extract the lorry and reconstruct the Arch. Further stretches of the
wall are preserved in the Bishop's Palace garden and also in Orchard
Street, together with the west gate.

Moving more to the centre of our area, and of England, the next
site is Leicester. Little is to be seen at the intermediate small Roman
towns of **Ancaster** (SK 984435), **Great Casterton** (TF 001901), or
Water Newton (TL 121969) except faint traces of their defences. Air
photographs taken in the right conditions can tell us a lot about the
street plans and buildings of such sites.

Leicester (SK 585046) was the tribal capital of the Coritani, hence
its Roman name *Ratae Coritanorum*. The most substantial visible
remains of Roman Leicester are beside St Nicholas' Church. Here
an immense piece of Roman wall rises, known as the Jewry Wall site.
It formed part of a large public building which has at times been described as a basilica on the east side of a forum, or a public bath. The
latter is the truer explanation and remains can still be seen of the great
halls of the building and of the hypocaust system that heated the rooms
to the required temperatures. The whole area is clearly laid out for
inspection and in the adjacent museum is a modern display of material
showing the archaeological history of Leicester. Several fine mosaics

have been found in the city over the years; several remain *in situ* (a good geometric pavement under the railway arches in Bath Lane), and others are exhibited in the Jewry Wall Museum. Notable are the Peacock pavement, so named from the fine bird, with its tail spread, depicted in the centre octagonal panel; the Blackfriars pavement of nine octagonal panels with geometric ornament; and the Cyparissus pavement, again an octagonal panel showing the youth Cyparissus with his arms about a stag and cupid aiming an arrow at them.

South-west of Leicester and on the east side of Birmingham is a concentration of six Iron Age hill forts: **Oldbury Camp** (SP 313947), **Burrow Hill** (SP 304851), **Wappenbury** (SP 376693), **Oakley Wood Camp** (SP 306592), **Beausale Camp** (SP 246701), and **Berry Ring** (SP 096778). Common to their type, they all command the areas around them, vary in size from about 3 to 11 acres, have single bank and ditch defences, and range in date roughly from the third century BC to the first century AD.

Right in the centre of this concentration, just outside Coventry on the A45, is **The Lunt**, Baginton (SP 345752). This is the site of a small Roman fort which has been the scene of very interesting archaeological excavations and experiments in recent years. The fort was long suspected to be in the area, but was only discovered in 1960. It is one of the early Roman forts constructed in Britain along the initial frontier of the Fosse Way. Excavation indicated that it had only been occupied between about AD 60 and 75. The area of the fort was on land scheduled by Coventry Corporation as a recreational area and the Corporation allowed the archaeological experiment of rebuilding the turf rampart and subsequently the main eastern gateway to be undertaken. Fifty-foot lengths of the turf rampart on either side of the gateway were reconstructed and, with the interested aid of soldiers from the local Royal Engineers Depot, the gateway was erected in just two days using only equipment that would have been available to the Roman army engineers. The result is an imposing double-leaved gate with a walkway over it, a tower fighting platform above that, and a palisade stretching away from it on either side on top of the turf ramparts. Main timbers for the gate were slotted into the original holes left by the Roman timbers and the whole is a highly accurate reconstruction of an early wooden-built fort, making The Lunt one of the most impressive and instructive Roman sites in the country. A barrack block building which housed 80 men, a century, has also been reconstructed along similar lines to house finds from the site. Where The Lunt stands apart from other similar forts of the period is in its unusual non-rectangular shape; the reason for this peculiarity is a large circular area on the east side, 105 ft in diameter, within the rampart. It seems to have had a palisade surrounding it and the interior had been levelled off. Exactly what purpose this curious structure served is not known; it is an arena of some sort and could well have been used as a training area for cavalrymen or schooling cavalry remounts, a *gyrus*, as mentioned in Xenophon's treatise on horsemanship. Excavations are still proceeding and it is hoped that they will provide even more useful and interesting information about the fort and its occupation at a period where our knowledge is sparse.

The principal Roman road in Britain was **Watling Street**, running from London (*Londinium*) to Wroxeter (*Viroconium*) just outside Shrewsbury. As an important road along which imperial messengers would travel at speed posting stations had to be provided rather as we find on the great coaching roads of the eighteenth century. Some stations would only be large enough to provide a change of horses, while other larger ones would also offer suitable overnight accommodation in a specially built hostel called a *mansio*. One of the posting stations in the Midlands about which we know something is the little Romano–British town at **Wall**, Staffordshire, whose Roman name was *Letocetum* (SK 098066). It lies on the modern A5 (which itself closely follows in many places the Roman Watling Street), 2 miles south-west of Lichfield and 14 miles north of Birmingham. Smaller stations merely for changing horses (*mutationes*) lay to the east at **Mancetter** and the west at **Penkridge**, 12 and 15 miles distant respectively.

The interesting aspect of the site at Wall is that, judging from sporadic finds over the years, it was the garrison fort of the Fourteenth Legion before it was transferred to Wroxeter *c*. AD 58. The town eventually spread over 20–30 acres and was obviously a prosperous little place, situated as it was on a main arterial road. Most of the remains

104 The Roman fort at The Lunt, near Coventry, where one of the most dramatic reconstructions following the archaeological record to be carried out in recent years was performed in 1970 by men of the Royal Engineers

105 A fine example of a Roman bath-house suite and its
hypocaust at Wall, Staffordshire

reported by antiquaries such as William Stukeley in the eighteenth
century have now disappeared, but excavations in this century have
produced interesting results. What were almost certainly the remains
of the *mansio*, the imperial posting hostel, were found in 1912–14, but
are now filled in. At the same time a bath-house was excavated and
has since been consolidated on the site. The bath-house went through
three principal phases of building, and what is seen today largely
represents the last phase. It is quite a complex structure, reflecting
the Roman love of bathing as a social function not to be entered into
lightly. A whole sequence of rooms conducted the bather through
varying degrees of temperature, ranging from hot, dry, or very hot,
humid rooms down to cold water plunge baths. The necessary heat
was conducted through hot air ducts from hypocausts beneath the
floors – an early form of ducted central heating. This sequence of
rooms and baths is very well preserved at Wall, and the bath-house
complex is one of the most complete to be seen in Britain. The site
museum contains material from a small Roman farmstead excavated
nearby at Shenstone, as well as material from Wall.

Between Wall and Wroxeter, towards which Watling Street runs,
is the major Iron Age hill fort of **The Wrekin** (SJ 630082), 4 miles
to the east of Wroxeter. It commands extensive views of the surrounding countryside and is steeped in local Shropshire legend. Probably
it was the tribal capital of the Cornovii who were later resettled at
Wroxeter, whose full Roman name is in fact *Viroconium Cornoviorum*.
The fort spreads along the crest of the hill and covers a total of just
over 10 acres, but the central strongpoint area is only 7 acres. This
central part was defended by a main rampart accentuated by the hillside below it having been cut to steepen it artificially. There were entrances at the east and west ends: the eastern one had additional protective banks and ditches, while the western one relied more on the

129

steep slope of the hill for protection. The fort was first built about 200 BC and subsequently underwent various modifications: some of the later dry stone walling appears rather hurried and shoddy – possibly the result of the need for rapid reorganization in the face of the Roman advance. The low mound at the south-west end of the fort is the remains of a Bronze Age round-barrow built some 1300 years before the fort.

At **Wroxeter**, *Viroconium* (SJ 565087), was established the garrison town of the Fourteenth Legion in *c.* AD 58. The legion had been moved up from Wall to assist with operations being conducted against the unruly Welsh tribes. About 30 years later the military presence, now represented by the Twentieth Legion (the Fourteenth having been withdrawn from Britain in AD 69), fell back to the new legionary headquarters at Chester (*Deva*). Wroxeter came under civil jurisdiction, being the tribal centre of the Cornovii, but it managed to maintain itself and expand on the firm basis of its having been a legionary garrison town for 30 years. It is larger and richer than other comparable tribal capitals and civic pride was represented in the large forum and baths. Information about the legionary town is gradually coming to light from excavations at times 10–12 ft below the present building remains. Much of the history of the early town is gleaned from the inscriptions on legionary tombstones found locally indicating the units involved, and which can be seen in Rowley's House Museum in Shrewsbury, 5 miles away. The most imposing part of the site today is the huge section of wall that was the entrance to the baths from the exercise hall (*palaestra*). This wall has been a feature of the site for centuries, but excavations have now revealed its situation within the plan of the whole complex. Wroxeter is the subject of a planned excavation programme over many years by Birmingham University, and gradually as each excavating season passes the amount of information about the site grows. The bath complex must have been one of the most imposing in Britain – its basilican aisled *palaestra* was 240 ft long and 65 ft wide. From here double doors led from the south side of the *palaestra* into the bath-house itself, in other words through the great gap in the present standing wall, into the cold room (*frigidarium*). Cold plunge baths followed, then dry heat followed by hot, humid heat of varying degrees. The foundations of many of these rooms around the great wall can be seen.

North of the wall, on the other side of the road and beneath some trees, is a length of the colonnade of the forum. The city seems to have been gradually abandoned in the fifth and sixth centuries and was used as a convenient quarry for stone in the Middle Ages. Today a certain amount of the Roman city is under the modern village but much more is still under the surrounding fields and shows up remarkably well in aerial photographs. The site museum contains many of these photographs clearly showing the plans of Roman streets and houses, along with actual material from the site.

About 20 miles from Wroxeter, just off the A488 from Shrewsbury before it joins the A489, are two Bronze Age stone circles; one, **Hem-**

106 View across the *palaestra* (exercise hall) at Wroxeter

ford (SO 324999) is 5½ miles north of Lydham and the other, **Mitchell's Fold** (SO 304983), is 5 miles north-west of Lydham. Hemford is a circle of 65 ft in diameter, set in low marshy ground. A lot of its stones have disappeared into the peat bog but at least 37 have survived and one of them is unusually placed in the centre of the circle. This stone is the tallest of the survivors, about 2 ft 6 ins. Mitchell's Fold is a much better placed circle, high up on the mountainside commanding a fine view to the west towards Wales. The circle is about 10 ft wider in diameter than Hemford – about 75 ft – but only 16 stones can be seen and these vary in height from 2 to 6 ft. As at Hemford, the stones are all natural and unworked.

Near this circle, to the south, is an interesting prehistoric 'industrial' site – the axe factory at **Cwm Mawr** (SO 304951). There are several such axe factories known in Britain, all sites that produced stone of high quality which was much esteemed and traded widely. The blanks of the axes were roughed out at the factory – and discards and other debris can still be found in the area – and then traded over quite long distances. By petrological examination of thin slices taken from the stone axes it is possible to ascribe them to individual factories, always assuming that the original outcrop and factory site are known. Study of the distribution of axes found away from their source gives us much useful information about trade in the Bronze Age and its influence on society at that time.

South of Mitchell's Fold there are at least 20 Iron Age hill forts

107 Mitchell's Fold stone circle has a magnificent setting looking out towards Wales

extending as far as the Herefordshire Beacon. Almost every river valley and open stretch of land going down through Shropshire into
Herefordshire is overlooked by a fort perched high on its hill. It would
be tedious and unnecessary to describe them all, since they only vary
in their internal size and combinations of banks and ditches.
A glance at the Ordnance Survey maps covering the National Grid
sj and so reveals them clearly, and the associated contours force home
the realization of how inaccessible the majority are even nowadays,
so how much more impregnable they must have been in the Iron Age.

Moving north from Mitchell's Fold there are fewer Iron Age hill
forts as one moves from Shropshire into Staffordshire. **The Berth**
(sj 788391), 8 miles north-west of Market Drayton, covers about 9
acres with a ditch and two banks, and **Bury Walls** (sj 576275) is
located east of Wem. Both date from the last centuries BC. (Old
Oswestry, to the west of these last named sites, is dealt with in the
next chapter, on p. 172.)

A fine example of a promontory fort in south Cheshire is **Maiden
Castle** (sj 498529) on Bickerton Hill. It has double ramparts except
on the north-west side where the sheer sides of the hill, artificially
steepened by scraping, protect it. The inner rampart was built of stone
which had great baulks of timber built into it, lacing the stone together.
This form of building with criss-cross timber lacing within a stone
wall is known as *murus gallicus*, as it is common on the Continent.
Many of these forts revealed on excavation that the timbers had been
fired and, burning fiercely, had vitrified the stone walls. It was thought
at one time that this might have been done deliberately to strengthen
the walls by making them into a fused mass, but the explanation now
more commonly accepted is that the burning was the result of an
enemy attack or accidental fire. The fort is small, only an acre and
a half, with an entrance through the ramparts 120 ft from their northern end. Starting at 16 ft wide, the entrance narrowed to half that
over a passageway 50 ft long. Its surface was cobbled and the wheel
ruts of traffic passing through it were found. This arrangement of the
entrance would have made it an extremely difficult gate to force in
time of attack.

At **Chester** (sj 405663), the Roman *Deva*, was the garrison of the
Twentieth Legion which was moved there from Wroxeter *c*. AD 88.
In 40 years it acted as watchdog in each of the three great legionary
fortresses facing the Welsh hill tribes; at Gloucester (*Glevum*) AD 48–
67, Wroxeter (*Viroconium*) AD 67–*c*. 88, and then at Chester. A
detachment also served at Inchtuthil in Perthshire *c*. AD 84–8. Despite all the knowledge we have of troop movements to and from *Deva*,
as with so many Roman cities that became prosperous in later medieval
times we only have sporadic finds from the Roman levels of the 60-
acre fortress appearing, as buildings that fell were quickly replaced.
The best view of Roman Chester is to be had from the collections
in the excellent Grosvenor Museum with its special emphasis on the
Roman army. Recent excavations have revealed the remains of the
amphitheatre which could accommodate about 8000 spectators. Only

half of the northern section can be seen because buildings still cover the rest, but outside Newgate are preserved the curve of the amphitheatre wall, the east entrance and a small shrine to the goddess of fate, Nemesis. Part of the Roman quay now stands overlooking the racecourse, itself set in the place from which Roman galleys once set sail to patrol the North Wales coast and keep a lookout for raiders from across the Irish Sea.

One of the best Iron Age hill forts to the north-east of Chester is **Castle Ditches** (SJ 553694). This fort had a long history, starting life about 600 BC. Its ultimate shape is a long oval with double banks and ditches enclosing 11 acres – a long way from the original simple wooden palisade. It was strengthened early in the first century BC when a second entrance was added on the north-west (the first was on the east side, approached by a hollow way). Dry stone walling with some timber was used but it was not of the true *murus gallicus* type; however all this was in vain as the fort was dismantled by men of the Twentieth Legion from Chester 10 miles away.

Moving more to the east into central England, Staffordshire merges into Derbyshire and the Peak District. In such a region it is to be expected that prehistoric man would find suitable caves for occupation – no doubt after he had first dispossessed any wild animals inhabiting them. At **Thor's Cave** (SK 099549), north-west of Ashbourne, a huge gash in the hillside overlooking the river Manifold is the cave entrance. This faces north-west, while a second, smaller and narrower entrance faces west. The interior of the cave contains several branching tunnels, and domestic refuse indicated that the cave had been lived in over a period of about 500 years from the second century BC into the third century AD. Obviously Romano–Britons appreciated a dry, warm cave as much as their forebears.

In quite a small area of the Peak District to the south of Bakewell are found some of the most important sites of the neolithic and Bronze Ages in the Midlands. On Harthill Moor (SK 225625) is the **Nine Stones** circle, of which only four stones remain, all upright. The circle was probably about 45 ft in diameter and its stones the largest uprights in Derbyshire; that on the south is 7 ft high and has another 4 ft 6 ins below ground level. Another moor north-east of Harthill, **Stanton Moor** (SK 247634), has an enormous concentration of Bronze Age monuments within an area of some 150 acres. There are at least 70 cairns, burial mounds, stone circles and a standing stone. The whole area must have been considered highly sacred by Bronze Age people in the locality to warrant so many monuments. **Doll Tor** (SK 238628) is a circle of four upright stones and two fallen ones joined by a ring of smaller stones. In cairns associated with it were found cremated remains and collared urns. Three-quarters of a mile away across the moor to the north-east is another stone circle, the **Nine Ladies** (SK 249635). Its stones, which are only 2–3 ft high, form a circle 33 ft in diameter. There is a slight mound in the centre and a low surrounding bank outside. A few yards south-west of the circle is an upright standing stone called the King Stone. This feature is found in many stone circles in Britain (cf. the King Stone, part of the Rollright Stones, p. 74). The moor between the two circles holds a very heavy concentration of cairns and mounds with diameters of up to 30 ft, and often standing between 2 and 3 ft high. Not all the mounds have been investigated, but those that have have produced a fine collection of interesting grave goods including collared urns, incense cups, flint and bronze knives, battle axes, and faience beads. Most of the excavations were carried out by members of the Heathcote family of Birchover and the finds are preserved in their private museum, but can be seen by appointment.

At **Arbor Low** (SK 161636), 5 miles south-west of Bakewell and 9 miles south-east of Buxton, is the foremost prehistoric monument of the Peak District. Often referred to as the Stonehenge of Derbyshire, it is a Bronze Age henge monument of classic type – a stone circle surrounded by a ditch and a bank on the outer side. The remoteness of its position has no doubt helped to preserve it from the ravages of man. It was first recorded in 1761 and various excavations have taken place since then. Within a circular bank of 250 ft diameter is an internal ditch about 5 ft deep around an earth plateau 160 ft in diameter. On this central plateau is a circle of stones, all of which are

108 The classic plan of a Bronze Age henge monument, an outer bank and an inner ditch surrounding a central plateau with a stone circle on it, is easily recognized at Arbor Low (cf. Illus. 62). Impinging on the bank is a later Bronze Age round barrow

now recumbent; presumably they did stand upright at one time, although there is no record of any of them having been seen thus except that of a local man, William Normanshaw, who told the antiquary the Revd Samuel Pegge that he remembered some of them standing in the early eighteenth century. Curiously enough, when excavations were carried out with the express intention of answering this question, no sockets were found into which the stones could be slotted – if they did at one time stand they were presumably held upright by blocking stones. In the centre of the circle are four stones, two large and two smaller ones, which probably formed a U-shaped setting such as those at Avebury and Stanton Drew. It is known as a cove, and a skeleton was found just to the east of it. The largest stone of the group is one of the central pieces which is 14 ft long; another in the circle itself is 13 ft long and 6 ft wide. The monument comprises a total of 56 stones. It has two entrances through the bank and ditch on the north and south. A round barrow of later date than the monument, and partly built of material taken from the bank, impinges on the south-east side of the south entrance. South-west of Arbor Low, about 350 yards away, is a large Bronze Age round barrow which still stands 15 ft high. It is called **Gib Hill,** its name apparently originating from the gibbet upon which a murderer was hanged in the early eighteenth century near the scene of his crime.

The largest hill fort in Derbyshire is **Mam Tor** (SK 128837); it is 16 acres in extent with a double bank and ditch that encloses within its circuit two Bronze Age round barrows at the south-west corner. They antedate the fort by about 1400 years.

Beyond Manchester to the north-east can be found the remains of the Roman road that ran from Manchester to Ilkley over **Blackstone Edge** (SD 973170 to SD 988184). It is one of the best-preserved sections of Roman road in Britain and quite an awe-inspiring sight, a tribute to Roman engineering, as it climbs up over the steep edge above Littleborough. Its surface is 16 ft wide and composed of large kerbstone blocks. Down the centre runs a shallow trough which was filled with turf so as to give some purchase to the hooves of horses pulling heavy carts up the hillside.

As the Roman road headed off towards Ilkley another minor road struck off for the fort at **Ribchester**, *Bremetennacum Veteranorum* (SD 650350). This was a small cavalry fort (590 × 450 ft) in the territory of the Brigantes tribe. When a group of Sarmatian cavalry veterans were given land to settle here on their retirement about AD 200 it was Brigantan land taken from the tribe. The excavated area beside the museum reveals part of the granaries, the north wall and gateway of the fort. The museum contains finds from the site but the most outstanding piece from here, found in the eighteenth century, is the Ribchester helmet now in the British Museum. It is a cavalryman's parade helmet made of thin bronze ornamented in relief with figures of cavalrymen and infantry in action. The visor mask is decorated with a relief representing a city wall with turrets above the forehead. Such a helmet could only have been used as a showpiece – similar parade helmets

109 The paved Roman road
running over Blackstone Edge

have been found in Norfolk (now in the Norwich Castle Museum)
and on the Continent at Straubing in Bavaria. They must have been
highly treasured possessions.

Across the other side of the Pennines at **York** (SE 603523) was the
legionary fortress of *Eburacum*, where the Ninth Legion was stationed
from AD 71 to *c*. 120, and the Sixth Legion after *c*. AD 120. Once again
occupation of the site has continued without a break into modern
times. As the Royal Commission said in its 'Report to the Queen's
Most Excellent Majesty' in 1961 – 'The visible monuments surviving
in situ are all fragmentary; many others have been excavated at some
time, by chance or design, and then covered, if not destroyed, and
the only evidences of them surviving for our use are written records
and surveys, varying greatly in competence and accuracy.' Despite
these problems the Royal Commission's first volume in its York series
is devoted entirely to Roman York.

York was very important in the administration of Roman Britain. When the province was divided into military and civil areas York became the capital of *Britannia Inferior* – Lower Britain, because that area was further away from Rome. The fortress expanded to cover an area of 50 acres, and a considerable civil settlement, a *vicus*, grew up outside the walls. The most prominent surviving parts of the fortress are its walls dating from the second to fourth centuries AD. They are still standing and visible at the east, west and south angles – the most important sections being the Multangular Tower and the east angle tower. The Multangular at the west angle is actually in the Yorkshire Museum gardens. It is mainly fourth-century work and is a projecting polygonal tower designed as a regular 14-sided figure with four sides omitted where the curve of the fortress wall joins it. Its interior diameter is 35 ft, and it still stands 35 ft high. Part of the military bath-house of the legionary fortress is preserved in the cellars of the

110 Exterior of the Multangular Tower, York

Roman Bath Inn (formerly the Mail Coach Inn) in St Sampson's Square. The bases of the *pilae* (piers) of a hypocaust can be seen through a glass panel in the saloon bar. They were supports under the floor of an apsidal room.

These rather meagre remains, together with a little Roman walling in the church of St Mary Bishophill Senior, were, until recently, all that existed of the fortress. However during the latest excavations archaeologists were astounded suddenly to discover the system of sewers that ran beneath the fortress in the area of Swinegate and Church Street. There are long sections, in good order, of well-built, narrow, low tunnels and it is possible to walk through some of them, bending double for much of the way. Because of the restricted entry to the sewers and the lack of space once underground they are not open generally to the public, but only to small parties on application.

Excavations in recent years by the York Archaeological Trust under the direction of Peter Addyman have revealed many more details about the Roman and medieval city. Under the Minster itself, in the Undercroft, there can now be seen preserved large sections of the walls of buildings within the legionary fortress and a magnificent expanse of brightly coloured Roman painted wall plaster. It is not often that Roman walls can be inspected rising neatly labelled from carpeted floors! The *principia* of the fortress lay askew to the plan of the later Minster and its remains are mixed with the walls and foundations of the Norman building. Elsewhere in the city some of the newly discovered remains will be preserved, such as the massive tower foundations near to the Multangular Tower on a new hotel site.

In the eighteenth century the remains of several practice camps could still be seen outside the fortress walls. It is easy to imagine a section of recruits being marched out from the garrison on exercise

111 Section of the recently discovered sewer system which runs beneath the Roman fortress at York

to throw up the rectangular defences of a temporary camp. Two can still be made out on the York to Helmsley Road (B1363), in the fields close to York airport. One is 88 × 145 yards, the other 133 × 75 yards, and ramparts up to 20 ins high can still be made out in the grass. A number of these practice camps have been found by air photography to the north of Hadrian's Wall – obviously a good place for army manoeuvres and training recruits.

Fifteen miles north-west of York near Boroughbridge at **Aldborough** is the Roman town of *Isurium Brigantium* (SE 405665) –

112 Part of the wall and an internal turret in the south-west corner of the Roman town at Aldborough
113 The Devil's Arrows, three Bronze Age standing stones at Boroughbridge

Isurium of the Brigantes, the tribe that lived in Yorkshire, Lancashire and the counties towards Hadrian's Wall. The town was quite small, about 55 acres, with a gate in the centre of each wall facing the cardinal points. Parts of the town wall and its turrets survive on the south-west side. Over the last 200 years parts of buildings have come to light, but the most interesting aspect of the town is the large number of mosaic pavements which are known to have existed there. Some were reburied after their discovery, while others have been destroyed, but two can still be seen *in situ*. They were part of a large town house found in 1832: one has a damaged scene of an animal sitting under a tree as a central motif set within borders of rope and guilloche decoration; the other, in almost perfect condition, has a multi-pointed star at its centre and guilloche and Greek key pattern borders. These are not in the museum on the site but in the more convivial surroundings of the local inn, the Aldborough Arms. In the Leeds City Museum is a section from another Aldborough mosaic pavement which shows the twins Romulus and Remus being suckled by the she-wolf – a scene unique amongst Romano–British pavements.

Close to Aldborough at Boroughbridge are three Bronze Age standing stones known as the **Devil's Arrows** (SE 391666). They stand almost in a north–south line at intervals of 200, 300 and 70 ft apart. The northern stone is 18 ft high and the other two 22 ft, which makes them taller than the uprights at Stonehenge, but just short of the Rudston Stone (p. 144). They are made of millstone grit and were quarried at Knaresborough which is over 6 miles away to the south-west. Blocks of this size must have presented great problems not only of transport but also in their initial cutting; the grooving seen on their tops and sides today is due to weathering.

A number of Bronze Age monuments can be found in this part of the moors and to the north of Ripon, which indicates that it was considered a very sacred area. Here, in an area 7 miles long, six sacred sites were constructed which attracted 28 round-barrows around them. There are three circles at Thornbrough and a circle each at Hutton Moor, Cana and Nunwick. The most impressive monuments of the group are the three **Thornbrough** henges. Each is about 800 ft in diameter; the northern one is the best preserved because of its trees – the other two, in open ground, have been damaged by ploughing. All the circles have the usual ditch on the inside of the bank which is a feature of henge monuments, and there is another ditch on the outside with entrances on the north-west and south-east. This is the direction in which all three circles are aligned lying about a half mile apart (SE 281801, SE 285795 and SE 289789). The longstanding sanctity of the site was demonstrated by aerial photography which showed an earlier cursus a mile in length that passes beneath the centre circle orientated north-east/south-west. The cursus belongs to the late Stone Age and is of a type known from several sites in Britain. On **Hutton Moor** (SE 353735) and at **Cana** (SE 361718) are two more circles – though less impressive because of plough damage, they are nevertheless part of this whole Bronze Age religious complex. A third circle at **Nunwick** (SE 323747) was first noticed by air photography and can still be traced on the ground. All these three circles are similar to the Thornbrough group in design except that here their entrances are orientated differently, being north and south.

Returning to the coastal area around Bridlington and Flamborough Head popular fancy has ascribed two Iron Age sites to the Danes. **Danes' Graves** (TA 018633), south-west of Bridlington, is a barrow cemetery of the mid-third century BC. There are over 200 round barrows here which are the remnants of a once much larger cemetery. The people buried under the mounds appear to have emigrated from northern France to the Yorkshire Wolds and brought the burial customs of their homeland with them. The barrows vary in size from 10 to 30 ft across and tend to be rather low, under 4 ft in height. Most of the dead were humble people crouched in an oblong grave beneath the mound and accompanied by a food offering, such as a joint of meat, and some everyday items – pins, brooches, beads, etc. One burial, however, was far richer. It contained the bodies of two men with their two-wheeled chariot and all its metal parts. The harness and snaffle bits of the horses had also been buried, but not, apparently, the horses themselves, probably because they were too valuable to kill.

The other site with 'Danes' in its name is at Flamborough Head. The headland is cut across by a massive bank and ditch and a counter-scarp ditch called **Danes' Dyke** (TA 216694), which isolates about 5 square miles of the headland as the Dyke runs from sea to sea. The bank is still 18 ft high in places and the ditch in front of it 60 ft wide, creating a formidable obstacle. The site probably dates from the first century BC and so, like the Graves, has nothing at all to do with the Danes as both precede them by several centuries.

Midway between the Danes' Graves and Dyke is **Rudston** (TA 097677) on the B1253. The usual memorials found in a churchyard are here dwarfed by the standing stone rising proudly in their midst. Composed of gritstone brought at least 10 miles from the nearest outcrop to the north at Cayton Bay, it is the largest monolith in Britain – 25 ft 6 ins high, 6 ft wide and 2 ft 3 ins thick. It is just one more illustration of the amount of labour that the Bronze Age people of the Yorkshire area were prepared to expend on their religious sites.

The Roman presence appears sporadically up the east side of the Pennines in Yorkshire; there was a signal station at **Scarborough** (TA 052892) with remains of fourth-century walls on the cliff near the castle; a series of practice camps in the area of **Cawthorn** (SE 784900), and just north of here a fine stretch of Roman road. Mistakenly dubbed **Wade's Causeway**, the Roman road runs for about a mile and a half over Wheeldale Moor towards Goathland, near Whitby (SE 793938 to SE 812988). It is 16 ft wide, with a kerbstone keeping the central paved slabs in position, and culverts and gutters for drainage. Although this stretch is located in a Roman military training area, exactly where it comes from or where it is heading is not known.

At **Stanwick** (NZ 180115), south-west of **Piercebridge** (itself a Roman fort) is one of the largest Iron Age fortified areas in Britain.

114 In the churchyard at Rudston amongst the graves stands the tallest monolith in Britain

115 Wade's Causeway, a paved Roman road running across Wheeldale Moor

It was built in three phases, each larger than the previous one, until in its final form it had grown to enclose about 850 acres. Its earliest phase, at the beginning of the first century AD, was a hill fort of 17 acres; about AD 50–60 another 130 acres was added and then about AD 72 a final 600 acres. Such an undertaking does not come about by chance, and the history of the site as elucidated by Sir Mortimer Wheeler's excavations in the early 1950s marks Stanwick as the rallying point of the Brigantes. For once historical characters can be set on a British archaeological 'stage'. Venutius and Cartimandua were king and queen of the Brigantes; he was anti-Roman and she pro-Roman, and the tribe divided between them in support. In AD 51 Caractacus, son of Cunobelin, asked Cartimandua for her protection – she handed him over to the Romans in chains. Now, or possibly in AD 57, Venutius broke with his queen and entrenched himself at Stanwick while Cartimandua courted the Roman might. In the turmoil following Nero's suicide in AD 68 ('the year of the four emperors') Venutius attacked his queen with such success that Rome had to rescue her. His action enhanced his prestige and cause, more men turned to him, and Stanwick had to be enlarged. It seems that some time before these last fortifications were finished between AD 71 and 74 the Ninth Legion marched north from York to the attack. Once this stronghold had fallen the way was clear for increased Roman influence in the north. Looking at the vast circuit of Stanwick, despite its deep ditches and stone-revetted defences it seems an impossible task to hold so large an area against disciplined Roman troops backed by heavy artillery.

Most of the monuments and sites to be seen between Stanwick and the Wall reflect a later age – the early days of Christianity with its monasteries and churches that still stand and are in use today.

On the west coast and inland there are a number of interesting sites. **Ravenglass** (SD 087959, also known as **Walls Castle**) was a port, and part of a bath-house has been preserved outside the 4-acre fort because it was later incorporated in a medieval building. It still retains traces of colour in some of the niches. From Ravenglass the Roman road went 9 miles up Eskdale to **Hardknott Castle** (NY 218014), the fort at its head, one of the remotest military installations in Britain, guarding the western end of Hardknott Pass. Eight hundred feet above sea level, it covers an area of $2\frac{3}{4}$ acres perched on the mountainside and commands a magnificent view on the rare occasions when the mist clears. The fort was built towards the end of the first century AD as part of the consolidation programme in the area. It had a bath-house and a parade ground, both outside the fort walls. So small is the shelf upon which the fort is sited that the parade ground had to be in part cut out of the mountainside so as to obtain a level area of suitable dimensions. The walls of the fort have been consolidated and partly rebuilt using the stones fallen from them; a thin line of slate in the walls indicates the new work carried out above it.

To the east, starting at the 50-ft contour on the north side of Great Langdale, is another example of a neolithic axe factory (NY 272072).

116 View down the Hardknott Pass from the Roman fort, Hardknott Castle, guarding its head

It is situated on the lower slopes leading up to the charmingly named Pike of Stickle and from here the axe blanks were traded far and wide. The rock is a volcanic tuff that flakes easily, is very hard, and grinds down to a fine, sharp edge. On the scree of the hillside roughed-out axe-heads, flakes and other debris can still be picked up, testifying to the great industry that was carried on here. The companion fort of Hardknott Castle was at **Ambleside** (*Galava*) and north of here is a magnificent stretch of Roman road called **High Street** making its way through the Lakeland mountains from NY 426070 to 504266 and on to the fort at **Brougham Castle**, *Brocavum* (NY 538289). The fort was on the south bank of the river Eamont and a twelfth-century castle was built on its site. Some of the Roman ramparts are still visible as grassy banks and there are a number of interesting inscribed Roman stones in the castle keep.

Near Brougham, just over a mile south of Penrith, are two Bronze Age henge monuments. **King Arthur's Round Table** (NY 523283) is just one of the many sites bearing that legendary association. This example is a circle of about 300 ft in diameter, with a ditch inside the bank which is up to 5 ft high and one surviving entrance (of two) on the south-east. The site was much disturbed in the nineteenth century and two standing stones shown on a seventeenth-century plan have disappeared, along with the entrance. The second henge monument, 500 yards away to the west, is called **Mayburgh** (NY 519284). This is better preserved than the Round Table; it encloses an acre and a half and is 360 ft in diameter. The rampart varies in height

117 Keswick Carles, a stone circle in a most dramatic setting east of Keswick

between 8 and 15 ft and it has a single entrance through it on the east side. In the centre is a standing stone 9 ft high which was once part of a rectangular setting with three other stones, while another quartet flanked the entrance. The site is very peaceful and in a beautiful setting, both of the sites being characteristically set close to a river.

Just to the east of Keswick is a stone circle variously known as **The Carles, Keswick Carles** or **Castlerigg** (NY 292236). It is a pear-shaped circle of 38 stones with a diameter of 110 ft. Inside this setting

and touching its edge on the east are another ten stones making a rect-
angle. There seems to have been an entrance through a gap on the
north side. This site is one of several in this area fairly close to each
other and they must have had great religious significance. Castlerigg
is probably the best known and has the grandest setting of them, but
Long Meg and her Daughters (NY 571373), 7 miles north-east of
Penrith, is the largest. The Daughters form an east–west oval,
360 × 305 ft, of 59 stones with 27 of them still standing. Originally

it comprised about 70 stones, mostly 10 ft tall. Long Meg is a 12-ft-high standing stone 60 ft outside the circle on the south-west. There are two other outlier stones, 28 ft apart, between Long Meg and the circle. Most of the larger stones seem to have been deliberately shaped and on the north-east face of Long Meg is cut a small cup mark surrounded by two concentric circles. Long Meg and her Daughters ranks high in the order of prehistoric circles in Britain, being considered fourth in importance after Avebury, Stonehenge and Stanton Drew.

Seven hundred yards to the north-east is another circle of 11 stones which were once set round a barrow. This is often called **Little Meg**, or the **Maughanby Circle**. Another circle 400 yards north-west of **Glassonby** (NY 573394) has a diameter of 45 ft, and 31 stones are set round a mound which covered a cist burial.

The concentration of stone circles in this area is of great interest. The new archaeological investigations that have taken place at a number of similar circles throughout Britain, coupled with the astronomical evidence emerging for their deliberate alignments, should in the not too distant future solve a number of the outstanding questions concerning them.

6 West of Offa's Dyke

Modern boundaries will, on occasion, follow a natural line such as a river, or an artificial one such as an arterial road or railway. Our ancestors did things on a grander scale; the Roman frontier of Hadrian's Wall is a prime example from the early second century AD, and six centuries later we find the Mercians employing a similar idea in the construction of Offa's Dyke in the eighth century AD. That line of earthworks, over 1000 years old, will be our delineation in this chapter between the 'middle lands' and the mountains of Wales, although almost everything described will be of an earlier date than the Dyke. But first to describe it: **Offa's Dyke** takes its name from Offa, king of Mercia, AD 757–96. He was the greatest of the Mercian kings and made his kingdom pre-eminent, conquering his neighbours, issuing silver pennies bearing his portrait, and finally making his western boundary with the Dyke, having driven the Britons further into Wales. Such was his standing that he was recognized by Charlemagne. The Dyke was a boundary line consisting of a bank at least 6 ft high and a ditch on the western side, with an overall average width across them both of about 60 ft. From Prestatyn in Flintshire in the north to Sedbury, east of the Wye, in the south, the Dyke ran for 149 miles,

118 Silver portrait penny of Offa, AD 757–96

a considerable undertaking in terms of physical labour and time. Its purpose was to control access to the lowlands on its east and in particular to protect the Mercian farmers from Welsh raids. Good sections of it will be pointed out from time to time and the survey of sites in this chapter will start in the southern area, although the section of the Dyke here, outside Chepstow within view of the Severn Bridge, is only of average quality.

In this southern area of Wales the Roman presence was quite strong, with a legionary fortress at Caerleon. There was a also a prosperous town at Caerwent and, going to the east of our appointed Dyke boundary in order to keep the Roman elements together, we come to Lydney.

Lydney (SO 615026) is a very interesting site on private land: it consists of a Roman temple and its precinct and a Roman iron mine. The temple was built high up on a spur overlooking the Severn estuary in the second half of the fourth century AD and was dedicated to the Celtic divinity Nodens. Although linked with the warrior god Mars he seems primarily to have been a god of healing. His temple, of which substantial traces remain, was basilican in plan like the early Christian churches. It was orientated north-west/south-east with the entrance up a flight of steps on the south-east and three sanctuaries at the back. Running at an oblique angle to the back wall of the temple is the 'Long Building'. This had a number of individual rooms where, it has been suggested, ritual incubation ('temple sleep') was practised as at the great healing centres in the Mediterranean world. The suppliant

119 The temple of the Romano–Celtic god Nodens at Lydney

would expect the god to appear to him in a dream. Dogs also seem to have been associated in some way with the cure judging by the number of small bronze votive statues of them found here. Possibly they licked wounds or otherwise affected parts of the suppliants. A public bath-house whose hypocaust is still visible catered for the need for cleanliness as well as the social aspect, and a series of small shops almost certainly supplied the religious votives and all the other commercial impedimenta that are always associated with shrines. To the south-east of the temple, between it and the ramparts around the site, is the narrow entrance to a Roman iron mine. The shaft is located under a trap-door among the ferns and the marks of the picks can still be seen on the walls.

Several interesting inscriptions were found on the site: one of them, inscribed on a plate of lead, was a curse by a certain Silvianus who had lost a gold ring at the temple. He promises half its value to Nodens upon its recovery, and hints darkly that one Senicianius was the culprit. Another inscription on a tessellated pavement, now destroyed, was a dedication to the god by Flavius Senilis, officer in charge of a naval supply depot which can only have been at Cardiff.

Further down the coast at **Caerwent** (ST 469905), 5 miles south-west of Chepstow on the A48, is the Roman city of *Venta Silurum*, 'the market town of the Silures'. The town was founded about AD 75 when it was felt a town was needed in the area now that the warlike Silures had quietened down and seemed ready to accept Roman administration and the benefits of the *Pax Romana*. It covered about $44\frac{1}{2}$ acres which were divided up into a grid of 20 blocks or *insulae*. The buildings seem to have been fairly dense, and it was certainly more crowded than Silchester (*Calleva Atrebatum*, p. 84) although half that city's size. Despite this it boasted all the accoutrements of civilized romanization: a forum, basilica, public baths and temples. The walls that surrounded it were built in the late second or early third century, replacing an earth rampart and ditch. A series of polygonal bastions were added to the wall about AD 340, probably because the inhabitants were frightened of Irish raiders. The bastions would provide a deadly cross-fire from *ballistae*, catapults that could fling a ball of stone of about 25 lb almost a quarter of a mile.

The west and the south walls are the best preserved, standing 9 ft high on average, 17 ft in some instances, and they were probably 25 ft high originally. The base courses of the wall were 10 ft thick and the wall reduced in width as it rose except at certain places on the inner face where, for sections approximately 13 ft in length, it maintained its full width all the way up. This is where, in all probability, wooden steps gave access to the wall walk. From the top of the walls the defenders looked out across two ditches that surrounded the town: the first ditch lay 13 ft from the wall, was about 30 ft wide and 7 ft 6 ins deep, and there was another similar ditch 27 ft beyond it. The external defences in all were in the region of 100 ft wide, all under direct fire from the bastions. It is very noticeable when walking round the walls that the bastions were added later, as they are not bonded into it which would have been the case had walls and bastions been contemporary. The offsets are another visible building feature: these occurred where sections of wall being built by different gangs met, and had to be disguised on the outer face since they would otherwise betray a weakness in the wall at that point to any attacking force. Each of the four walls had a principal gate, those in the north and south walls not being centrally placed. Remains of all four gates can be seen, but the south gate is the best preserved with the springing of its arch still standing on projecting piers. At some time during the fourth century the gateway, 8 ft 9 ins wide, was blocked by a well-built wall of regularly coursed masonry with a run-off culvert left through the lower three courses to allow water to escape. This blocking may have been carried out at the same time as the bastions were built in an effort to concentrate the defences.

Although the plan of the town within the walls has been recovered in some detail in excavations and casual digging since the sixteenth century, the only part now open to view is part of the *insula* excavated in 1947–8 to the west of the forum beside Pound Lane. The outlines of a couple of houses are marked, one a combined house and shop, the other a courtyard house where a mosaic with a hypocaust underneath it was found. One other building can be visited, a small octagonal Romano–Celtic temple which stood just outside the east wall and is now by the caravan site next to the Coach and Horses Inn. Much of the Roman town still lies beneath the fields, but some 30 modern houses have been built within the town walls. In the church porch (now dedicated to St Stephen but once to St Tathan, the Irish saint) are two inscribed stones. One is a small altar stone dedicated to Mars Ocelus, a composite Romano–Celtic deity, but the other is rather unusual. It records a dedication to Claudius Paulinus, legate of the Second Augustan Legion at Caerleon, who rose to be governor of two provinces in Gaul, Narbonne and Lyon. The inscription, and presumably a statue as the stone is a pedestal, were set up by order of the tribal senate of the Silures tribe community – an interesting sidelight on local tribal self-government in Roman Britain.

Not far from Caerwent, just 2 miles outside Newport, is **Caerleon**, *Isca* (ST 339906), the legionary fortress of the Second Augustan Legion. It is the third of the three permanent legionary fortresses, its companions being Chester and York. Apparently its name stems from the Latin *castra legiones*, the camp of the legions, which has been transmuted into Caerleon. Like a number of British sites it has legends of Arthurian romance linked with it; it is said that Arthur was crowned here, and Tennyson's *Idylls of the King* embellished the stories further for Victorian audiences.

The prosaic Roman fortress, as against the medieval fantasy, covered about 50 acres and was rectangular in plan, 540 × 450 yards. The centre point of the fortress, the headquarters building, is marked by the later church as is seen elsewhere in Roman Britain. A portion of the site known as Prysg Field – the angle of the fortress formed by the south-west and north-west walls – has been fully excavated and

120 The Roman walls at Caerwent. The bastions were added at a later date and not bonded into the main wall structure

121 Part of the excavated area of the Roman fortress of Caerleon known as Prysg Field. The church in the background stands over the headquarters building

gives a very good idea of a military layout. The original earthen rampart of the fortress was strengthened in the second century by the addition of a stone revetment on the outside, and the internal barrack blocks, headquarters building, etc. were rebuilt in masonry at the same time. Within the wall angle at Prysg Field and backing up against it are the remains of a number of round army ovens, 8 ft in diameter. They were subsequently superseded by stone-built square cookhouses. Nearby, outlined in the grass by their foundations, are four barrack blocks (out of a total of 64 that would have occupied the interior of the fortress). Roman military architecture was very regular and neatly laid out here are 24 small rooms in 12 pairs, each pair allocated for the use of six legionaries; the larger of the rooms was for living in and the smaller for stacking arms and equipment when not in use. The larger accommodation at the north-west end was for the centurion and his immediate staff. Each barrack block held 80 men, a *centuria*; the full complement of the fortress would have been 5–6000 legionaries.

Entertainment for the troops, and for the civilian population that lived in the town outside the walls, was provided in the amphitheatre that was built about AD 80 (contemporary with the great Flavian Colosseum in Rome). It was excavated in the late twenties by Sir Mortimer Wheeler and is the only completely excavated amphitheatre to be seen in Britain; many portions of amphitheatres are extant, or overgrown remains such as those outside Richborough and Chester, but no other example exists such as this. The arena was hollowed out of the hillside and the earth thrown up to create the banks which supported additional seating for spectators. Overall the area was 180 ft × 136 ft 6 ins with a 12-ft-high internal stone wall surrounding it; behind this the bank rose to 28 ft and the external holding wall to 32 ft. In the usual fashion of any such large undertaking, sections were built by individual units and they were only joined together on completion. Several of the slabs recording this work are still extant and tell us that, amongst others, the ninth and tenth cohorts were involved and also the centuries of Fulvus Macer and Sadius Tiro. There were eight entrances into the arena, now lettered A to H, the main ones being at either end of the oval area at B and F. The two centre entrances in each of the long sides (at D and H) are far more elaborate than the others, and above H was the equivalent of the 'royal box'. Two of the inscribed stones mentioned above can be seen in the arena wall on either side of this entrance: the tenth cohort to the north, and Tiro's century to the south. Though gladiatorial combats and the like were almost certainly featured in the amphitheatre from time to time, it probably saw more use as an area for weapon handling, drill and military displays, and as a convenient place to muster the full legion. Near the church is a small museum containing material from the site.

Although **Cardiff** was an important Roman supply depot little remains to be seen. The walls of the medieval castle (ST 181766) follow the line of their Roman predecessor and their upper reaches are nineteenth-century restoration work by Lord Bute. Here in Cardiff

122 The Roman amphitheatre at Caerleon, the finest example
to be seen in Britain

123 Tinkinswood long cairn, from the east, with its entrance
set deep between prominent 'horn works'

the National Museum of Wales (ST 183769) is located, which is a
treasure house of archaeological material from Wales of all periods.

Five miles south-west of Cardiff is an interesting group of mega-
lithic remains. The two of principal interest are the Tinkinswood and
St Lythans long cairns. They are good examples of dolmen tombs –
generally called cromlechs in Wales. Both of them, like so many other
Welsh cromlechs, are known locally as *Gwâl-y-filiast*, 'Kennel of the
Greyhound Bitch', which apparently has connections with Arthurian

157

legend via a Welsh variant. The **Tinkinswood** cairn (ST 092733), standing in a small copse, is the better preserved of the two as it was carefully excavated in 1914 by John Ward. It consists of a chamber formed by five upright slabs which support a huge capstone, 23 ft 6 ins × 15 ft, which weighs about 40 tons. The chamber was located at the eastern end of a cairn about 140 ft long, and set back between 'horn works'. At the entrance to the chamber a stone specially chosen for its L-shape was tipped to one side to narrow the entry. The remains of at least 50 bodies were found inside, together with fragments of pottery that indicated a date between 2500 and 2000 BC for the cairn being in use for communal burial. About halfway along the north side of the cairn is a rectangular enclosure, 10 × 9 ft, that might have served as a place for exposing the corpses before they were placed in the burial chamber. About a mile away from Tinkinswood long cairn is another of similar type at **St Lythans** (ST 101723). Here the cairn that once covered the burial chamber has almost disappeared, leaving the three uprights supporting the capstone standing out clearly. The existing cairn is only 80 ft long but was probably much longer originally.

Christianity came to the Glamorgan peninsula area fairly early, and the **Margam Stones Museum** (SS 802862) at Margam Abbey, east of Swansea, contains a remarkable collection of early inscribed stones and crosses from the region. The earliest is a Roman milestone from Port Talbot erected between AD 309 and 313 and subsequently re-used in the sixth century as a Christian memorial stone for one Cantusus, erected by his father Paulinus. Other early stones commemorate people named Pumpeius and Boduoc, the former having a Latin and two Ogham inscriptions cut on it.

The Gower Peninsula to the west of Swansea is rich in archaeological remains. The earliest is the **Goat's Hole** cave, **Paviland** (SS 437859), a most distinguished site in the history of British archaeology.

In 1823 Dean William Buckland, who conveniently combined Holy Orders and the first chair in geology at Oxford, excavated the cave. He found traces of wild horses, hyaenas, cave bears, rhinoceroses and mammoths. Among these bones of long extinct animals he also discovered a human skeleton with a number of ivory amulets buried in a deposit strongly tinted red by iron oxide. He was in a quandary – his geological self said that here were human remains associated with extinct animals that must therefore be far older than the biblical account of the creation. This was obviously at variance with his religious calling, and eventually he solved the problem by asserting that the burial was a later intrusion of a Romano–British lady! From this, and the red ochre, this first Stone Age burial became known as the Red Lady of Paviland. It was only when the Bible came to be interpreted less literally, and modern methods of investigation were applied to the remains, that research showed the Red Lady actually to be a well-built palaeolithic hunter about 25 years old! The site itself is not easy to get to as it is a cave that opens from a deep rock-cleft, and the visitor can be trapped by incoming tides. When the cave was used by palaeolithic man as his home *c.* 16,500 BC there was a low plain

124 Arthur's Stone, or Maen Ceti, a 25-ton boulder, conceals two
burial chambers beneath it

between the cave entrance and the sea and the situation was ideal for
spying game.

There are several other caves on the peninsula that were inhabited
in upper palaeolithic (late Stone Age) times – **Bacon Hole** (SS 560868),
Cat's Hole (SS 538900) and **Long Hole**. The last of these is quite
near Goat's Hole and has an entrance on top of the cliff (SS 452851).
Of the other monuments on Gower the two most interesting, even
spectacular in terms of the area if one excludes the ramparts and
ditches of Iron Age hill forts, are the Parc Cwm long cairn and
Arthur's Stone. **Parc Cwm** (SS 537899) is a neolithic chambered tomb
of the Severn–Cotswold group. The cairn is about 75 ft long, orientated south to north with a deep entrance between horn works at the
south end that leads to a long gallery with two pairs of facing side
chambers off it, rather like Hetty Pegler's Tump (p. 68). In the
chambers the remains of about two dozen people were found, and the
tomb had obviously been used for communal burial over a fairly long
period. Not far away to the west, **Arthur's Stone** (SS 491905), also
called **Maen Ceti**, is a very unusual megalithic tomb. The capstone
is a huge 25-ton glacial boulder, supported on nine uprights that form
between them two irregular shaped burial chambers below the capstone. It gets its name from the local legend that King Arthur, out
walking one day near Llanelli in Carmarthenshire, found a stone in his
shoe. He removed it and flung it towards the Gower Peninsula where
it was used as the capstone for Maen Ceti.

Some way inland from Gower, up in the Black Mountains, is **Cerrig
Duon** (SN 852229). A stone circle 55 ft in diameter has 20 stones fairly
regularly spaced around its circumference, all under 2 ft high. Going
away from the circle in a north-easterly direction is an avenue of stones
and to the north of the circle, 30 ft away, is a 6-ft-tall standing stone.

125 The south gate of the Roman fort at Brecon Gaer, a
double entry flanked by guard-chambers

While stone circles are relatively common in Wales, stone alignments
are not, and it is curious that another exists not far away to the south-
west of Cerrig Duon at **Saeth Maen** (SN 833154). Others occur in
Breconshire and Radnorshire, but all are in fairly inaccessible spots
and little is known about them save that they are ascribed a Bronze
Age date, usually on no certain evidence.

Further into the mountains north of Cerrig Duon are several interesting Roman sites. They are in remote areas and one cannot help
but admire the tenacity of the Roman legionary and military engineer
who pushed into these regions against the hostile Silures. At **Brecon
Gaer** (SL 002297), west of Brecon itself, are the remains of a 5-acre
cavalry fort established about AD 80 and garrisoned by 500 Spanish
Vettones. Sixty years later the earth ramparts were replaced by stone,
and both the south and west gates still present substantial remains
of the second-century rebuilding. The south gate is particularly well
preserved; the walls of its guard-chambers still stand 6–7 ft high on
either side of the double carriageway. A central pier in the middle
of the gateway gave added strength to the gates, and two of their pivot
holes remain. The layout of the west gate is similar. In places the fort
wall still stands to an imposing height of 10 ft and is constructed of
well finished masonry.

From Brecon Gaer the Roman road heads west towards **Y Pigwn**
(SN 828313) where there are two marching camps, temporary ones in
use early in the Roman campaigns in Wales and probably even then
only for a couple of seasons. One fort is partly superimposed on the
other. The earlier fort is the larger one, and about 3½ acres of it underlie
the later, slightly smaller fort. Their outlines can be picked out by
the ditches and, at the right time of year, discolouration in the grass
over them.

Julius Caesar mentions the mineral wealth of Britain and this was
especially so in terms of tin and lead; several inscribed lead pigs of

Roman date are known. One of the best areas for lead mining was in the Mendips but at **Dolaucothi** (SN 665403) is the only Roman gold mine known in Roman Britain. It lies on the A482 near the village of Pumpsaint. The area is rather a jumble of workings – Roman, medieval and modern – but some of the old mining tunnels can still be seen. Both opencast and tunnel mining were carried on to win the precious metal. Mining was very much a state enterprise and under military control, although the actual work would have been done by civilians. To give some idea of the intensive industrial activity at the workings, water was brought by means of three separate aqueducts, the longest being 7 miles. Large quantities of water were needed to assist in crushing and washing the ore – part of a Roman wooden water wheel from here can be seen in the National Museum, Cardiff.

Turning towards the west, prehistoric sites become more and more abundant around St David's Peninsula and Milford Haven. There are large numbers of small hill forts and megalithic remains which bear study on the Ordnance Survey maps for the area (SM and SN). **Gors Fawr** stone circle (SN 135293) is not particularly impressive but it is fairly typical of a number of Welsh circles. Some 16 stones remain from the original setting and all are small, under 3 ft, set in a circle about 70 ft in diameter. Outside the circle to the north-east are two stones that may be connected with the setting of the stones as outlier markers. Among many megalithic remains in the area of St David's are **Carn Llidi** (SM 735279), with two chambers and roofing slabs partly supported by the edges of pits cut into the rock; **Carreg Samson** or **Longhouse** (SM 846334) has seven uprights forming a polygonal chamber but only three actually support the huge capstone; and **Rhos y Clegryn** (SM 913354) is a single 9-ft standing stone near a flattened round cairn.

126 Only three of the upright stones actually support the massive capstone of Carreg Samson

127 *Right* The Pentre Ifan burial chamber, all that remains of a denuded mound, is one of the finest examples of its type in Wales

The area around Newport and its bay is backed by the Prescelly Mountains. At the head of the Nevern Valley the **Pentre Ifan** burial chamber (SN 099370) is one of the finest megalithic tombs in Wales. It has the distinction in historical terms, along with Arthur's Stone in Gower, of being the first burial chamber to be taken into guardianship by the first of the Ancient Monuments Protection Acts in 1882. The burial chamber is a communal tomb and has characteristics more usually found in North Wales, Ireland and north-west Scotland. As seen today the monument is at once impressive and deceptive. Its impressiveness comes from the remains of the chamber and its capstone, a huge monolith weighing about 17 tons appearing to be only lightly balanced on the tips of four tapering uprights. It is deceptive because the seemingly impossible feat of balance performed by the uprights makes one forget that they were only part of a monument originally consisting of a 120-ft-long cairn orientated north to south with the entrance at the south end set back deep within the projecting side horns of the cairn, and with a large forecourt in front. Within the body of the cairn, and therefore originally hidden from view, was a series of small upright stones on the eastern and western sides flanking the area of the burial chamber. Between the eastern line and the east side of the burial chamber is a large fallen monolith that excavation indicated had been deliberately toppled before the cairn was raised. Further back along the eastern side of the cairn were two ritual pits of unknown use. Another megalithic tomb with Irish connections in its architecture lies a mile away south-east of Pentre Ifan and is known as **Bedd yr Afranc**, the **Dwarf's Grave** (SN 113346). It has a long, narrow chamber, unusual for its 30-ft length, which tapers from 6 to 3 ft wide.

It was from this area of the Prescelly Mountains that the blue stones came which were used at Stonehenge. A broad ridge known as **Fleming's Way** is the probable route that they took to Milford Haven to be loaded on to rafts. On the ridge is the **Meini Gwyr** circle (SN 142266). Only two of its original 17 stones remain but it is the sole example of a stone circle in South Wales where the stones were set on an embanked circle.

At **Castell Collen** (SO 055628), north of Llandrindod Wells, is one of the better preserved Roman forts in the network that criss-crossed Wales, maintaining a watch on roads and people. An auxiliary fort, originally about 5 acres in area, it was reduced to about $3\frac{1}{2}$ acres in the early fourth century. Ramparts, part of the headquarters building, a granary and a bath-house can still be made out.

Nearer the coast but still inland from Aberystwyth near Devil's Bridge on the A4120 is **Ysbyty Cynfyn** (SN 752791). As at the Knowlton Circles in Dorset (p. 52) the Church took a poor view of a Bronze Age pagan stone circle. Within the embanked stone circle a church was built and a number of the circle's stones were incorporated in the churchyard wall; two others were moved to be used as gateposts and only one 11-ft-high stone to the north seems to stand in its original position. There are very few sites in this desolate area of Mont-

128 Concealed beneath the bumps, hollows and ridges at Castell Collen is the complete layout of a Roman fort

gomeryshire in central Wales, and one can sympathize with the legionary detachment stationed in the little fort at **Cae Gaer** (SN 824819), literally stationed in the middle of nowhere.

Towards the northern end of Cardigan Bay, and north of Barmouth, are two long cairns called the **Carneddau Hengwm** (SH 614205). They lie side by side, the southern one being the larger of the two, 200 ft in length. It has a damaged chamber at the east end with three tall standing uprights that once supported a capstone which has now slid down behind them. This cairn is very reminiscent of the dolmen at Pentre Ifan. Set into the northern side of the mound, at the end of a short passageway, is a small chamber. The northern mound, the smaller of the two, also had a burial chamber at its eastern end – there may have been two of them, back to back. A small chamber is set into the side, but it no longer has a capstone; this however might be the largish slab lying on the mound towards the west end opposite to the burial chamber. Nearby, and bearing the same name, are the remains of two stone circles. Once the stones stood on a raised embankment but little remains now of either stones or bank.

Near Porthmadog – better known perhaps for the Ffestiniog railway – is a remote Roman auxiliary fort at **Tomen y Mur** (SH 707387). If one considers the fort at Cae Gaer remote, Tomen y Mur

163

129 The Roman fort at Tomen y Mur is one of
the remotest in Britain

must have been regarded by any legionary as the end of the world.
The interest of the site lies not in its stonework, which has now all
disappeared, but in the remains that can be seen by a little intelligent
fieldwork and realizing, once you 'get your eye in', what the landscape
can tell and the story behind it. On all sides the views are magnificent,
either down the valley towards the sea or up into the mountains. But
this was small compensation for the bleak hours spent on duty here
by the legionaries attached to the fort and so, a little way off to the
north-east of the fort, we find an amphitheatre. It is the only known
example attached to an auxiliary fort, and one cannot help speculating
as to whether a special dispensation was granted here in the provision
of the amphitheatre to boost the troops' morale. A Norman motte was
built within the fort itself and its top provides a useful platform from
which to make out the features of the fort and its adjacent buildings.
Standing on top of the motte it is easy to pick out the surrounding
banks of the fort built by Agricola in about AD 78. Then, from this
vantage point, you realize that the motte itself stands astride a Roman
rampart that passes right underneath it. This rampart represents a
later phase of the fort, built probably during the reign of Hadrian in
about AD 110, when it was curtailed by the addition of this cross rampart which sliced off about a quarter of the west end of the fort. At
this juncture the fort was given a stone wall, most of which has since
been re-used as dry stone walling in the surrounding area – such a rich
and convenient quarry was not to be missed. Since the Norman motte
stands in the centre of the early second-century AD additonal rampart,
it is possible that a complete Roman gate might still be preserved
within its bulk.

About 30 years after it was rebuilt in stone the fort appears to
have been abandoned for some unknown reason. During its life,

however, the surrounding countryside tells us that the legionaries were not left idle. Apart from the amphitheatre already mentioned there are all sorts of remains: about 100 yards to the north-west of the fort are traces of two earthworks that look as if they were practice camps – quite a few of these are known in Wales and to the north of Hadrian's Wall. South-east of the fort, between its walls and a small stream, lay a *vicus* (civil settlement) and the fort bath-house – all now just mounds. East of the fort was the parade ground, which involved much earth-moving to level it up: the load had to be carried down the hillside to build up the lower side, and in the end it remained unfinished. The amphitheatre lies some way north-east of the fort in a now rather marshy area; a couple of mounds near it are probably tombs.

High above Beddgelert on a hill which rises from the Gwynant Valley is one of the few known princely sites in Wales, a defended dwelling rather than a hill fort, at **Dinas Emrys** (SH 606492). It was occupied from the early Iron Age into the Roman period and down into the fifth century AD. It has double ramparts and an original entrance on the west; the pool within the ramparts was dug during the first century AD and the foundations near it are Roman. The site's setting is quite idyllic and it is small wonder that the site has attracted local legends. Myth connects the pool with Vortigern, a fifth-century British king, and the magician Merlin. The Emrys of the site name is Ambrosius Aurelianus, Vortigern's adversary, and it is either an odd coincidence, or evidence of the continuity of folk-memory over the centuries, that excavations at Dinas Emrys produced evidence of its occupation at a fifth-century date contemporary with Vortigern. Fragments of pottery imported from the Mediterranean world have been found here and in other hill forts occupied at this date, such as South Cadbury in Somerset. Once again Arthurian legend is connected with a site that can be shown archaeologically to have been occupied around the relevant time in the fifth century AD.

One of the most spectacular of the Iron Age hill forts in northern Wales is at **Tre'r Ceiri** (SH 374447), nearly 2000 feet above sea level looking out over Caernarvon Bay. A stronghold of the local Ordovices tribe, it follows the summit of Yr Eifl and is therefore curiously long and narrow for a hill fort. It is orientated north-east/south-west. The main rampart is stone-built in a most skilful manner – loose stones were piled up, not mortared together, and still stand up to 12 ft high with ramps leading up to a rampart walk protected by a parapet. Inside is an absolute profusion of stone-built huts of two types. The round huts date from the pre-Roman Iron Age; many of them were later adapted into a rectangular plan, and others of similar plan were built during the Roman period. Access to the fort was by two gates at the south-west end, both quite well preserved, and by three lesser passage-ways. Outside the fort are traces of terracing and what may be cattle pounds, but this high, remote place seems an odd and impractical one in which to practise agriculture or stockbreeding.

Passing round the coast, megalithic and Iron Age sites become denser as Anglesey is approached. At **Caernarvon** lies the Roman

130 Two thousand feet above sea level the Iron Age hill fort of Tre'r Ceiri
well merits its name of 'the town of the giants'

fort of *Segontium* (SH 485624), 150 ft above sea level and guarding
the Menai Strait. The Romans had suffered at the hands of the Ordovices, and Tacitus tells us (*Agricola* 18) that just prior to the arrival
of the general, Agricola, in AD 78, a squadron of cavalry had been
almost wiped out by them. Agricola decided to hit back hard. He cut
most of the Ordovican forces to pieces in hill fighting and then decided
to capture the island where their sacred shrines lay – *Mona* or
Anglesey.

Agricola picked out the best of his auxiliaries, who had experience of fords
and had been trained to swim with arms and horses under control beside them,
and made them discard their whole equipment. He then launched them on
a surprise attack, and the enemy, who had been thinking in terms of fleet,
ships and naval warfare, completely lost their heads. . . . They sued for peace
and surrendered the island.

Evidence of pottery from the excavations at *Segontium* shows that
occupation of the fort began about AD 75–80, and in view of Tacitus'
remarks AD 78 seems a very probable date for the fort's foundation.
It then appears to have been garrisoned with only a few breaks for
about the next 300 years.

   Its last years enter the realm of fairy tales woven about the usurper
emperor in Britain, Magnus Maximus (AD 383–8), who features in
the Welsh national folktale of the Mabinogian as Macsen Wledig,
'Lord Maximus', the same character who appears in Kipling's *Puck
of Pook's Hill*. The small museum on the site gives a good introduction
to the history of the fort and the remains of the northern half at present
exposed. Much excavation remains to be done as parts of the fort are
still undug or concealed beneath adjacent roads and the reservoir. The

131 View across the interior of the Roman fort of *Segontium*
just outside Caernarvon

Caernarvon to Beddgelert road (A487) cuts through the site, and has
obliterated beneath its surface the south-east gate of the fort. The
other three gates, each set in the centre of their respective walls, survive in varying degrees. The best place to view the site is from the
headquarters building to the left (west) of the museum. From here
can be seen the outlined foundations of the commandant's house and
sections of the barrack blocks that lay to the north and south of it.
On the north end of the headquarters building was a chapel to house
the standards and beneath this, in the third century, a strongroom
was built with steps leading down into it. Unfortunately it suffered
from the high water table and was often damp, so it was filled in in
the fourth century. Seen today as excavated it still has the same problem, and the floor is frequently wet. Sixty yards away, by the north-
east gateway and close to the reservoir, was a forage store. The garrison
seems to have been a mixed one of cavalry and an infantry cohort,
a combination often found on Hadrian's Wall.

The religious needs of the garrison were catered for by a temple
of Mithras, 150 yards east of the fort, which was excavated in 1959.
It is of the normal type, a long narrow building (48 ft × 21 ft 6 ins)
with a low bench on either side of the nave and a sanctuary at the north-
east end where the sculptured relief depicting Mithras slaying the bull
would have been set. The temple was built about AD 200, abandoned at about the same time that the sculptures in the London Mith-
raem were concealed, and then destroyed late in the fourth century.
Ten Mithraea are known in Britain: all except the London one are
in the military zone as Mithraism was a cult that appealed particularly
to soldiers as a solely male-orientated cult promising a splendid life
after death (see pp. 24, 182). Only five of these ten known Mithras

167

temples have been excavated. On the west side of the fort, also about 150 yards away, is a walled enclosure known as Hen Waliau, whose southern wall still stands almost 20 ft high. It appears to have been a stores compound as it lacks bastions and the blocked gateway had no gate towers which would be expected with a defensive installation.

From the fort at *Segontium* Agricola's trained auxiliaries moved out against the Druids who had made Anglesey a sacred island and who, as Tacitus tells us, 'deemed it indeed a duty to cover their altars with the blood of captives and to consult their deities through human entrails'. Few traces of the Druids as such have been found on Anglesey – the most important was the accidental discovery during the Second World War of a huge votive deposit at Llyn Cerrig Bach, 5 miles south-east of Holyhead. The large accumulation of metal objects recovered from a small area of peat indicated that they had been thrown into a lake as offerings. The site no longer exists and the objects are in the National Museum of Wales in Cardiff. The monuments and sites to be seen on Anglesey are, in the main, of much earlier origin than the Druids with whom the island is now indelibly linked. It contains some of the finest and most interesting monuments in Britain of the neolithic period and Bronze Age.

Crossing the Menai Bridge and turning to the south, the first monument reached is the **Bryn Celli Ddu** burial chamber (SH 507702), just off the A4080. The name means the 'Mound of the Dark Grove'. A passage grave and a henge monument are combined at this site: both were built between 4000 and 2000 BC. The henge monument was erected first and comprised a circular ditch 69 ft in diameter with 14 upright stones standing within this area. Only two of these, on opposite sides of the cairn, now remain. All the stones used in the circle appear to have been deliberately damaged or slighted in some way by the people who built the passage grave about 2000 BC. Stones were broken, toppled over, deliberately removed and sometimes buried within the cairn after being broken.

The passage grave consists of a polygonal chamber formed by six uprights. There is a seventh, free-standing, stone just inside the burial chamber on the right and, because of its almost circular shape and careful finishing, it is thought to have some phallic significance. From the chamber a passageway 27 ft long and 3 ft wide led to the outside on the north-east side of the cairn. The inner 16 ft of the passage was covered by large slabs, and the outer end was left uncovered. At the junction of the roofed and unroofed parts was a doorway formed by two uprights supporting a lintel. The right-hand upright is now broken and the lintel gone. A low bench can be seen on the right beyond the portal: this structure is generally rare in megalithic tombs, but is known from similar tombs in the Orkneys and in Spain. Near the centre was found a 5-ft-long stone: it had a pattern picked out on it which started on one side and continued up and across the stone on to the other side. A cast of it is now shown on the site, and the original is in the National Museum, Cardiff. The cairn erected over the earlier henge monument was 85 ft in diameter and swallowed it

132 The passage leading
to the burial chamber in
Bryn Celli Ddu

up. Its edge was marked by a double row of kerb stones, the inner line of which swings in at the entrance to the passageway and abuts on to the portal stones. In front of the passage entrance was a forecourt for ceremonial purposes, and just in front of it the skeleton of a small ox was found buried in a three-sided stone enclosure. The tomb was obviously in use over a long period of time as a communal burial place until the final blocking of the outer passage. The inner passage was never filled up to seal it.

An interesting memorial stone of the early seventh century AD, known as the **Catamanus Stone**, is preserved in Llangadwaladr church (SH 383692). Its Latin inscription commemorates Cadfan, who died *c*. AD 625, as 'the wisest and most illustrious of rulers'. Cadfan was the grandfather of St Cadwaladr.

Not far away from Llangadwaladr on a headland on the north side of Port Trecastell is the remarkable chambered cairn of **Barclodiad y Gawres**, 'the Giantess's Apronful' (SH 329708). It consists of a burial chamber set in a mound 90 ft in diameter. The entrance to the chamber, on the north side of the mound, is a 20-ft-long passage-way lined with stone uprights. The burial chamber itself is a polygonal structure about 12 ft across at its widest point, with three subsidiary chambers opening off it on its east, south and west sides. These chambers are more like widenings of the main chamber than truly separate ones. During excavations and restoration carried out in 1952–3 five of the stones used in the construction of the side walls of the passageway and chambers were found to be decorated with pecked linear designs. Three of the decorated stones occur at the junction of the passageway with the burial chamber – two on the east side and one on the west. They all incorporate zigzag lines and lozenges, the stone on the west being the larger and more heavily decorated of the three. The designs are very abstract, but it has been suggested that

169

they represent extremely stylized human figures. The other two decorated stones are at the back of the eastern and western side chambers respectively. The one on the west has a decoration consisting of four spirals, while the other one, rather more weathered, has only faint traces of spirals and a possible pecked 'cup mark'. Such megalithic art has parallels in similar tombs in Ireland, notably at New Grange on the river Boyne south of Dublin, and the discovery of these decorated stones made a notable addition to the known examples of British megalithic art. Parallels occur also in north-west Spain. They are all indicative of a seaborne wave of migrants bringing their ideas of megalithic architecture and decoration with them some time between 2000 and 1500 BC.

Another fine megalithic tomb occurs a little further along Anglesey's south-west coast at **Trefignath** (SH 259805), south-east of Holyhead. It is a rare type of tomb known as a segmented cist because its passageway, 45 ft long, was originally divided up by cross slabs into three, possibly four, segments. Such tombs are better known in Ulster and south-west Scotland; only two other tombs of this kind are known in Anglesey (the burial chambers of **Din Dryfol**, SH 395725, and **Presaddfed,** SH 347808), and none at all in the rest of England and Wales. Of the chambers at Trefignath the eastern one is the best preserved and has two 7-ft-tall portal stones standing at an angle. There is a double capstone over the chamber and the other chambers further along the passage are represented by huge tumbled stones. No trace remains of the covering which would once have overlain the structure of the passageway, hidden within a mound.

Out on Holyhead Mountain Iron Age peoples found a marvellous site for their hill fort of **Caer y Twr** (SH 219831) and a group of huts forming a settlement site nearby at **Ty Mawr** (SH 212820). The fort is so situated that no defensive ramparts are needed at its southern end – the steep drop over the cliff edge makes a more than adequate defence. The hut group at Ty Mawr consists of about 20 round huts in two groups spread over some 12 acres. They are quite easy to pick out in plan, and a number still have the visible remains of hearths. Curiously, like many other hut settlement sites in North Wales, their local name is Cytiau Gwyddelod – 'Huts of the Irishmen'. There is a tradition, totally unsupported by archaeological evidence, that they were the huts of the Goidels, the Irish driven out in the fifth century by the Brythonic Celts.

Roman presence was enforced in the area from the fort at **Caer Gybi** (SH 246827). Built on the edge of the harbour about AD 300 it is quite a small fort, only 250 × 175 ft. Circular towers are still extant at three of its four corners, and the walls stand up to 15 ft high on the outside and ten on the inside. Enclosed within the walls are St Cybi's church and churchyard.

On the other side of Anglesey, in the north-east corner by Moelfre Bay, are two sites situated close together but of very widely separated periods. The earlier of the two is the **Lligwy** burial chamber. Its huge capstone, 18 × 15 ft and weighing around 25 tons, sits oddly on a series

133 Both sides of the passage leading to the burial chamber of Barclodiad y Gawres are lined with large stone uprights
134 The Trefignath burial chamber is a rare example of a segmented cist grave
135 Almost two-thirds of the Lligwy burial chamber is underground beneath the huge 25-ton capstone

of small uprights. The chamber itself makes use of a natural crevice in the rock surface and thus about two-thirds of its height is underground, giving the monument a rather stunted appearance. It was used as a communal burial place and the remains of some 30 bodies were found when it was excavated in 1908. From the pottery evidence, as well as the skeletal remains, it seems to have been in use over a considerable period from neolithic times into the early Bronze Age. A couple of hundred yards away is the settlement site of **Din Lligwy** (SH 496862). A well-preserved group of two round huts and seven rectangular workshops (?) are all set within a strongly built pentagonal enclosure. There is an entrance in the north-east wall of the pentagon, and the whole site gives the impression of being the fortified house of a local chieftain during the fourth century AD, as indicated by small finds from the excavation in 1905 and later years.

Back on the mainland, on the other side of Conway Bay and along the high ground of Flintshire, is a long line of Iron Age hill forts. They are all situated on high ground which, in many instances, provides their defence by virtue of steep cliff faces rather than strong walls. While for the avid collector of hill forts they are in most instances worth visiting, there is little to describe except the number of their ramparts and the extent of their acreage. The notable ones amongst this series running from Colwyn Bay are: **Pen y Corddynmawr** (SH 915764); **Parc y meirch** (SH 967757), better known perhaps for the Dark Age site of **Dinorben**; **Moel Hiraddug** (SJ 064782); **Moel y Gaer, Flint** (SJ 095707); **Pen y cloddiau** (SJ 128677); **Moel y Gaer, Ruthin** (SJ 148617), and **Foel Fenlli** (SJ 163600). Behind this line of forts runs **Offa's Dyke**, coming inland from the sea at Prestatyn as far as the A55 to Holywell which crosses it. After a break it can be picked up again at Treuddyn (SJ 267577), and then it leads away south towards Breiddin Hill (SJ 297140). Running almost parallel to Offa's Dyke, except that it starts at the sea coast near Holywell, is the earlier **Wat's Dyke**. This was built in the early eighth century AD and runs through Wrexham to just beyond the hill fort of **Old Oswestry** (SJ 295310). This is one of the great Iron Age hill forts to be found in the Welsh Marches. Its long and complicated history goes through several stages from its origins in the mid-third century BC, through various restrengthenings when the west gate was redesigned, and to the new series of earthworks that enclosed the whole. As so often happened it was abandoned after the Roman conquest, but evidence has been found of squatters moving in during the Dark Ages before it was deserted again for good.

Returning to the line of Offa's Dyke, a quarter mile north of Valle Crucis Abbey at Llantysilio-yn-Ial (SJ 203445) is an interesting monument erected in the century following the building of the Dyke. It is known as **Eliseg's Pillar** and is the most famous of the inscribed stones in Wales. It commemorates Eliseg, a king of Powys and contemporary and opponent of Offa, and was put up by his great-grandson, Prince Cyngen of Powys, who is known to have died at Rome in AD 854. It records the lineage of Cyngen and claims his descent from Vor-

136 The elongated shape of the Herefordshire Beacon Iron Age hill fort running along a narrow ridge make it one of the most spectacular hill forts in Britain when seen from the air

tigern and Magnus Maximus, the Macsen Wledig already encountered in North Wales at *Segontium*. The long inscription is now illegible and it is thanks to the Welsh antiquary Edward Lhuyd who copied the inscription in 1696 that it is still known.

At **Breiddin Hill** (sj 297140) Offa's Dyke meets another hill fort in a superb situation. The Breiddin has a double line of ramparts and once again makes good use of the hill contours for its defence. Like so many other hill forts in the area it was refortified against the Romans, deserted and then reoccupied some time in the fourth century. Following the line of the Dyke to the south and the Severn are two sites that insist on being linked by name with Arthur but have nothing to do with him or with the Dark Ages. **Arthur's Stone** (SO 318431) is a neolithic chambered tomb that was at least 85 ft long and orientated north–south with a passage and chamber at its south end. The burial chamber, under a huge capstone supported on nine uprights, is about 18 × 7 ft. On the north side of the burial chamber are three stones which cannot really be explained. The site has not yet been excavated, and this would probably answer a number of questions posed by the present appearance of the site, not least the curious right-angled change in direction of the entrance passage, which suggests that there may have been an antechamber approached by the passage.

Near Ross-on-Wye is the second site in this general area laying claim to a connection with Arthur – **King Arthur's Grave** (SO 545155). This is even older than his Stone, for it is a cave that has produced evidence of occupation from the late Stone Age through most periods down to Roman times. A good, warm, dry cave was always appreciated and this cave has two chambers very adequately protected from the weather by a broad pillar of natural rock standing within the wide entrance. A large number of flint and bone artifacts were found here during excavations.

Of the small group of Iron Age hill forts that lie close to Offa's Dyke on the east at its southern end one, although a little distance away, is pre-eminent and falls more readily into place in this chapter than in the Midlands – it is the **Herefordshire Beacon** (SO 760399). It sits on a ridge of the Malvern Hills and surveys the countryside for miles around. Its long history started in the third century BC when it enclosed about 8 acres within a single bank and ditch; it then grew to take in the whole of the ridge with extra earthworks that brought it up to 32 acres in extent. By that time it had become so large that it needed four entrances facing east, west, north-east and south-east respectively. The extension seems to have been completed during the first century BC, after which there is little evidence until the site once more became a defensive one with the building of a Norman castle within an enclosure that utilizes much of the area of the earlier phases of the third-century Iron Age fort. In many fortified sites in Britain it is interesting to note how often, after the passage of centuries, the military significance of a site is recognized by later builders and once more comes into its own despite the radical changes that have taken place in the meantime in tactics and armament.

7 The North

In northern Britain geographical considerations affect the locations of archaeological sites far more than in any other part of the country, except for the mountainous terrain of Wales. The boundary between north and south was conveniently drawn in Roman times, with an eye for geographical considerations, between the mouth of the river Tyne and the Solway Firth. The building of Hadrian's Wall along that line 'to separate the Romans from the barbarians', as Hadrian's biographer, Aurelius Victor, laconically put it, gave physical emphasis to the division. Like Offa's Dyke in the last chapter a man-made division here forms a convenient line of demarcation for our purposes. The best approach to the sites of this part of Britain is to follow Hadrian's Wall from east to west and then to note the sites of interest between Hadrian's Wall and the Antonine Wall which runs from the Firth of Clyde to the Firth of Forth. North of this second line the archaeological sites divide into those on the Scottish mainland and the sites beyond the mainland on the Orkney and Shetland Islands.

Hadrian's Wall takes its name from the emperor who instituted its building and who himself visited Britain in AD 122. It was finished six years later and is a monument to Roman singlemindedness, running up hill and down dale, across rivers, marshy ground and lofty crags for a distance of 73 miles (80 Roman miles) from Wallsend across to Bowness. It was not simply an isolated linear structure: there were 16 forts along its length with two mile castles between each pair of forts, turrets between them, back-up forts and supply depots in the hinterland, and a series of watch-towers extending down the east and west coasts to the south to make sure that the Wall could not be out-flanked from the north.

Before starting to describe a number of the more important sites on Hadrian's Wall it makes sense to give some idea of its history viewed overall as simply one huge and very long site. The Romans always needed to have a tidy frontier to the various far-flung parts of the empire. Where possible natural features would serve to mark the limit which could be suitably patrolled and held by the Roman military

137 A larger than life-size bronze head of the emperor Hadrian. It probably formed part of an equestrian or similar statue erected in *Londinium* to commemorate his visit to the province of *Britannia* in A D 122. Dredged from the Thames near London Bridge in 1834, it is now in the British Museum

presence. In parts of Europe the great rivers such as the Danube and the Rhine served the Roman boundary purpose, and a series of forts along their banks marked the limit of the *Pax Romana*. The Roman conquest of Britain was pushed north by the legions under Agricola, but he was recalled to Rome by the emperor Domitian in AD 85 for service in Germany. Agricola had managed to get as far as Inchtuthil in Perthshire, but a few years after his recall the fort was abandoned. So a very untidy situation was left in Rome's newest province and northernmost frontier – it had to be remedied and a tangible frontier produced. Hadrian's Wall was the answer to that nagging untidiness of the northern frontier.

The Wall was built in three phases: from Newcastle to the river Irthing its foundations were 10 (Roman) ft wide, but before it could be completed there was a change of orders and the width was reduced to 8 (Roman) ft. This meant quite a saving in manpower and materials and in places it is still possible to see the 8-ft-wide wall sitting on the larger and earlier foundations. From the river Irthing, due to the initial lack of suitable quantities of limestone for building, the Wall was built of laid turves on a base 20 ft wide – this was later to be replaced by stone. The initial stretch was then built which took the Wall east from Newcastle to Wallsend. Forts to accommodate aux-iliary army units were added to the Wall in the face of mounting hos-tility to the Romans from both sides of it. Previously there had been a series of back-up forts along what is known as the Stanegate line behind the Wall, but now forts such as Chesters and Housesteads were built right on it, relegating the Stanegate forts to store depot status. The Wall had flanking ditches: one in front to the north some 20 ft away was about 10 ft deep and 28 ft wide. On the south side of the Wall was another ditch, also about 10 ft deep, but starting at the top around 20 ft wide and narrowing to a width of about 8 ft at the bottom. This is known as the *vallum*; it was not a defensive structure as such but more a delineation of the military zone on the south side of the Wall. The civilian population could only cross into this zone across the *vallum* at specially controlled points.

The Wall's fortunes fluctuated a lot. It was abandoned in Antoninus Pius' reign when the Antonine Wall was built in AD 139 (p. 199); then it was reoccupied in about 159. In 197 it was overrun by barbarians when Clodius Albinus withdrew large numbers of troops in his unsuccessful bid to gain the empire near Lyons in France. Septimius Severus restored Britain to the empire and died at York in 211; then in 287 another usurper emperor, Carausius, set himself up only to be murdered in his turn six years later by his chief minister Allectus. The latter had also drawn troops from the Wall, leaving the way open for invasion from the north. Allectus died in battle in 296 against the rightful heir Constantius Chlorus, who rebuilt the Wall and died at York in 306. In 367 a great invasion swept south, slaughtered garrisons and even killed the count of the Saxon Shore, the high Roman official in charge of the line of forts from Brancaster to Carisbrooke Castle. Despite being restored yet again, this time by Theodosius, the Wall was at risk once more in 383 when Magnus Maximus, another British emperor, arose and held out for five years against the rightful emperor, Gratian. Maximus was defeated and executed, and somehow the Wall had now lost its *raison d'être* – dark clouds were looming from across the North Sea that threatened 'barbarian' and Roman to the north and south of the Wall alike.

It is only possible to draw attention to some of the more notable sites on and adjacent to Hadrian's Wall, but the classic guide, in great detail, is still J. Collingwood Bruce's *Handbook to the Roman Wall*, revised by Professor Ian Richmond, and ably supported by the special Ordnance Survey *Map of Hadrian's Wall* drawn on a scale of 2 ins to the mile.

The first substantial remains to see at the eastern end of the wall are those of the little Celtic temple that lay outside the fort at **Benwell**, *Condercum* (NZ 217646), 2 miles west of Newcastle. The fort itself is now buried partly under the Denhill Park housing estate and partly under the adjacent Benwell High Reservoir. The temple was fortunate in being outside the fort walls to the east, and it has been preserved in Broomridge Avenue. Its dedication was to the god Antenociticus,

138 The powerful head of the Celtic god Antenociticus from his temple at Benwell. University Museum of Antiquities, Newcastle

and three altars were found in the building: two had the god's name inscribed in full on them, and the third had a shortened version, Antociticus. The building was only 27 ft long with an apsidal end within which, presumably, stood the statue of the god. His head and a few pieces of his arms were found in the temple and they, together with the three altars, are now in the Museum of Antiquities at the University of Newcastle; copies are exhibited on the actual site of the altars. The head of the god is a powerful piece of sculpture and bears comparison in its typically Celtic brooding look with such pieces as the famous head in the Gloucester Museum and other recently found pieces from that area.

Following the line of the Wall to the west various stretches can be seen from time to time, but it is best now to leave it and move a little to the south to the site of **Corbridge**, *Corstopitum* (NY 982648), which served as a fort, supply base and arsenal on the Stanegate. It lies between Newcastle and Hexham on the A69, half a mile west of the modern town of Corbridge. The site is on the north bank of the Tyne, about 60 ft above the river – an ideal situation from which to command the crossing and the bridge that was erected here. When the river is low the piers of the bridge can still be seen. The fort was rebuilt many times over: the first one, built by Agricola in AD 79–80, was burnt, only to be rebuilt 20 years later and abandoned 20 years after that when the garrisons were moved up to the Wall. When the next Roman push into Scotland came under Antoninus Pius the fort was rebuilt yet again, but in stone, about AD 139.

The remains seen on the site today are largely those of the fourth-century layout, and the coin evidence indicates occupation until the last years of the fourth century. At first glance the site appears confusing because of the large areas of foundations that remain. The Stanegate itself bisects the settlement, and on the north side are the substantial foundations of two granaries, a fountain and a water tank. In front of the granaries are the lower parts of a series of columns and brick pilasters which supported the porch. When the granaries were rebuilt, the bottoms of the columns and pilasters were buried within the metalling of the new and higher road. Excavation has revealed them down to their bases and this is why they look rather odd – which indeed is true elsewhere on the site where different levels reveal the various building periods.

The granaries behind the porch are considered the finest existing examples in Roman Britain. Here it is possible to get an idea of how such buildings worked. Both are very large – the west granary is 92 ft 6 ins × 23 ft 6 ins and the east granary 86 ft × 25 ft 6 ins. Their heavy stone slab floors are supported on sleeper walls; buttresses on the outside take the weight of the stone slab roofs and also allow air to circulate beneath the floors to keep the granaries dry. One of the ventilation grids between the buttresses is still *in situ* in the east granary.

Beside the east granary was a large fountain fed by a covered aqueduct to a well-house which then discharged into an oblong tank. The

139 The granaries and column bases of earlier buildings at Corbridge
140 At Corbridge the underground strongroom located below the chapel of
the legionary standards in the West Compound is still well preserved

well-house was designed to look like a small shrine and was built by
the Twentieth Legion. Beyond the fountain was an immense store-
house covering more than an acre, with four wings set around a central
courtyard. It does not seem to have been finished, but was converted
c. AD 160 into the headquarters building of the second-century fort.
Later this was to move to the other side of the Stanegate where there
are two military compounds: the West and East Compounds. Within
these compounds, joined together in the early fourth century by a
common wall with an entrance on the Stanegate, were various

workshops, officers' quarters, temples etc. Before they were unified each compound had its own headquarters building, but later the West Compound, which was rather more impressively built, became pre-eminent. It boasted a chapel for the legionary standards, flanked by offices, and from the front part of the chapel a flight of well-preserved steps leads down into the barrel-vaulted strongroom below ground. The apsidal buildings behind the headquarters in both compounds seem to have been clubrooms – the equivalent of the modern NCOs' mess – and are called *scholae*.

Just outside the walls of each compound there were temples: three beyond the East Compound that fronted on to the Stanegate, and two, set one behind the other, to the west of the West Compound. Despite the number of temples found at Corbridge, the gods or goddesses to whom they were dedicated have not been identified. A clay mould found in the East Compound was for making figures of the Celtic god Taranis. He is an amusing-looking amalgam of Roman and Celt – he carries a Roman-type shield and is helmeted, but his Celtic attributes of a wheel and a crooked stick are also much in evidence. His crooked stick made him known affectionately as 'Harry Lauder', after the famous comedian whose 'badge' was a similar stick. *Corstopitum* has produced many finds, perhaps the most notable being a hoard of 160 Roman gold coins, the largest hoard of such coins ever found in Britain. Artistically the most important piece is the so-called Corbridge lion, a three-dimensional sculpture of a lion devouring a stag, justly famous as a remarkable piece of Romano–Celtic carving. It is displayed in the site museum along with many other carved stones, altars, pieces of metalwork etc. from the fort. One of the most human of the tombstone inscriptions is that of Barates, who came from Palmyra in sunny Syria, so different a climate from that on the Wall. His wife, a British girl named Regina, is commemorated on an elaborate tombstone found at South Shields and now in the museum there.

Returning to the Wall itself the next site is **Chesters**, *Cilurnum* (NY 911701), mainly excavated by John Clayton and his nephew Nathaniel in the nineteenth century. Chesters is one of the best examples of a Hadrianic cavalry fort – though unfortunately its presentation in a series of parts enclosed in wire cages makes it a little difficult to appreciate the site fully. While the basic plan of an infantry fort and a cavalry fort were much alike, except for such obvious requirements as stabling, it is interesting to note that the *élan* and inbred superiority of cavalry already existed in Roman times – the headquarters building of the cavalry commandant is always somewhat superior to an infantry commander's, and that at Chesters is no exception. The fort had four main gates, each double-leaved. Three of these lay to the north of the Wall to allow squadrons of the 500-strong cavalry garrison to make quick sorties. The fourth gate, the south one, faced the civil area, and there was a narrower, subsidiary single gate in the east and west walls south of the Wall. These opened on to a cross street that went behind the headquarters building and took a lot of the local traffic away from the *via principalis* in front of it. At a later date, probably in the fourth century, several of the portals in the main gates were blocked, indicating that there was no further need for cavalry to make a speedy exit. The fort had by then become more of a solid fortified area, merely consolidating its position as a village stronghold.

The headquarters building is still very impressive. It followed the usual plan of a verandahed courtyard, entered from the *via principalis*, which gave on to a large hall beyond which lay the regimental chapel flanked by two pairs of rooms. The western pair housed the adjutant and his staff, and the eastern pair the standard-bearers who also had the responsibility of keeping the men's records, and organizing their pay, deductions etc. A stairway leads down from the chapel ante-room to a strongroom located beneath the chief standard-bearer's office. The roof that still covers it dates from the third century, and when it was found by accident in 1803 the room still had its strong, heavy wooden door armoured with iron plates held by large square nails. To the west of the headquarters building were granaries and workshops, now no longer visible. On the east side was the commandant's house with attached bath-house suite, and the substantial remains here include a good hypocaust system with part of the floor above the *pilae* still in position. Among the other buildings that can be seen within the fort complex are some barrack blocks in the north-

141 The strongroom at Chesters Roman fort still retains its barrel vault. Beyond it is the commandant's house

east corner of the fort. As Roman forts were always built to the same basic plan it is relatively simple to fill in where missing buildings once stood, and probably still lie merely awaiting the excavator's spade. There would have been two groups of stable blocks, one pair fronting on to the *via principalis* from the north facing the headquarters building and commandant's house, and another pair inside the south wall by the south gate. Between the south-eastern stable block and the commandant's house was the probable site of the hospital.

Outside the fort can be seen the abutments of the very solid bridge that crossed the North Tyne here. The western abutment, the one nearest the fort, is now under water as the river has changed its course since Roman times and now flows nearer the fort. Some of the piers can be seen when the river is unusually low. The eastern abutment (NY 913700), due to the river shift, is now a massive affair completely on dry land. It is built of huge blocks of very carefully dressed stone. On the northern side the builders carved a phallus for good luck, and beneath the tower a special channel was constructed through which the water rushed and operated an undershot water mill.

Downstream from the bridge in the usual situation outside the actual fort area was the bath-house. Parts of the walls here still stand 10 ft high, and on the west side of the large changing room a series of seven round-headed niches probably represent lockers, once provided with wooden doors, where the bathers could leave their clothes and valuables. They would then pass through a lobby from where they could make their way into a dry hot room or a cold room, and then on through the full ritual of the bath so close to a Roman's heart. The baths served other functions besides the simple one of cleanliness. In a fort such as Chesters they gave the soldier an opportunity to relax, to talk to his comrades – in short they were a kind of club with pleasant amenities.

Further along the Wall at **Carrawburgh**, *Brocolitia* (NY 859711), is the seventh fort from the east along the line of Hadrian's Wall. An earth rampart is the only evidence of the fort, but it is the small building 30 yards outside the fort to the south-west that is of interest. During the severe drought of 1949 when the marshy ground here dried up and shrank, the protruding top of an altar was noticed. Investigation showed it to be the tallest of a trio of altars dedicated to Mithras, standing before a three-sided apse at the north end of a 36-ft-long Mithraeum. Like the London example (p. 23) it had been built on flat, rather boggy ground, with no attempt to place it even partly underground as is the case with many of the Continental examples. The building was excavated in 1950 and found to be of two periods: the first structure was quite a small affair, only 26 ft long, which was then apparently enlarged to 36 × 15 ft in the third century. It follows the basic plan of a small Mithraeum – a narthex led, via a screen, into the nave which was flanked on either side by low benches for the worshippers. The head of the nave was guarded by statues of Cautes on the right and Cautopates on the left, each holding his torch respectively tilted up and tilted down. They are dressed in Persian clothes,

142 Downstream from the main fort at Chesters is the bath-house, a well-preserved building which has niches that were originally lockers for the bathers' clothes

143 The Mithras temple at Carrawburgh. Replica altars stand in place of the originals which are in the University Museum of Antiquities, Newcastle. The altar on the left has Mithras' radiate halo cut through to allow a light to be shone from behind *(cf. Illus. 6)*

similar to Mithras, and are his constant companions, symbolizing the rising and the setting sun; Mithras himself is the sun at midday. Of the three main altars to Mithras, the one on the left is the most interesting. It bears an inscription on the lower half, above which is a half-length representation of the god himself. He is shown with a radiate halo around his head, and this is pierced so that a torch, placed behind the figure, would let its light shine through the radiate crown into the semi-darkness of the temple. The three altars were set up by prefects from the nearby fort: Aulus Cluentius Habitus, Lucius Antonius Proculus and Marcus Simplicius Simplex. Behind the altars, in the apse on a ledge, there would have been a relief of Mithras slaying the bull – the usual decoration of such sanctuaries. The original altars are in the University Museum, Newcastle, which also has a full size reconstruction of the temple. Copies of the altars are on the site.

Initiates to Mithraism were required at certain stages to undergo various ordeals or tests, and an interesting feature of the later phase of the temple was the coffin-shaped ordeal pit dug in the southern half of the narthex. The pit, which could be sealed with flat stones above an initiate who would lie full-length in it, was probably used to simulate the initiate's death, burial and rebirth. The temple was desecrated early in the fourth century, probably about AD 324, and then the wet marshy area gradually overcame it until its rediscovery 1600 years later.

In the boggy ground close to the temple was a well sacred to the Celtic water nymph Coventina. There is little to see here now but this site has produced several thousand Roman coins, as well as other offerings, all tossed into the water. Old habits die hard – people still frequently drop a coin into a pool or well for good luck, and the ornamental fountain in the Greek and Roman Life Room in the British Museum is never without its coins from many lands!

The next fort, 4 miles to the west and perched dramatically high on a crag, is **Housesteads**, *Borcovicium* (NY 789687), one of the most visited of all the Wall forts. Its name actually means 'hilly place' and it is admirably sited on a ridge of basalt to command all the various roads that met here. Housesteads was a 5-acre infantry fort with a 1000-strong garrison; we know that it was garrisoned in the third century by the first cohort of Tungrians (from an area now in Belgium), and there also seems to have been a small unit of cavalry there – the *cuneus Hnaudifridi* is how it was described on an altar found in 1920. The main gate (*porta praetoria*) is the east gate which opens on to a direct road to the headquarters building in the centre of the fort. Its opposite number, the west gate, is the best preserved of the four. Only one of the gates, the north gate, opened beyond the Wall, and the Wall itself abutted on the fort at its north-east and north-west corners – thus the area of the fort itself lay south of the Wall, not astride it as at Chesters where three gates opened to the north of the wall. This is the basic difference in plan between cavalry and infantry forts. All four gates were partly blocked in the later Roman period, and quite a large part of them still remains. The commandant's house which

144 The communal latrine in the south-east corner of
the Roman fort at Housesteads

lay just inside the south gate has recently been excavated. The headquarters building, immediately to the north of it, is not very well preserved due to the activities of stone-robbers. It followed the basic plan
for such buildings, known so well from other sites.

Another recently excavated building is the hospital, lying behind
the headquarters building and between it and the west gate. Although
once again the basic plan of such military hospitals is well known,
it is the only actual example to be seen at present in Roman Britain.
To the north and south of the hospital are barrack blocks, and the
remains of a substantial granary lie between the north gate and the
headquarters building. Other barrack blocks lie in the eastern half of
the fort, and in the south-east corner can be seen the best preserved
Roman military latrine in Britain. Like many Roman public lavatories
seen in town ruins throughout the empire it was a communal establishment. Considering the problems of water supply from the basalt upon
which the fort is built, the provision of fully flushing latrines on such
a scale was a major achievement. The other communal gathering place,
the bath-house, was, as usual, outside the fort and has not yet been
excavated.

Associated with the fort on its south side was an extensive civilian
settlement built on the hillside in a series of terraces. Several of the
houses had the remains of their walls consolidated after excavation
and were left open to view, while the others have been covered up
again. In one of the houses a grim story came to light during excavations in 1932. The house was actually a shop fronting on to the street,
with living accommodation behind. Beneath the floor of the living-
room the excavators found the skeletons of a middle-aged man and

145 An impressive section of Hadrian's Wall near Housesteads
making its way west, up and over the crags

woman. They had been murdered – the man had the broken-off point of a sword within his ribs – and the crime had been concealed by laying a new clay floor above them. Roman law was most particular that no burials should be made within the confines of a settlement except for infants of up to nine months – so the only possible explanation (together with the evidence of the sword point) is that of murder, and the site of the house is accordingly labelled 'Murder House'. A small museum on the site houses many of the finds from the fort and civilian settlement.

Beyond Housesteads is some of the wildest, most spectacular scenery to be seen along the entire length of the Wall. Here are the famous Cuddy's Crag, Hotbank Crags and Crag Lough where the Wall goes steadily on, up and over them, taking all, literally, in its military stride.

Moving back from the Wall to the line of the Stanegate and south of the Milking Gap we come to a site that has recently produced some of the most startling finds from the Wall area for many years. It is **Chesterholm** (NY 357766) now more commonly known by its Roman name of *Vindolanda*. The fort itself was largely excavated in the 1930s and the principal remains to be seen are the north and west gates, the headquarters building and some store rooms with parts of their stone-flagged flooring still in place. It is in the civilian settlement outside the fort, the *vicus*, where extensive work has been carried out, that important finds are being made. In due course, time and especially money permitting, it is hoped to uncover the whole of this area; it is already shedding great light on domestic life in a military area in Roman Britain. By a curious quirk of nature the local conditions have preserved huge quantities of organic material that would under normal conditions have perished by this time. All sorts of domestic equipment have been found in the waterlogged deposits of brushwood sealed beneath floors and domestic rubbish. Particularly important are the large quantities of leather goods of all varieties, including fine leather shoes and ladies' slippers. Some writing tablets have been preserved, and a number of small altars that have provided much evidence of the many and various minor gods and goddesses that the common folk worshipped. Within the area of the *vicus* there was the usual bathhouse for use by civilians and troops, married quarters for the troops and a large *mansio*, an imperial posting house. The results of the continuing excavations at this site under Professor Robin Birley are going to be the most important in Roman Britain for some while to come.

Returning to the Wall there are good stretches with turrets at regular intervals along most of the route to the west. The next fort, **Great Chesters** (NY 704667), *Aesica*, is very overgrown and neglected compared with the other forts already visited. **Birdoswald** (NY 615662), *Camboglanna*, about 10 miles west of *Vindolanda*, is the next important and finely preserved fort along the Wall. *Camboglanna* means the 'crooked bend', and it aptly describes the fort's situation on a bluff high above a bend in the river Irthing which almost forms an oxbow lake at this point. A farm now covers almost a quarter of the fort's

146 Excavations in progress at the Roman fort of
Vindolanda (Chesterholm)

$5\frac{1}{3}$ acres but there are still impressive remains to be seen. Its north
gate lies beneath the modern roadway and the west gate is still buried
under the farm area. The remaining two gates, the south and the east,
are still quite substantial: they are both double-portalled and the pivot
sockets for their double gates are still there. The north side of the
east gate was blocked up in the fourth century to make it into a guardroom, and part of this still stands to the height of its springer arch
over the gate. Large sections of the walls still stand, much of it the
work of restoration carried out between 205 and 208 by the first Dacian
cohort and the first cohort of Thracians, and recorded in an inscription
found in 1929. Towards the end of the third century other restorations
were carried out on the headquarters building and commandant's
house. In an unusual moment of candour for a Roman inscription –
usually so prosaic and full of stereotyped abbreviations – it confides
that the commandant's house had 'fallen into ruin' and was 'covered
by earth'. Evidence of accidental covering by earth was found in 1949,
when a bronze arm-purse containing 28 silver denarii was excavated
from the soil forming the rampart-backing to the east wall between
the gate and an internal tower. Its owner had obviously put it down
for a moment, and another labourer then unwittingly buried it under
the soil for the rampart before its loss was discovered. The coins represented a considerable amount in those days, and one can easily imagine
the uproar that ensued when the loss was discovered!

147 The east gate of the fort at Birdoswald. It has been
partly blocked on the north side where the beginning
of the springer arch can be seen (*right*)

In many of the quarries of the area can be seen rough inscriptions
left by the men who cut the stone for the Wall. They are a very personal
reminder of the 'blood, sweat and tears' that went into such a massive
undertaking. Two miles west of Birdoswald on Coombe Crag several
inscriptions can be seen, but the best series are on the **Rock of Gelt**
(NY 526587), to the south of Brampton. Mostly the inscriptions are
short, and often undated, but each records the men and their gangs.
The longest one at Gelt, dated to AD 207, records 'a *vexilla* [62 men]
of the Second Legion, under the *optio* [a junior-ranking post to the
centurion] of Agricola, in the consulate of Aper and Maximus'. Only
odd small portions of the Wall can be seen as it heads on through
Carlisle, *Petriana*, to its termination at Bowness-on-Firth and small
forts on the coast to prevent outflanking.

To the north of the Wall there were a number of outlier forts at
certain strategic points. The area was also used for manoeuvres: aerial
photography in recent years has revealed numerous practice camps,
and new ones are still being reported. Because of the terrain north
of Birdoswald a forward fort was built at **Bewcastle** (NY 565745) as
a lookout post against raiders creeping down on to the Wall. Bewcastle
is better known, however, for its Dark Ages remains than its Roman
ones. The **Bewcastle Cross** is actually only a cross-shaft, 14 ft 6 ins
high, standing in the churchyard. Together with the Ruthwell Cross,
Dumfriesshire, which it much resembles, it forms the finest pair of
surviving rune-inscribed monuments in Britain. On its north and
south faces are panels of interlaced work, chequer patterns and foliage
scrolls, with five lines of runes on the horizontal bands between the
panels. The east face is decorated with a continuous foliage scroll from
top to bottom, with animals but no inscriptions. The west side is
sculptured with panels showing Christ, a man carrying the Agnus Dei,
and a man carrying a hawk. Inscriptions now virtually illegible on this
face indicate a date in the second half of the seventh century.

148 The south and east faces of the Bewcastle Cross
149 *Right* The west and south faces of the Ruthwell Cross

150 The bank and ditch of the Roman fort on the south side of Burnswark. The mound in the centre, one of the 'Three Brethren', was a base for a catapult

Not far from Locherbie in Dumfriesshire is the Iron Age hill fort of **Burnswark** (NY 186788). Covering 17 acres, it dominates the area for miles around. The history of the fort has given rise to some argument, because below the hill on its north-west and south-east sides the outlines of two Roman siege camps can be made out. At one time this visual evidence was taken to mean that Burnswark had been the site of a stand against Roman arms, and that it might have been the *oppidum*, tribal centre, of the Novantae tribe. Why else should Roman siege works be built up against a hill fort, apparently investing it? The Roman fort on the south side is exceptionally well preserved – it is very easy to pick out the ramparts with their typical playing-card shape and the gates in their walls. Additionally, by the northern rampart there are three large mounds called the Three Brethren – they were the bases for Roman catapults. In the corner of this Roman fort is a much smaller fort of mid-second-century date, and the camp around it, in fact, was built after the fort. Excavations 70 years ago on the hill top produced 67 Roman lead sling bolts and evidence that the fort was demobilized in the first century AD. The excavation evidence from the forts in 1967–70 showed that the Roman camps were much later than the abandonment of the ramparts of the hill fort and, anyway, the Roman camp on the north side was too far away to be very effective. So the original explanation of Romans mounting an attack on a stubborn native hill fort falls down – the excavation evidence reveals that it is only a case of the Roman army on manoeuvres making two practice camps below an abandoned hill fort and, for once, using 'live ammo' against it to simulate battle conditions.

In the little parish church at **Ruthwell** (NW 101682), south-east of Dumfries on the Solway Firth, stands one of the most important monuments of Anglo-Saxon art in Britain – the **Ruthwell Cross**. Fifteen feet high, it stands in a small side apse rescued from oblivion after it had been smashed during post-Reformation arguments in the seventeenth century. It still has its cross at the head of the shaft, unlike the Bewcastle Cross, and, unlike the Irish high crosses, its arms are not enclosed in a ring (although the cross arms are in fact modern restorations). Like Bewcastle it is carved with scenes: those on its west side depict Saints John the Evangelist and the Baptist, Christ, Saints Anthony and Paul of Egypt, the flight into Egypt, and the Nativity. Around the edges of the panels are Latin inscriptions. On the east side are an eagle, an archer, Mary Magdalene washing Christ's feet, the healing of the blind man, the Annunciation, and the Crucifixion. These panels are also surrounded by Latin. The north and south sides are decorated with running scrolls of foliage ornament inhabited by animals and birds. The cross dates from about AD 750, and inscribed on it in runes along the edges of its east and west faces around the sculptured panels are parts of the first 78 lines of *The Dream of the Rood* – the first and most moving of early English religious poems. Christ's cross appears in a dream to the poet and tells him of the suffering that it saw and how, after being thrown away after the execution, it was rescued by Christians, honoured and decked with gold, silver and jewels. A manuscript of *The Dream of the Rood* written between AD 950 and 1000 is preserved in the Cathedral Library of Vercelli, Italy, but the Ruthwell Cross gives us a text of 200 years earlier.

Along the south coast of Kirkcudbrightshire and Wigtownshire are a large number of Iron Age and Dark Ages sites. Scottish sites of the Iron Age tend to carry on to a much later date than their English counterparts because there was no proper Roman occupation in Scotland. Many of the sites are in quite spectacular situations but there is little else that can be said about them without being unduly repetitious. They are all marked on the Ordnance Survey maps of the national grid NX area. I shall describe only three sites in this area, but each of these is pre-eminent in its own way above its fellows.

151 The horn-shaped forecourt of Cairnholy, a Clyde–Carlingford-type tomb, with its large uprights and narrow entrance between the centre pair

152 Bronze Age cup-and-ring markings on the natural rock surface at Drumtroddan Farm

153 Auchagallon stone circle and Bronze Age cairn

Cairnholy (NX 517538), 4 miles south-east of Creetown, overlooks the eastern shore of Wigtown Bay. There are two monuments here, both neolithic chambered cairns, about 150 yards apart. Both are of a type known as Clyde–Carlingford tombs – this is a group of megalithic tombs that occur largely in northern Ireland and south-west Scotland. Their characteristics are a long, oval cairn with a rectangular gallery running into the cairn from a horn-shaped forecourt. Invariably there are two or three chambers off the gallery. In many respects they are like the megalithic tombs of the Severn–Cotswold group (e.g. Nympsfield, p. 69, and Stoney Littleton, p. 66). The southern cairn at Cairnholy is a good example of the type. Its covering cairn has now gone, and so the stones of the horn-shaped forecourt stand out clearly; behind them is a ruined chamber in two sections, front and back. The mound was about 170 ft long and 50 ft wide. Its companion to the north was much shorter – only about 70 ft long but 40 ft wide. The burial chamber here was also divided into two sections. Excavations in 1949 found that both burial chambers had been robbed, but interesting and valuable finds for dating purposes produced sherds of neolithic Peterborough ware and fragments of Bronze Age beaker pottery that belong to a later phase of the monument, about 1800 BC.

At **Torhousekie**, on the opposite side of the bay from Cairnholy and 3 miles west of Wigtown, is a Bronze Age stone circle (NX 382564). It consists of 19 granite boulders standing up on end forming a circle 60 ft in diameter, and is a perfect example of this kind of circle. Near the centre of the circle are three boulders standing in a line. Also of

Bronze Age date are the curious groups of cup-and-ring markings on several parts of the natural rock face at **Drumtroddan Farm** (NX 363447), north-east of Port William on the A714 road. Similar markings occur at other sites nearby and elsewhere in Scotland, but their significance remains unknown. Four hundred yards south of the marked rocks are three stones, two upright and one fallen – all that survive of an alignment of stones that may have some connection with the markings and the sacred nature of the area.

While in this area of Wigtownshire some fine early Christian inscribed stones can be seen in the museum at **Whithorn Priory** (NX 445403). They include the **Latinus Stone** of *c*. AD 450, set up by Barrovadus to commemorate his grandfather, which is the earliest known Christian memorial in Scotland, and the **St Peter Stone** of late seventh- or early eighth-century date. At **Kirkmadrine** (NX 081484) on the other side of Luce Bay are three other very early Christian memorial stones with inscriptions and the *Chi Rho* symbol.

North of Kircudbrightshire into Ayrshire and Lanarkshire along the western seaboard and hinterland there are only a few sites, and most of these are in rather inaccessible places and in widely scattered locations. On the Isle of Arran there are several neolithic sites – Clyde–Carlingford chambered cairns at **Cairn Ban** (NR 991262), the **Giants' Graves** (NS 043246), and **Tormore** (NR 903310). Cairn Ban is the best preserved of the three. At **Auchagallon** (NR 893349) in the centre of the island's west coast is a Bronze Age circular cairn surrounded by a circle of 15 standing stones.

There are no other noteworthy sites before the west end of the Antonine Wall is reached at Dumbarton on the Firth of Clyde, and it is best now to return to the eastern half of Scotland, north of Hadrian's Wall. In Roxburghshire, noted mainly for its great abbeys of Jedburgh, Kelso and Melrose, there is quite a concentration of monuments 9 miles south-east of Jedburgh. The Roman Dere Street runs up from **High Rochester** (NY 833986), where the most substantial stone Roman remains north of the Wall can be seen, comprising a strong west gate with walls still around 6 ft high, and other foundations of walls in the north-west corner of the fort. According to Roman law the dead had to be buried outside the inhabited area, and so tombs will generally be found lining roads outside cities – the Via Appia outside Rome itself is the classic example. Here at High Rochester, on the extreme outposts of empire, the law was upheld and followed. Along Dere Street as it skirted the fort on its east side 750 yards away there were several large tombs – the lower courses of one fine circular tomb, called the Roman Well, can still be seen. The fort produced a large number of inscriptions and reliefs which can now be seen in the University Museum at Newcastle; the best-known piece from the site is the naively crude relief of a Celtic Venus, her hair in two long braids, bathing with two water nymphs in attendance.

Dere Street runs on to **Chew Green** (NT 787085), a most complex area of four Roman forts and fortlets. This area was a staging post for troops heading north in convoy into the wilds of Scotland – the forts are defended by ramparts still clearly visible, and must have resembled the stagecoach posts of frontier days in the American West. Three miles north of Chew Green is the native fort of **Woden Law** (NT 768125). The hill fort is not a particularly strong one, and it could quite easily have been taken by storm by the disciplined Roman troops, but all round it is evidence of Roman siege works. On three sides, and a regular distance of 70 ft away from the ramparts, is a well-preserved complex of two banks and three ditches; these in turn are backed by three other siege lines, all independent of each other and unfinished. The only conclusion possible is that Roman troops, probably stationed at the large temporary camps at **Pennymuir** (NT 755138) to the north of Woden Law, used the fort for training exercises, and it is easy to imagine the disgust of the regulars having to throw up such earthworks simply as a military exercise.

With Woden Law as a focal point there are a number of native hill forts of the Iron Age within quite a narrow radius: **Shaw Craigs** (NT 673095), **Bonchester Hill** (NT 596120), **Hownam Law** (NT 796219), **Hownam Rings** (NT 790194), **Blackbrough Hill** (NT 809177), **Swindon Castles** (NT 829192), and **Park Law** (NT 850197). All are quite small *oppida*, but their close concentration is rather intriguing.

North of these *oppida*, and a mile south-east of Melrose, is **Eildon Hill North** (NT 554328). This, the largest hill fort in Scotland, matches Traprain Law (p. 198) in enclosing an area of about 40 acres. Also like Traprain Law, Eildon Hill was the *oppidum* of a tribe – here the

Selgovae – but, unlike Traprain, its use as a stronghold seems to have ended in the face of the Roman advance of AD 79. Apparently there were three phases of building at Eildon Hill; the first merely enclosed the area of the top of the hill, creating a fort 600 × 170 ft. This was subsequently enlarged to an area of about 9 acres that included the flanks of the hill to the north, previously outside the earlier wall. The last phase created a town perched on the hill top, about 1500 ft in diameter and covering some 40 acres, all enclosed within a double rampart. Within this area the large numbers of flat platforms that can still be picked out – over 300 – indicate the arrangement of the wooden houses. After the abandonment of the hill as an *oppidum* about AD 79 it remained desolate except for a small Roman signal station located on the west just below the hill summit; its site is indicated today by an almost circular, shallow ditch. The Romans themselves took up occupation at the foot of the hill at Newstead, in the fort of *Trimontium*.

There is a thin spread of Iron Age forts and settlements in Berwickshire and East Lothian in what was the territory of the Votadini. Two of the best sites in this area to visit are Edinshall broch and settlement, and Traprain Law. **Edinshall** (NT 772604) lies on the north-eastern slope of Cockburn Laws, about 4 miles from Granthouse. An Iron Age fort was built here in the late first century BC or in the early years AD but, curiously enough, not crowning a hill top in the normal place

154 Edinshall broch and hill fort

one would expect. It is situated on sloping ground with double ramparts and ditches and an entrance at the west end. Probably 100 or so years later, in the eastern half, a broch, together with its outerworks, was built. This stone-built broch is only one of ten known examples in Lowland Scotland. It is a substantial building, 55 ft in diameter with walls 17 ft thick. Within the walls are three sets of rooms and also guardrooms flanking the narrow entrance passage. Rather like later Norman motte and bailey castles set in the Iron Age hill forts, it was placed to make the best use of already existing defences as an outer bailey. From the late second century onwards there was more general settlement in the western half of fort and, in fact, this later settlement has destroyed a lot of the earlier defences on the north-west.

Traprain Law (NT 581747), 2 miles south-east of East Linton, is an absolutely magnificent hill fort – it has been described as 'a harpooned whale', and it certainly is an apt description when its huge bulk is seen rising 500 ft above the plain on the south side of the river Tyne. Although the site was occupied for about 1000 years in all from *c.* 500 BC, its historical surface, figuratively, has hardly been scratched. Like many hill forts it began life in a small way, a mere quarter of its ultimate size. Curiously, it then appears to have grown in 10-acre jumps – the next expansion made it up to 20 acres and a third brought it to 30 acres. At this point it now included the whole of the hill top except for the northern end, and when these 10 acres were incorporated, making a total of 40 acres, it could vie with Eildon Hill North (p. 196) as the largest hill fort in Scotland. With so large an area within its ramparts it must have been a hive of industry – as the *oppidum* of the warlike Votadini it held sway over vast areas and numerous smaller forts. It achieved its greatest extent in the late first century AD, but problems obviously arose in defending so vast an area and there is evidence of raids and destruction in the late second and third centuries.

Some time in the fourth century it was decided to curtail the huge area, and the northern end of the hill became once more outside the defences. A huge wall, still most impressive and striking, was built to exclude 10 acres, bringing the town area down to about 30 acres. Still standing today is the 12-ft-thick wall built of turf and faced with stone, that ran for 1200 yards cutting off the unwanted part of the town. Some 60 years ago, workmen digging on the west slope of the hill found a huge treasure of Roman silver plate, now in the National Museum of Antiquities, Edinburgh. It was apparently loot from pirate raids, possibly made into Roman Britain or even Gaul. Most of the pieces were actually fragments of over 100 high-quality silver vessels that had escaped being melted down into bullion by some chance occurrence that led to their being buried in the early fifth century. Amongst the smaller items which had not been broken up were flasks, goblets, spoons and a ladle in the form of dolphin holding the rim of the bowl in his mouth – there are five similar ladles from the great Mildenhall Treasure, Suffolk, now in the British Museum.

155 The great hill fort of Traprain Law, capital of the Votadini

The Roman presence, somewhat tenuous in this part of Britain, appears along the south edge of the Firth of Forth as it cut in towards Bowness and the start of the Antonine Wall. At **Inveresk,** just north of Edinburgh, there was a fort with a bath-house attached and at **Cramond** (NT 190768), 6 miles west of Edinburgh, there was another fort which stood above the harbour. Parts of the buildings within the fort can be seen near the church and down by the harbour is the so-called **Eagle Rock** (NT 184774). Here, on its east face, is a very worn sculpture once thought to be an eagle but now more probably considered to have been a carved figure of Mercury. He would be more appropriate than an eagle in such a setting, as guardian of travellers approaching the harbour.

Cramond would have acted as the supply depot for servicing the **Antonine Wall** by sea. The fort was built about AD 142 and was ideally situated as a naval supply base. The Antonine Wall was built on the orders of Antoninus Pius (AD 138–61) under the direction of the newly appointed governor of Britain, Quintus Lollius Urbicus. Work started in the late 130s and the defensive line was moved forward from Hadrian's Wall. The Antonine Wall was used as a jumping-off place for a series of campaigns into North Britain which culminated in Roman victories in 142–3. For the next 15 years, until AD 158, the Antonine Wall was held and then abandoned and the frontier line fell back to Hadrian's Wall.

The Antonine Wall ran from Bowness to Old Kilpatrick on the Firth of Forth, a distance of 37 miles (half the length of Hadrian's

156 Rough Castle, one of the best preserved forts on the short-lived Antonine Wall

Wall). It was built of turf with a rampart about 12 ft high; about 20 ft in front of it, in other words on the northern side, was a ditch 40 ft wide and 12 ft deep. This is still the most salient feature of the Antonine Wall and, although traces of many of its 16 known forts (19 are presumed to have existed) can be seen, the best preserved is **Rough Castle** (NS 843799), near Bonnybridge. The fort is only about an acre in area with well-preserved earth ramparts and ditches on three of its four sides. The buildings within the fort were built of stone and included the usual commandant's house, headquarters building, granary and barracks – some of these can be seen as foundations. On the east side of the fort was an annexe, defended by a rampart and ditch, which contained the bath-house. Crossing over the Wall and the flat berm between it and the ditch, and about 20 yards beyond the ditch into hostile territory, the small Roman garrison left a nasty surprise for any attackers. Excavations revealed a series of ten rows of small pits which, from descriptions in Dio Cassius and Julius Caesar, were called lilies (*lilia*) by the troops. In each pit five sharpened stakes were arranged like the five dots on the face of a dice. Carefully concealed by twigs and brushwood, such traps would create havoc amongst a charging foe. The examples at Rough Castle, where some have been left open to view, are the only ones known as yet in Britain. New archaeological survey methods, mostly relying on electrical impulses and resistivity, will no doubt reveal more of these sites in due course.

Returning a little from the Antonine Wall to the south-east we find the very important site of **Cairnpapple Hill** (NS 987717), near Torpichen and 3 miles north of Bathgate. The hill stands over 1000 ft above sea level, with extensive views over the countryside for miles around. It is a complex site that includes a henge monument, and cairns and burials were found here. The history of the site begins about 2700 BC with three large boulders in a group associated with a half-

157 Cairnpapple Hill, a cairn surrounded
by a circle of standing stones

dozen cremations in pits. Subsequently 24 standing stones were
erected in an arc enclosed by a rock-cut ditch, making it into a henge
monument with two entrances. The stone circle enclosed two Bronze
Age beaker folk burials – one of these has now been reconstructed on
the site under a concrete dome. The burial was crouched in a pit with
a standing stone at the west end, and accompanied by two beakers.
Within a short while a complete new plan for the site was put into
operation. In the western half of the henge monument a huge cairn
40 ft in diameter was erected. In places it passed over the stones of
the earlier circle and they were removed to make way for it. The northern of the two beaker graves disappeared into it completely. An inhumation burial was made in a cist grave at the cairn's centre, and
a stone used in the construction was decorated with three cup marks.
Around the edge of the cairn was a 'kerb' of boulders. The size of
the cairn was then doubled to 100 ft in diameter with a new kerb of
boulders, and two cremations in cinerary urns were placed in it. A
final, fourth, phase of the site is represented by four full-length graves
being dug into the east side of the cairn to take four inhumation
burials. These probably belong to the early Iron Age.

It is evident, therefore, that Cairnpapple was considered a sacred
site for about 1600 years, from around 3000 BC down to 1400 BC – from
the neolithic period through the Bronze Age and into the early Iron
Age. Few Christian sites can claim such longevity.

Crossing back over the Antonine Wall at Rough Castle and 18 miles
directly to the north is the Roman fort of **Ardoch** (NN 839099), near
to Braco. It is one of a series of forts thrown forward into hostile territory on a line going up into Angus. As such they must have resembled
the French Foreign Legion forts in Algeria in the 1930s. There is not
a stone building or wall to be seen at Ardoch, but for all that it is
one of the most spectacular Roman sites in Britain. The ramparts were

158 The Roman fort at Ardoch, a forward base
18 miles – a day's march – from the Antonine Wall

built of turf on a stone base, like the Antonine Wall. They followed
the usual playing card shape and had an area of 75 × 70 yards with
the customary military buildings within. Outside the fort area on the
north and east side are a series of five parallel ditches; presumably
there was a similar system on the south and west sides, but here the
evidence has been largely obliterated. A turf rampart further out
encloses the whole defence system. The ground to the east and south
of the fort was marshy, which meant that there was less chance of
attack from those directions; consequently the ditches on these two
sides are closer together than those on the north side. The fort itself
served as a permanent legionary base but beyond it, to the north, are
the remains of five larger temporary camps of varying dates. Two of
them – 13 acres and 20 acres respectively, the second one being an en-
largement of the smaller – date from Agricola's advance into Scotland.
Even larger camps in the group can be ascribed to the campaigns
of Septimius Severus in AD 208–9. All the camps overlie each other
to a greater or lesser degree, and this does make their interpretation
at ground level rather difficult.

The northernmost Roman site in Scotland (except for a few marching camps) is the fort at **Inchtuthil** (NO 125397) about 4 miles west
of Meikleour. Agricola had intended this legionary fort standing above
the river Tay to be the focal point of his expanding campaigns into
Scotland. The ambition was, however, shortlived. Work started on
the fort about AD 83, and the typical plan and buildings of a legionary

159 White Caterthun
hill fort

fortress began to appear – the headquarters building, accommodation for junior officers, a hospital, barracks, granaries and workshops. All these features were revealed in the excavations carried out by Sir Ian Richmond and Professor J. K. S. St Joseph in the thirteen seasons from 1952 to 1965. Agricola was recalled to Rome in the winter of AD 84–5 by the emperor Domitian, and his conquest of Britain remained unfinished. Within four years of starting to build at Inchtuthil the order came to dismantle everything and move back; not even the commandant's house had been built. The outlines of the ditches and ramparts seen today give little indication of the calculated withdrawal that was made, but the excavations revealed the story – the whole fortress was deliberately dismantled. Nothing was to be left that could be of use in hostile hands – glass and pottery were smashed to smithereens, timber dismantled and nails removed and the record swept clean, except for just one thing. In a pit the excavators found a million unused iron nails of all sizes – they weighed nearly 12 tons. It was obviously just too much of a dead weight to be carried off as the last troops turned south and marched away.

In the north-east are several hill forts of Iron Age date: the most interesting are two known as the White Caterthun and the Brown Caterthun. They are two hill forts 5 miles north-west of Brechin on sites a mile apart. The **White Caterthun** (NO 547660) is the more spectacular of the two and stands about 35 ft higher than its Brown neighbour. Two massive circuits of stone walls surround an area about

500 × 220 ft. The fallen stone from these walls spreads out over a vast area; probably the inside wall was originally about 40 feet thick and the outside one 20 ft, though debris from them now spreads over 100 ft. An entrance is noticeable on the south-east, but little else is known of this site with its spectacular ruined walls because it has not been excavated. Its companion, **Brown Caterthun** (NO555668), is much smaller, the interior area being about 260 × 200 ft. The curious feature of this fort is its complex defences – six ramparts in all with a very odd system of entrances. The innermost rampart surrounding the living area has only one entrance, on the north on the summit of the hill; the next three ramparts, the first of them massively built of stone, each have nine entrances, and the outer two ramparts have eight entrances apiece. Once more, lack of excavation simply leaves us with an impressive but enigmatic site.

Among the antiquities of Aberdeenshire are a number of Pictish symbol stones. They are remarkable monuments, and can be divided into three classes according to the symbols carved on them: the first class has purely Pictish symbols, while the second has, additionally, Christian symbols such as crosses. The chronological division between the two classes seems to fall about AD 700; the third class, with Christian symbols only, appears to continue from about AD 850 (the fall of the Pictish Kingdom) into the twelfth century. A number of the stones have been removed from their original sites and gathered together – there are good collections in the National Museum, Edinburgh, the Meigle Museum, Perth, and St Vigeans Museum, Arbroath. Very many, however, still remain *in situ* in out-of-the-way places such as odd corners of fields, gardens and churchyards. A number of these can be found in Angus and up into Aberdeenshire, together with other Iron Age sites which are mainly to the north-west of Aberdeen.

Almost in the centre between the two museums of Pictish stones in Meigle and Arbroath is **Glamis** (NO 385466). Here, in the garden of the Glamis manse, is a 9-ft-high stone carved on both the front and back. The main motif on the front is a finely cut Celtic cross with a complicated interlace pattern. Around the cross are carved a centaur brandishing two axes, a hound's head with three disc symbols, two men facing each other holding axes aloft, with a cauldron above them, and a four-legged beast. The back has purely Pictish symbols incised into the stone: a snake, fish and mirror symbol. Because of the mixed Christian and Pictish symbols it apparently belongs to class 2, but was probably converted, both literally and metaphorically, from a class 1 stone by the addition of the cross. Other examples of Pictish stones *in situ* in the area are four at **Kirriemuir** (NO 386545; two of class 2, two of class 3) in the cemetery on the north side of the town, and another class 2 cross-slab stone decorated on front and back in the churchyard at **Eassie** (NO 353475), off the A94 Glamis to Meigle road.

Five miles north-east of Forfar at **Aberlemno** (NO 523555) is a group of stones consisting of an upright cross slab in the churchyard and three stones beside the B9134 road. The cross on the slab is in-

160, 161 The front and back of the Glamis Stone with its mixture
of Christian and pagan Pictish symbols

tricately carved with interlace and spiral patterns and flanked by inter-
twined beasts. On the back is a representation of Pictish infantry and
cavalry engaged in a battle; various symbols are cut at the top of the
slab. Three hundred yards away, in a field beside the road, are two
stones, while a third lies on the verge; these are stones of classes 1
and 2. The cross on the latter is flanked by praying angels.

Another group of monuments centres on the area around Inverurie,
north-west of Aberdeen. At Chapel of Garrioch (NJ703247) is the
Maiden Stone, the most famous Pictish stone in Aberdeenshire.
Several legends are associated with it. The Stone is decorated not only
on the front and back but also on the side panels. The front of the
cross, which has itself been defaced, has five decorated panels including what might be interpreted as Jonah and the whale. On the back
are four panels of mixed symbols that include the so-called Pictish
'elephant' and geometrical designs. The sides are filled with an inter-
woven pattern of knots and cross lacing. Closer to Inverurie is the
Brandsbutt Ogham Stone (NJ760224) which has Pictish symbols
(class 1) and a line of writing in Ogham.

A little to the north of the stone on Brandsbutt Farm are two stone
circles. The first is at **Easter Aquhorthies** (NJ733208), where nine
stones form a 60-ft diameter circle; just inside the circle on the south
side is a recumbent stone with two standing flanking stones. The
Loanhead of Daviot stone circle (NJ747288) is similar in that it
has nine recumbent stones in a circle about 65 ft in diameter. Within
the circle are the remains of a Bronze Age cairn; the five standing

162 The Maiden Stone with 'elephant', mirror and comb Pictish symbols
163 The rear face of Sueno's Stone covered in elaborate Christian decoration which is later than AD 850

stones outside the circle on its west and south-east sides may be an indication of its use as an astronomical observatory. Round about these are a number of Iron Age forts, but they are of no great significance in themselves.

A very important carved stone stands at Elgin in Morayshire – the **Sueno Stone** (NJ 047595). This 23-ft-high cross slab of sandstone is a class 3 stone, in other words post AD 850, with Christian symbols only. All four of its faces are carved, the front with a tall wheel cross, and the sides with beasts interlaced in foliage that owes much to the tenth-century East Anglian school of carving, while the back has four detailed panels. The uppermost panel is rather eroded but the subjects of all four relate to a battle and a victory to judge by the cavalry and infantry represented, and also the several decapitated bodies. A last Pictish symbol stone, the **Boar Stone,** is at Knocknagel (NH 656413), south-east of Inverness.

Up the east coast from the Moray Firth are a scatter of mainly Iron Age forts, with occasional neolithic sites, but most are in very inaccessible country.

Swinging back over to the west coast, down the long peninsula of Argyllshire to the north of Lochgilphead, we find a heavy concentration of sites of all ages, only a few of which can be described here. To the south of Kilmartin there are two stone circles at **Temple Wood** (NR 826979), where 13 of the original 20 stones still stand.

Nearby are the **Nether Largie** standing stones (NR 831985), comprising five stones arranged as two pairs and a single stone running north-east/south-west. On the centre stone between the two pairs are a series of cup marks. These stones may be part of an astronomical setting coupled with others in the Temple Wood circle. Next to these circles is a series of five cairns of neolithic and Bronze Age date set in a linear cemetery. This kind of line is unique in Scotland, although perfectly familiar from the Wessex area around Stonehenge. The earliest cairn of the group is of neolithic date; the other four running away from it are of early Bronze Age date from the evidence of pottery and decoration such as flat axes on the undersides of some of the capstones.

Scattered in this area, and on the islands, are numerous Iron Age fortifications, many occupied into the Dark Ages, and all incorporating the word 'dun' in their name. They have a basic circular plan, walls up to 10 ft thick and some, with interiors larger than the others, may have been built deliberately to that size so that cattle could be accommodated inside and family and possessions could be safe from marauders.

On the small island of Eigg is **An Sgurr** (NM 462847), one of the most impressive Iron Age forts in Scotland. It occupies an area of over 9 acres – 1320 × 300 ft – on top of a 400-ft-high mass of pitchstone. On the north, south and east sides the rock falls sheer, and only on the west is there a means of approach up a steep and rocky slope. Here the way is barred by a stone wall 10 ft thick and 250 ft long, running between the precipices on the north and south to create an impregnable fortress.

On the mainland west coast of Inverness-shire a pair of Iron Age brochs can be found a mile and a half south-east of Glenelg. The broch is a curious and distinctive structure peculiar to Iron Age Scotland, and generally dated around the beginning of the Christian era. Some 500–600 examples are known, nearly all of them situated on the northern mainland of Scotland and the western and northern isles. They are the typical fortified homestead of these areas, just as the dun or hill fort is in the southern highlands: brochs and duns are almost mutually exclusive in their distribution pattern. Confusingly, many brochs also have 'dun' as part of their name, as will be seen. The basic structure is a tall stone-built tower with a single entrance, often with passages and rooms built within the walls. The finest extant example is the Broch of Mousa on Shetland (p. 222) but the two near Glenelg are acknowledged as second only to Mousa.

Dun Telve (NG 829173) is a mile and a half south-east of Glenelg and **Dun Troddan** (NG 834172) a quarter of a mile beyond it. With walls still standing to maximum heights of 33 ft 6 ins and 25 ft they are respectively the second and third largest specimens of brochs. At Dun Telve the circular wall is 13 ft 6 ins thick at its base, enclosing an inner courtyard 32 ft in diameter. Passages, stairs and rooms are contained within the thickness of the walls. Dun Troddan has a wall of similar thickness, but the courtyard is slightly smaller than Dun Telve, being only 28 ft in diameter. Like its neighbour, the thick

164 Only half the walls of
Dun Troddan broch remain, but it is
still an impressive site

circular wall hides internal constructions. More excavation has been
carried out at this broch than at its companion and in the courtyard
there is some evidence of internal wooden structures – post holes –
that could indicate the presence of an internal gallery. Only a mile
and a half further on in the south-east direction is **Dun Grugaig**
(NG 852159), which is a dun and not a broch. It is quite well preserved,
with a wall 8 ft high and 14 ft thick. Like the brochs it has chambers
set in the walls, but these are now very ruined. Its interior area is
a flattened oval about 47 ft in length at its widest part – this is partly
filled with tumble debris from the walls.

In the Outer Hebrides there are a number of Iron Age sites, as well
as a few neolithic ones. They are scattered on the islands of South
Uist, North Uist and Lewis. Two of the most important and interesting sites in this area are both on Lewis: Callanish and Dun Carloway.
Callanish (NB 213330) is a site spectacular for both its content and
its setting; in terms of prehistoric stone circles it ranks second after
Stonehenge in importance. It stands on a promontory reaching out
into Loch Roag 13 miles to the west of Stornoway. Here is an arrangement of megaliths that is unique in Britain, and associated with them
are two stone cairns. The alignments of the megaliths take the basic
form of a cross: there is a central pillar stone 15 ft 7 ins tall × 5 ft
wide × 1 ft thick in a circle of 13 standing stones with an average height
of 10 ft. Running north from the circle is an avenue 27 ft wide with
a double line of megaliths, ten standing on the west side and nine on
the east (originally there were probably 20 a side). This avenue is 270 ft
in length. From the east, south and west sides of the circle run single
lines of standing stones consisting of four, five and four megaliths
respectively. Two of the stones on the east side of the circle, together
with the central pillar, are located on the perimeter of a chambered

165 Callanish stone circle is one of the most important of its kind in Britain because of its interesting juxtaposition of stone cairns and alignments

cairn that has its roofless chamber at the mid-point between the pillar and the outer circumference of the circle. The cairn is of neolithic type and would therefore predate the circle setting, but it was obviously taken into consideration in the geometry of the circle when it was set up. There is another cairn north-east of the chambered cairn and one of the circle megaliths is part of it. This site has been the subject of intense astronomical study by Professors Thom and Hawkins, because it does provide excellent sighting lines on nearby Mount Clisham to the south in order to determine moon settings using this feature as a horizon marker. The mathematical arguments involved in ascertaining the mean declination of the moon are very complicated. However, given that Thom and Hawkins' calculations are correct, they add even greater weight to their postulated theory of such stone settings being used as astronomical observatories, and more and more archaeologists are accepting this theory. It does make Callanish one of the most important monuments of this type in Britain.

There are six other stone circles around Loch Roag and two of them at least, **Cnoc Ceann** (NB 222326) and **Cnoc Fillibhir Bheag** (NB 226326), can be seen and sighted on from Callanish and seem to be part of the overall concept of the 'observatory'. In all there are eight stone circles on Lewis within a 4-mile radius of Callanish.

About 6 miles north of Callanish is a well preserved Iron Age broch, **Dun Carloway** (NB 190412). Its walls still rise to almost 30 ft in places and it has an 11-ft-thick wall surrounding a 25-ft-wide courtyard. The internal arrangements of one of these fortified dwellings can be seen far better here than on many other similar sites. Its main door faces north-west, and just inside on the left is a guardroom within the thickness of the wall. From the central area four doorways give on to the rooms and a stair within the walls, and in several places the large slabs

166 Cut from one huge block of sandstone, the Dwarfie Stane is a rock-cut tomb unique in Britain

that cross between the inner and outer skins of the wall bonding them together are clearly visible. Only the doorway on the south-east side of the inner court opens on to an internal staircase, and well into the last century the remains of upper galleries were still preserved.

One last area remains to be described – the Orkney and Shetland Islands. The wonder is that prehistoric man should choose two areas where for most of the year the weather is harsh and inhospitable. On these two small groups of islands there is a larger concentration of important archaeological monuments from every period of British prehistory than anywhere else in Britain, apart from the Salisbury Plain area.

On Hoy, one of the southernmost of the Orkney group, is the **Dwarfie Stane** (HY 243004). This huge block of sandstone, 28 ft long, 14 ft wide and 9 ft deep, is a rock-cut tomb unique in Britain. An entrance cut into its west face gives on to a narrow, low passage 7 ft 6 ins in length. On either side of the passage is a small cell 5 ft wide × 3 ft deep × 2 ft 6 ins high. To enter them from the passageway you must step up, because their floors are 7 ins above the passage floor and there is a kerb of rock a foot high at the entrance to each of them. The right-hand cell has an uncut ledge of rock against its inner wall, almost like a pillow. Lying just outside the entrance to the passage is a slab of stone, 5 ft × 2 ft 9 ins × 2 ft, which acted as the door block. These rock-cut tombs are common around the Mediterranean, but it is unlikely that Mediterranean influence would have reached that far north, and the Dwarfie Stane is generally accepted as being of neolithic date, about 2000 BC.

The mainland island of Orkney itself has a magnificent collection of prehistoric remains. The passage grave of **Maes Howe** (HY 318127), 9 miles west of Kirkwall, is without doubt the finest

167 Interior of the burial chamber at Maes Howe, showing one of the four monoliths in the corners and the beginning of the corbelled roof above the wall junction

megalithic tomb in the British Isles. Its only near rival in Britain is New Grange on the river Boyne near Dublin in Eire, and in continental Europe the Treasury of Atreus at Mycenae. From the exterior it is, nowadays, merely a grass-covered mound 24 ft high, about 110 ft in diameter and surrounded by a ditch that lies, on average, about 50 ft away from the base of the mound. The ditch itself varies in width, generally being about 40 ft wide. Beneath the grass covering of the mound the structure itself is probably carefully built dry stone walling. The entrance lies on the south-west side where there is a passage 36 ft 6 ins long. Just inside the entrance, about 6 ft 6 ins along the passage-way, is a door whose closing slab lies just beyond it in a wall recess. Until the door is reached the masonry of the passage is of the normal coursed type but after the doorway the walls and roof are formed by huge slabs 18 ft 6 ins long, 4 ft 4 ins wide and 7 ins thick. Three of these blocks complete the length of the passage to where it enters the central chamber. This is 15 ft square and was once about 18 ft high. The walls still stand to a height of 12 ft 6 ins, the last 5 ft above this being modern restoration where the mound was severely damaged in 1861. In each corner of the chamber stands a monolith which helps to hold the roof in place because above 4 ft 6 ins from the ground the side walls begin to converge, each course overlapping the previous lower one to form a magnificent corbelled roof. Eventually the gap would have been made so narrow by this overlapping that a single stone could have sealed the roof and chamber. Small rooms open off the central chamber on the north, east and west sides. The openings giving access to them are about 3 ft above the chamber floor; outside each opening on the central chamber floor is a massive blocking stone, obviously displaced from its sealing place when the tomb was robbed.

Maes Howe dates from about 1800 BC and was broken into many times during the course of its history before it found protection under the Ancient Monuments Act. Some raiders left their mark in inscriptions, graffiti and drawings. At various spots throughout the monument there are 24 runic inscriptions left by raiding Vikings. Four of the inscriptions refer to the mound being broken into and treasure being removed. None of them is very explicit – each gives a tantalizing glimpse of what might have been there, but is certainly there no more: '. . . treasure was carried off in the course of three nights', 'Away to the north-west is a great treasure hidden . . .' and so on. The main robbery seems to have been carried out by a pirate gang led by Rognwald and Eindrid the Younger in the winter of 1150–1. In January 1153, Earl Harold and his men sheltered in Maes Howe 'while a snow-storm drove over them, and there two men of their band lost their wits'. Among the various animal carvings and scratchings there is a note-worthy 'dragon', beautifully engraved on the stone; on stylistic grounds it is ascribed to the early twelfth century.

To the west of Maes Howe, and about 4 miles north-east of Stromness, is an important group of Bronze Age stone circles that comprise the Ring of Brodgar (HY 294134), and the Ring or Stones of Stenness (HY 306126) together with various associated cairns. The first site reached, coming from Maes Howe, is the **Ring of Stenness.** Like its companion, Brodgar, it was originally a henge monument although the bank with the ditch on its inner face is difficult to pick out. There are four large upright stones (17 ft, 15 ft 6 ins, 15 ft and 6 ft high respectively) which stand at irregular intervals on the arc of a circle. The diameter of the henge was about 200 ft but the stones stand on the arc of a circle 104 ft in diameter. Away from the circle at the south end of the Bridge of Brodgar stands a single impressive monolith 18 ft 6 ins high. Probably once part of a circle, it does appear to be in some relationship to Stenness.

Beyond the Bridge is the **Ring of Brodgar,** the largest and finest stone circle in Scotland. It stands on a low neck of land between Lochs Harray and Stenness, a classic example of a class 2 henge monument (that is, with two entrances through its bank and ditch). Originally there were 60 upright stones and nearly half (27) still stand, averaging 7 ft in height. The circle was 360 ft in diameter and the containing ditch 10 ft further out. The entrances on the north-west and south-east that cut through the bank and ditch are 10 and 12 ft wide respectively. Several of the stones have carvings on them, comprising an un-deciphered runic inscription, a cross, an anvil and an Ogham inscription (they are on stones 3, 4, 8 and 9 moving east from the north-west entrance). This site is another of those which Professor Alexander Thom has studied in detail, and associates with the nearby island of Hoy to give lunar sightings from the circle.

Over on the west coast of mainland Orkney, 7 miles north of Stromness among the sand dunes on the south shore of the Bay of Skaill is a settlement site unique in Europe – **Skara Brae** (HY 231 187). It has an intriguing history – on a wild and stormy night in the winter of 1850 the wind stripped off the covering of a high dune at the south end of the Bay of Skaill, to reveal a series of ancient ruins. It must have been just such a night that drove the inhabitants away, whipping up the sea and sand against them – one woman in her haste broke her necklace, and the beads fell in a line behind her as she ran.

The site at Skara Brae is a stone-built village: not only the walls, doorways and passageways but even the furniture – the beds, cup-boards and dressers – are made of stone. It is so complete that it could almost be dubbed the British Pompeii, but the natural catastrophe that drove out the inhabitants took place nearly 1500 years before the eruption of Vesuvius in AD 79. Skara Brae is a neolithic village in the proper sense of the word – there was nothing amongst the great numbers of finds to indicate that the villagers knew about metals. Their economy seems to have been based on stock-raising and fishing, but their lifestyle was highly sophisticated. The village consists of a group of huts built largely with good-sized flat blocks of stone readily available from the seashore, and the roofs were also of stone. No cement or mortar was used for bonding the walls: clay was used to fill up holes and to form a coating over exposed outer surfaces. Some of the walls still stand 8 ft high; above this the roof was corbelled, with the eventual central opening probably left free to allow smoke to escape from the well-built central hearths that were provided in each hut. Low doorways, generally 3–4 ft high, gave on to a narrow passage in the thickness of the hut wall. The slots on either side of the door jamb took a bar to hold the stone door slab in position. Once inside the hut their plans all followed a similar arrangement around the central hearth, with a series of 'box' beds of upright stone slabs around the walls, often with cupboards in the walls above them. Each hut also contained on the back wall a statutory piece of furniture that can only be described as a kind of Welsh dresser, more familiar in nineteenth-century AD settings. These stone cupboards stood on three stone legs and invariably had two levels of shelving.

In the thickness of the walls of some huts there are small round chambers, some of which appear to have been used as store rooms

168 Hut no.1 at Skara Brae, with sleeping areas and a 'sideboard' on the right

or even treasuries, to judge from the well-made implements and carefully finished beads found in them. Although most of the huts, when excavated, produced large quantities of animal and fish bones and other domestic debris littering the floors, the inhabitants had taken the trouble to construct shallow, stone-lined, roofed drains. Between the huts ran a series of alleyways and covered streets, so that in bad weather no one need venture outside the large mound that formed the village proper.

Despite the numerous finds made sporadically and in excavations over the last 100 years, Skara Brae is difficult to date because of its sheer isolation. Nothing in any of the finds came from anywhere else except the immediate vicinity, so there is no chance of dates from that source. The pottery used in the village was very poor, but is similar to some neolithic pottery of southern Britain, and it does seem that the settlement was occupied intermittently: at least three phases have been recognized, from between about 1600 and 1400 BC.

North of Skara Brae, and 20 miles north-west of Kirkwall, is the tidal island of the **Brough of Birsay** (HY 239285). It lies 200 yards off the north-west coast of the Orkney mainland and can only be reached on foot at low tide. It has a fascinating history extending well

169 The Birsay Stone probably commemorates three warriors. National Museum of Antiquities of Scotland, Edinburgh

into early medieval times but it is the remains on the slopes above the ruined eleventh- and twelfth-century cathedral that concern us here. These long houses (one of them 56 ft long and 15 ft wide) are the evidence of the first Norse settlement in the Orkneys, and the ruins of a great hall, suitable for a Norse earl, can also be seen. Before the coming of the Norsemen the island had been a Celtic retreat, and a cemetery was found surrounding a small Celtic church. The cemetery yielded an early cross, an Ogham inscription and, most important of all, a broken Pictish symbol stone engraved with symbols: a mirror, a crescent, a V-shaped rod, an elephant above an eagle, and a row of three men wearing long coats, each man carrying a spear and a small square shield. The fragments of this stone (the Birsay Stone, now in the National Museum, Edinburgh; a copy is exhibited on the site) were found at the west end of a large, triple grave. It had stood at the head of the graves and so must have commemorated their occupants, probably high-ranking officers to judge from their appearance on the stone and their accoutrements. The first in the series has more elaborate decoration on his shield than that on his companions' shields and this might indicate his precedence. The find of the stone, although in fragments, in close association with the grave in an early Celtic

170 The Broch of Gurness, seen from the landward side, with its rock-cut ditch and outer enclosure. Most of the northern side has been eroded away by the sea

cemetery, is unique. It is also of great importance in the arguments about how Christian the Pictish symbols are and whether Christian masons would carry on carving them on purely Christian memorials and monumental stones.

Eleven miles north-west of Kirkwall on the coast at Aikerness, near Evie, is the **Broch of Gurness** (HY 382268). This broch, like others in the islands, is of Iron Age date and it is of interest because it continued to be used into later Viking times. There were a number of brochs in the Aikerness area; at one time it is said that eleven could be seen from Gurness alone. Now the Gurness broch stands 10 ft high and rather forlorn on the edge of the sea, though once it stood clear away from the shore. The sea has eroded the land away so close to it that part of the northern defensive earthworks have gone, and even part of the stone buildings.

The plan of the broch is basically the usual one except for one difference: an additional passage runs through the thickness of the wall at ground level, as well as the one higher up, which is the more usual arrangement. A ladder must have been used to reach the gallery at first-floor level as there is no trace of an internal stairway. Externally the structure is complex – a number of enclosures abut against the broch and enclosing them was a great rock-cut ditch, one of three that encircled the broch. On the inner side of the ditch the earlier rampart was removed and a new defensive wall built with bastions projecting out into the ditch. This very strong defensive feature is unique among the defences of Iron Age Britain. The last phase of the broch's occupation was in the Viking period when the defensive nature of the establishment seems to have been abandoned in favour of a more domestic structure built on top of the debris of the earlier broch and adjacent enclosures. To the north-east there was a typical Viking long house, and in the ruined outer courtyard on the seaward side of the broch the burial of a ninth-century Viking lady was discovered. She was dressed in woollen clothes with two bronze brooches, a necklace, knife, shears and an iron sickle. She had been peacefully laid to rest, but elsewhere in the broch more violent happenings were revealed by the excavations: in the debris of a kitchen midden inside the rampart wall were found five bronze finger rings – the macabre thing was that they were still on the fingers of the skeletons of two severed hands that had been tossed into the rubbish of the midden!

On the island of Rousay there are four prehistoric cairns and a broch. Almost opposite Gurness, on the other side of the Eynhallow Sound, and west of Brinyan pier, is the four-stalled neolithic cairn of **Taversoe Tuack** (HY 426275). This is a most unusual site, one of only two known examples of double-decker cairns (the other is Huntersquoy, on Eday). It stands over 200 ft above sea level, commanding extensive views. The lower chamber is below ground level and has a 19-ft-long entrance passage opening on the south. This passage, instead of approaching the chamber and entering it on its long axis in the normal manner, enters the chamber at right-angles to its length. The chamber is divided into four stalls, or cells, by upright slabs that stand forward from the back wall; the entire chamber is 12 ft 3 ins long × 5 ft wide. During excavations in 1937 several skeletons, some fragments of pottery and a perforated granite mace-head were found. The upper chamber was at ground level but most of it, save for the stumps of the walls, has disappeared. Its entrance passage, only 11 ft long, approached the chamber from the north. The burial chamber opens off on either side of the passage, which continues for a further 4 ft 6 ins beyond it. Thus the burial chamber is really in two halves: 9 ft 6 ins × 6 ft 6 ins, and 4 ft 3 ins × 3 ft 8 ins. Cremated bone was found in the upper chamber, and sherds of Unstan ware pottery in the lower chamber. In 1937 an area in front of the lower southern entrance was cleared and about 20 ft away the excavators found a small

171 Interior of the cairn of Taversoe Tuack showing its double-decker structure

172 Some of the 12 sections, or stalls, in the Mid Howe cairn. Those on the left (the east side) have a stone platform in them

underground room, 5 ft × 3 ft 9 ins, carefully lined and covered with stone slabs. It was only 3 ft high and had a narrow sloping entrance. Round the walls were four upright stone slabs projecting into the chamber; two complete neolithic pots and fragments of a third were found. It seems to be a classic example of the so-called Orkney earth-houses.

Not far away is the **Blackhammer** chambered cairn (HY 414276); it is four-stalled like Taversoe Tuack and has its entrance passage in the long side of the burial chamber.

On the north-west coast of Rousay by the cliffs of Scabra Head are two imposing monuments: the **Mid Howe stalled cairn** and Mid Howe broch. The cairn (HY 372306) is located on the seashore under an immense shed which protects it and enables visitors to walk round the cairn and view it from above. It is the largest known stalled cairn, being 106 ft 9 ins long and 42 ft 6 ins wide. The entrance at the south end leads to the burial chamber, which is 76 ft long and 7 ft wide down the centre of the cairn. Its length is broken up into 12 sections on each side by tall upright slabs, the tallest of which is 7 ft high. Most of the 12 compartments on the east side have a stone bench or platform about 10 ins above floor level, and scattered on them were the bones of at least 25 people, including six adolescents and two children less than four years old. Strangely enough, on the west side of the burial chamber the remains of only one person were found. Many animal and bird bones were also present, including those of oxen, sheep and voles, together with quantities of limpet shells which seem to have been a major element of the diet in neolithic and later times in the islands.

Only a few yards away from the stalled cairn is **Mid Howe broch** (HY 371308). Within a radius of 500 yards there were actually three brochs of which Mid Howe is the centre one; it was excavated in 1930–3.

Located on a spur between two creeks (Stenchna Geo and Geo of Brough), it is protected on three sides by water at high tide; on the landward side a defensive ditch cuts across the narrow neck of land on which it stands. Between this ditch and the actual broch walls are a strong wall, another ditch and then a confused mass of secondary buildings. The broch rises from these to a height of 14 ft, and is 59 ft in diameter with walls 15 ft thick at the base. Its one entrance, on the west side, is guarded by two chambers just inside the passage. The guard chamber on the left (north) of the passage gives access to the lower gallery within the walls. Further round the inside wall a door about 6 ft off the ground leads into the other gallery and rooms. Also particularly clearly preserved in this broch are the door checks (with holes through which spears could be thrust at attackers), and holes for the crossbars securing the doors against intruders.

On the **Holm of Papa Westray**, the northernmost island of the Orkney group, is a massive chambered cairn (HY 509518) of the same name. It is 104 ft long, while the island upon which it stands is only 2415 ft in length. The chamber within the mound is 67 ft long and 5 ft wide (the whole mound is 41 ft wide). It has an entrance on the south-east side which led into the long side of the burial chamber; the chamber's two cross walls divide it up into three sections respec-

173 Interior of the chambered cairn on the Holm of Papa Westray. It is entered via ladders through the modern protective concrete roof

tively 12 ft, 45 ft and 7 ft long. The passage is now closed and access to the monument is only possible through manhole covers in the concrete roof which has been placed over it for protection. Opening off the burial chamber are 12 small side chambers, each 4 ft in diameter and height and each with a corbelled roof. This arrangement is unique amongst the known cairns in the Orkneys. There are some crude engravings on the walls of the chamber, comprising zigzags, circles and rectangles. Such examples of megalithic art are rare on Scottish monuments.

On the southern tip of Shetland, 22 miles south of Lerwick, is **Jarlshof** (HU 398096), a site which covers some 3 acres in area and the Bronze, Iron and Dark Ages in its occupation. It is one of the most remarkable sites in Britain. Like Skara Brae, Jarlshof was discovered after a series of violent storms in 1897 had revealed massive stone walls in the mound above the beach. The site contains remains of three prehistoric villages and a medieval settlement in successive levels like a layer cake, forming a mound of occupation debris. The answer to the question as to why so remote a site should reveal evidence of such a long sequence of occupation seems to lie in the safe harbour provided by the West Voe on the east of the site, and good, well-watered land for stockbreeding.

The earliest remains on the site, on the landward side of the museum, only consist of an irregular wall and a very few fragments of the walls of an oval hut. Pottery and tools from these levels indicate a date of around 1800 BC. The late Bronze Age remains are more substantial, and there are four houses which are oval in plan with a large chamber at the back which faces on to a central courtyard area. The best-preserved house is no. 3, an oval about 17 ft long and 18 ft wide; an entrance passage on the south side leads into the central courtyard, which has two small rooms on either side and a large room set at right-angles to the courtyard at the back. Just inside the entrance are a quern and stone for grinding corn *in situ*.

The next layer of occupation on the site came after a short interlude when windblown sand had drifted across it; the newcomers levelled any walls of earlier buildings protruding through the sand and then built their houses on top of the earlier courtyard houses. The new ones were circular in plan with piers of stone which projected into the interior and made a series of divisions in the house. It is possible to stand in some of these later houses and see the plan of the earlier house beneath the floor, which has been removed in excavation. Once again the site was abandoned long enough for the sand to find its way back.

The site was next occupied in the late Iron Age, during the first few centuries AD. This settlement had a broch, but it has been much damaged by sea erosion and now only measures 30 ft in diameter; it may have been as high as 40 ft originally. On its west side was a courtyard, half of which has been claimed by the sea. Within the courtyard are the remains of an aisled round house but this has been largely lost under two large wheel-houses built later. A third wheel-house

174 Iron Age wheel-houses in the settlement at Jarlshof

was built within the by now abandoned broch tower, and a fourth outside the broch to the south-east. The wheel-houses were built about AD 200 and the second one is the best preserved. Its central court, 24 ft in diameter, has seven bays around it, all roofed about 8 or 9 ft above ground level except for the one facing north-west which was the entrance passage. Each compartment was paved and had a kerb separating it from the central court. Probably this type of building was pioneered at Jarlshof and spread from there to the rest of the Shetlands and Hebrides. Another example can be seen at Clettraval, North Uist.

In the ninth century the Norsemen took an interest in the site and an entire Viking settlement is preserved, the most complete example known in Britain. Possibly the new settlers came from the Møre-Trondelag districts of Norway as an incised picture of a ship found in the oldest house is very like ships from those areas. The Viking farmstead was quite extensive with outhouses, a bath-house and stables. There are eight Viking houses in all and finds associated with them indicate occupation down to the twelfth and thirteenth centuries. At this latter date a medieval farm was laid out, which was in use for the next 300 years. The history of the site was still not finished – in the seventeenth century a Laird's house (the Jarlshof) was built; it is described by Sir Walter Scott in his novel *The Pirate*, set in the Shetlands.

About a mile south-west of Jarlshof on the tip of Scatness and across the Voe on the **Ness of Burgi** is an Iron Age promontory fort (HU 388084). A massive wall still 6 ft high was built across the promontory and flanked by a deep ditch on either side. Within this defended area is a blockhouse of dry stone walling, one of only three known examples (the other two are on Whalsay Island, Loch of Huxter, and Clickhimin, p. 224). They appear to be earlier than the brochs and may have been the germ of the idea that later led to the broch. The basic plan

175 The Iron Age blockhouse
on the Ness of Burgi

of the Ness of Burgi is rectangular, with an entrance passage through
the centre dividing the building in two. Each half has an internal
chamber: the one on the east is entered from the entrance passage
and the other one directly from the exterior on the south-east. The
remains of another chamber can be seen at the south end, but most
of it has long since disappeared over the cliff edge.

Fifteen miles to the south of Lerwick, opposite Sandwick on the
small island of **Mousa**, stands the broch of that name (HU 457236).
Of all the brochs concentrated in the north of Britain (and especially
in north-east Scotland and on Orkney and Shetland) this is the finest
preserved of the 500 or so examples known. Mousa is pre-eminent
in preservation, height and plan and it is from here, together with
the evidence from the site of Clickhimin, that the origins of the brochs
become evident. They developed out of timberlaced rampart forts
(often referred to as vitrified or *murus gallicus* forts). The gradual need
for higher outer walls to protect the interior domestic units from in-
creasingly powerful armaments, often including firebrands, led to the
elevation of the wall, its interior galleries and rooms, and the overall
protection of a tall, stout, easily defended tower. Thus the broch was
brought into being as a major feature of Iron Age military architecture.

At Mousa the broch stands 43 ft 6 ins high and is 40 ft wide at
the top. Its diameter at the base is 50 ft and the walls swell out above
the base before they taper off to the top. The secret of the broch's
survival in such good order – apart from its remoteness – seems to lie
in its compact form and the fact that at the base its wall is solid for
the first 10 ft. This gives great stability to the structure, which other
brochs have lacked. Its entrance is on the west side, the seaward side,
and a passage 16 ft long and at first 4 ft wide leads into the central
area which is 20 ft in diameter. Along the passageway there is a defensive door whose barhole can still be seen; beyond this the passage
widens slightly, to 5 ft. There is a hearth in the centre of the court
and in the walls six openings: three are merely recesses but the other
three lead into quite large horizontal rooms within the thickness of
the walls, each room provided with three or four wall cupboards. In

176 The Broch of Mousa, the finest example
extant of this type of architecture

the interior walls there are two ledges or scarcements which would
have supported timber galleries: one is 7 ft above ground level and
the second is 12 ft. Above the second ledge the walls of the broch
are no longer solid-built but are hollow – double-skinned with cross-
bonding at 6- or 7-ft intervals; in conjunction with the slab floors,
this forms six circular galleries one above the other up to the existing
height of the broch. A narrow stairway leads up through these galleries
to the wall top; it is only 3 ft wide and, like the stairways in other
brochs, its entrance was above ground level and had to be reached
by ladder, thus ensuring greater protection.

Brochs continued in use as fortified places long after their initial
building and occupation. As strongholds they could hardly be bettered
and Mousa proved its continuing strength in a charmingly romantic
story. The *Orkneyinga Saga* relates how, in AD 1153, a man named
Erland fled from Orkney, taking with him Margaret, the mother of
Earl Harold Maddadson. He made for the broch of Mousa which he
had suitably provisioned beforehand. Earl Harold pursued his
mother's abductor and laid siege to Erland and his men within the
broch but, as the *Saga* says, he found it 'an unhandy place to get at'.
The stalemate was overcome by a reconciliation between the parties:
Erland married Margaret, Earl Harold got a stepfather, and the broch
of Mousa weathered the storm.

Clickhimin (HU 464408), in many ways the companion site to
Mousa, lies 15 miles north just outside Lerwick on a promontory on
the loch's southern shore. Until the excavations carried out by the
Ministry of Public Building and Works (now the Department of the
Environment) in 1953–7, there was no real core of hard facts known
about brochs, their origins or even their dates, except in a few rare
instances. The excavations at Clickhimin were exceptionally important because here, for the first time, an Iron Age fort was found under-
lying the broch. Its occupation actually extended from the Bronze Age
to the Dark Ages. There was a farmstead here in the Bronze Age (*c.*
700–500 BC) and some of its remains can be seen on the west side
of the broch – a small house with two sleeping areas around a central

223

hearth, and outside the back of the house, on the north, part of an outhouse with its paved flooring. Iron Age farmers succeeded the Bronze Age ones but little remains to be seen of this place. It is in the third period, that of the Iron Age fort (*c.* 500–300 BC) that the remains begin to make a more coherent picture for the visitor.

The fort consisted of a ring of dry stone walling round the islet (it was not yet a promontory) with a landing stage in front of the entrance on the south-east side, and just inside the entrance a blockhouse like that at Ness of Burgi (p. 221). The blockhouse was originally three storeys high, but it only survives today to the first-floor level. It was entered by the usual central passage, suitably blocked and barred by a wooden door. There were large rooms to right and left of the passage but not entered from it. A door at first-floor level gave access to the living quarters. Behind the blockhouse in the interior of the fort were a large communal hut and cattle byres. Some time around the end of the fourth century BC the seaward mouth of the loch became blocked and it changed into a freshwater loch. This had adverse effects on the Iron Age settlement which was badly flooded by the rise in the loch's water level. A breakwater was built – clearly the inhabitants had no intention of being forced out of their fort. Other steps taken included building an inner ring wall, never completed, and plugging the entrance to the fort. The work was apparently left unfinished because newcomers arrived who pointed out the advantages of broch construction; the first project was therefore abandoned in favour of a combined effort on the broch.

The base of the broch was 65 ft in diameter and it probably rose to a height of about 40–50 ft; only just over 17 ft of this now remains. The entrance was by a 17-ft-long passage on the west side, with the usual fortified wooden door. At the end of the passage was a central

177 The site of the Broch of Clickhimin has been occupied from the Bronze Age down into the Dark Ages. The remains at present most in evidence are the Iron Age defensive structures of the broch itself and the blockhouse on the right

court, 33 ft in diameter, with two rooms in the walls on the east and south sides entered from ground level. All the other rooms and galleries had to be reached by a wooden ladder up to the first-floor level. The blockhouse was reconstituted and became a valuable element in the forward defences of the broch, as the entrance was still in front of it on the south-east side. Times must have been difficult if such defensive measures were called for, and it has been estimated that the community here only numbered about 30–50 people.

Things settled down in due course; the source of the danger seems to have passed – possibly because the previously hostile elements were now too busy harrying the Roman province of *Britannia* to the south to worry about small fry like the inhabitants of Clickhimin. Anyway, the defensive nature of the site was toned down and a wheel-house like those at Jarlshof was built in the interior courtyard. The typical stone 'spokes' of its construction were built out into the courtyard from the interior wall of the broch, using stones from outside constructions. This all occurred during the second century AD, and dating evidence for this is provided by the pottery and some fragments of Roman glass vessels. Life continued much the same for the next 400 years – the islet became a promontory as the shallow strait silted up and a causeway 80 ft long was formed. A general decline took place in the people's lifestyle, and no care seems to have been taken of the basic structure which simply fell into disrepair: drains got blocked and stayed that way, and walls began to slide and topple over.

Associated with this last period, but not necessarily contemporary with it as it may be earlier, is a stone sunk into the causeway at the islet end and now under a nineteenth-century gateway. Outlined in the stone by pecking is a pair of footprints. Such footprints are very important symbolically – the implication is that whoever stood within them asserted their intention to follow their predecessors. There is a single print in a stone at Dunadd in Argyllshire and both these occurrences have overtones of a high king. As the Clickhimin example is located almost carelessly, in a humble place, it is probably out of context and therefore belongs to an earlier period than the causeway where it was used when its significance was either forgotten or overlooked. (In such a context it is intriguing to recall the footprint in the Church of Domine Quo Vadis on the Appian Way outside Rome, and the story of Cinderella's glass slipper – all have a common ancestry in folk myth.)

One last site remains to be described. Many prehistoric remains can be explained in religious terms, and the site at **Stanydale** (HU 285502) falls into this category. The site is 2¾ miles north-east of Walls, and some way north-west of Clickhimin. The structure has been described as a neolithic 'temple', and the 1949 excavations produced fragments of late neolithic pottery, Bronze Age urns and a piece of possibly Iron Age pottery. Externally the building is heel-shaped with a 12-ft-thick wall that encloses a large oval chamber 40 × 20 ft. Its entrance is in the facade that forms the flattened element of the heel-shape, on the south-west. On the interior wall opposite the entrance

178 The neolithic 'temple' at Stanydale

(i.e. the north-east) are six shallow recesses, built with the same concern for fine stonework as is evident throughout the entire structure. From the plan, and from the care and attention lavished on its building, the designation 'temple' seems reasonable, and it certainly has no parallels elsewhere.

The 'temple' stands within a group of five houses with another four quite close by. About 40 ft away on the south side is an arc of several standing stones. Assuming that all the structures and stones are contemporary – and there is no reason why they should not be – the layout of the site may have further significance in the context of the astronomical sitings mentioned previously with other circles and standing stones.

Further Reading

The Department of the Environment (formerly the Ministry of Public Building and Works) publishes numerous guidebooks and pamphlets on monuments and sites in its care. They are listed in Government Publications Sectional List No. 27: Ancient Monuments and Historic Buildings. Six illustrated regional guides are also published by the Department:

Vol. 1, *Northern England* (ninth impression 1971)
Vol. 2, *Southern England* (fifth edition 1973)
Vol. 3, *East Anglia and the Midlands* (third edition 1967)
Vol. 4, *Wales* (second edition 1973)
Vol. 5, *North Wales* (ninth impression 1972)
Vol. 6, *Scotland* (sixth edition 1970)

Bruce, J. Collingwood. *Handbook to the Roman Wall* (revised edition 1970)
Clarke, R. Rainbird. *East Anglia* (1960)
Dyer, James. *Southern England: An Archaeological Guide* (1973)
Feachem, Richard. *A Guide to Prehistoric Scotland* (1963)
Fox, Aileen. *South-West England* (second edition 1973)
Hawkes, Jacquetta. *A Guide to the Prehistoric and Roman Monuments in England and Wales* (revised edition 1973)
Houlder, Christopher. *Wales: An Archaeological Guide* (1974)
Jessup, Ronald. *South-East England* (1970)
MacKie, Euan W. *Scotland: An Archaeological Guide* (1975)
Ordnance Survey. *Map of Ancient Britain: North Sheet* (second edition 1964)
— *Map of Ancient Britain: South Sheet* (second edition 1964)
Stone, J. F. S. *Wessex Before the Celts* (1958)
Thomas, Nicholas. *A Guide to Prehistoric England* (1960)
Wilson, Roger J. A. *A Guide to the Roman Remains in Britain* (1975)
Wood, Eric S. *Collins Field Guide to Archaeology in Britain* (second edition 1974)

Glossary

agger	raised mound upon which a Roman road was laid.
bailey	*see* motte and bailey.
barrow	mound of earth raised over a burial; used in neolithic, Bronze Age, Iron Age, Roman and Saxon times. *See* p. oo for diagrams of neolithic and Bronze Age types of barrows.
basilica	long building, often with an apsidal end, which was the focal point of legal and municipal life in a Roman town or city. Its basic plan is followed in many early Christian churches, such as the one at Silchester.
bastion	forward construction from a defensive wall to provide enfilading fire against attackers. Also used as a base for heavy artillery such as catapults.
berm	levelled area of ground between a bank of earth and a ditch.
broch	circular fortified tower built of dry stone walling, having internal galleries and rooms within the thickness of the walls. Found in north-west Scotland, and especially in north-east Scotland and the Orkney and Shetland Isles; *see* particularly Mousa.
Bronze Age	period from about 1900 to 500 BC when bronze was the main metal used for tools and weapons.
chert	stone with a flint-like quartz quality.
cist	stone-lined burial pit.
corbelling	method of roofing a stone-built chamber by making each succeeding course of stones project forward over the preceding course until a small gap only is left which can be covered by a single slab to complete the roof; *see* Maes Howe.
cove	setting of stones found in some prehistoric henge monuments; *see* index entry.
cromlech	megalithic tomb chamber that has been denuded of its covering of earth; a term generally used in south-east England and Wales for such monuments in those areas.
cup and ring markings	decoration of a small hollow surrounded by pecked markings in concentric rings; generally found on megaliths of the Bronze Age in northern Britain.
cursus	term first applied by the antiquary William Stukeley (1687–1765) to an avenue of neolithic date bounded by banks and ditches near Stonehenge; *see* index entry.
dolmen	ruined burial chamber which has lost its covering of earth, and generally also its shape or plan.
door check	projection in a passageway into a broch against which an internal door would be shut.
dun	small Scottish Iron Age fort, not having the tall circular walls of a broch.
entrance grave	circular cairn covering a small rectangular burial chamber with an entrance in one side; found in Cornwall and the Scilly Isles.
forum	market place of a Roman town or city.
henge monument	sacred or ceremonial area of the neolithic and Bronze Ages enclosed by a ditch with an earthen bank on its outer side.
horn works	protective formation thrown forward in front of and around the gate of an Iron Age hill fort or the entrance to a burial mound.
inhumation	uncremated burial.

Iron Age	period after about 500 BC when iron was the primary metal used for tools and weapons.
keep	strong point of a medieval castle which held the main apartments and where a last stand might be made in the event of attack.
megalithic	term describing a structure such as a burial chamber, or stone circle, made of large blocks of stone.
mesolithic	literally the middle Stone Age, c. 10,000–4000 BC, typified by a hunter–fisher economy and the use of microlithic flints.
midden	prehistoric rubbish pit or dump.
monolith	single, large standing stone.
motte and bailey	early Norman castle consisting of a tall mound (motte) with fortifications built on it, standing within a defended enclosure (bailey).
murus gallicus	fort – *see* vitrified fort.
narthex	separate area before the entrance to a shrine; in a Christian church it is found at the western end.
neolithic	literally new Stone Age, c. 4000–2000 BC. Typified by the introduction of settled communities, the use of pottery and the production of highly polished and finished stone tools and weapons.
Ogham	alphabet written by using vertical and diagonal strokes on or across a straight line. Generally fifth century AD or later in Scotland.
palaeolithic	literally the old Stone Age, c. 500,000–10,000 BC. The era of the Ice Ages when man used crude or simple stone tools and maintained a precarious existence by hunting.
passage grave	vaulted burial chamber beneath a cairn entered by a straight passage. Generally found on the Atlantic coasts of Europe.
radio-carbon dating (C-14)	method of obtaining dates by measuring the carbon-14 element remaining in organic material. This should give the date of death, e.g. when the tree was felled from which a plank of wood was later hewn.
revetment	construction, generally of wood or stone, used to hold earth back and to prevent its slipping.
sarsen	basically a sandstone rock, often found as a 'boulder erratic', i.e. stones left behind by the retreating ice sheets of the glacial periods. Much used in the erection of stone circles and monuments such as Stonehenge.
sleeper walls	walls not fully load-bearing, often of wattle and daub, and always internal walls in a building.
stele	upright stone slab, usually inscribed in commemoration, e.g. a gravestone.
Stone Age	period before the discovery of metals, when stone was the major material used for the manufacture of tools and weapons. It divides into three: palaeolithic, mesolithic and neolithic (*q.v.*).
tessellated	floor made up of tesserae (*q.v.*), generally all of one colour such as red tile.
tesserae	small blocks of coloured stone, pottery, or glass used to make up a mosaic floor in a Roman house.
trilithon	two upright stones with a third laid across their tops, as at Stonehenge.
tumulus	*see* barrow.
vitrified fort	fort with dry stone walling laced with timbers which have been fired, and this produced an accidental fusing together of the stone (also known as *murus gallicus*; *see* index entry).
wheel-house	circular house of the Scottish Iron Age with internal stone piers radiating from the walls to support the roof.

Some Museums to Visit

Many of the sites described have small museums attached to them, and they have been mentioned in the relevant places in the text. The following list excludes these smaller museums and draws attention to the larger or more important collections which are not associated with a particular site and might therefore be overlooked. An indication of opening times is given although these may vary slightly seasonally.

1 THE SOUTH-EAST

London

British Museum, Great Russell Street, WC1 (weekdays 10–5, Sundays 2.30–6). The national collection of antiquities; of special relevance are the galleries of the Department of Prehistoric and Romano-British Antiquities which exhibit material from the earliest periods of British prehistory down to the fifth century AD.

British Museum (Natural History), Cromwell Road, SW7 (weekdays 10–5, Sundays 2.30–6). The Sub-department of Anthropology deals with the prehistory of man; major British finds exhibited here include the Swanscombe skull.

Museum of London, Aldersgate Street, EC1 (at the time of writing, not yet opened). This museum has recently been formed by amalgamating the former Guildhall Museum with the former London Museum. It covers the history of London and finds from the City of London and its environs. Among the major finds on display are the sculptures from the temple of Mithras in Walbrook and objects of everyday life from Roman and medieval London.

Brighton

The Brighton Museum and Art Gallery, Church Street (weekdays 10–6, Sundays 2–5). Collection relating to the archaeology of Sussex; includes the Hove amber cup.

Canterbury

Canterbury Royal Museum, High Street (weekdays 9.30–5.30). Local archaeological material; especially strong in Roman finds.

Dover

Dover Corporation Museum, Lady-well (weekdays 10–5, except Wednes-days). Large collection of Roman and Anglo-Saxon material.

Maidstone

Museum and Art Gallery, St Faith's Street (weekdays 10–5). Material from Kent, especially Anglo-Saxon.

St Albans

Verulamium Museum, St Michael's (weekdays 10–4, Sundays 2–4). Very fine collection from the Roman city including magnificent mosaics and a hypocaust with mosaic *in situ* in the park nearby.

2 SOUTHERN ENGLAND

Avebury

Alexander Keiller Museum (weekdays 9.30–5.30, Sundays 2–4). Material from Avebury and Windmill Hill excavations. Includes the remains of the medieval barber surgeon trapped under a falling sarsen.

Bath

Bath Roman Museum, Abbey Church-yard (daily 9–5). Includes Roman material from elsewhere as well as the Great Bath. Famous Medusa stone sculpture from temple pediment of Sul-Minerva, bronze head of Minerva and Bath 'curse'.

Bristol

Bristol City Museum, Queen's Road (weekdays 10–5.30). Emphasis on West of England finds and especially on barrows in the area.

Cheltenham

Cheltenham Art Gallery and Museum, Clarence Street (weekdays 10–6). Archaeological collections from the Cotswolds; includes Belas Knap material.

Cirencester

Corinium Museum, Park Street

(weekdays 10–5). Magnificently displayed collections in a new museum that includes large selection of fine mosaics, objects of everyday life, reconstruction of a Roman *triclinium* (dining-room), and the unique Cirencester acrostic.

Devizes
Devizes Museum, Long Street (Tuesday–Saturday 11–5). Premier collection of material relating to Wiltshire archaeology. Includes Sir Richard Colt Hoare's collection of prehistoric material from his excavations.

Dorchester
Dorset County Museum, (weekdays 10–1, 2–5). Major collections from all periods of British prehistory; includes the finds from Maiden Castle and the war cemetery at the east gate.

Gloucester
City Museum and Art Gallery, Brunswick Road (weekdays 10–5.30). Interesting material of all periods from the area; note especially the Celtic head from Gloucester and other local sculptures, the Birdlip mirror, and Roman inscribed stones, especially the tombstone of the cavalryman Rufus Sita.

Oxford
Ashmolean Museum, Beaumont Street (weekdays 10–4, Sundays 2–4). Major collection for Oxfordshire; particularly strong in prehistoric material of the Bronze and Iron Ages.

Reading
Museum and Art Gallery, Blagrave Street (weekdays 10–5.30). Contains the Roman collection from Silchester and other prehistoric material from the Thames Valley; note especially the gold Moulsford torc.

Salisbury
Salisbury and South Wiltshire Museum, St Ann Street (weekdays 10–5). Important collection from Salisbury Plain and south Wiltshire.

Taunton
Somerset County Museum, Taunton Castle (weekdays 10–5.30). Especially rich in material from the lake villages of Glastonbury and Meare, finds from South Cadbury and the Low Ham Roman bath mosaic.

3 THE SOUTH-WEST

Exeter
Rougemont House Museum, Castle Street (weekdays 10–5.30). Important collections of prehistoric material from Exeter and Devon.

4 EAST ANGLIA

Cambridge
University Museum of Archaeology and Ethnology, Downing Street (weekdays 2–4). Important material from Cambridgeshire, especially Iron Age chieftain burials.

Colchester
Colchester and Essex Museum, The Castle (weekdays 10–5, Sundays 2.30–5). One of the finest Roman collections in the country; beautifully displayed in the largest Norman keep known, set on the foundations of the Roman temple to Claudius.

Ipswich
Ipswich Museum, High Street (weekdays 10–5, Sundays 2.30–4.30). Suffolk archaeological material of all periods; includes copies of the Ipswich torcs.

Norwich
Norwich Castle Museum, The Castle (weekdays 10–5, Sundays 2–5). Very rich in East Anglian material; note finds from Grimes Graves, Iron Age torcs and ornaments, part of the Snettisham treasure (the rest is in the British Museum), and Roman parade helmets.

5 THE MIDLANDS

Chester
Grosvenor Museum, Grosvenor Street (weekdays 10–5, Sundays 2–5). Rich collection of Roman antiquities from the legionary fortress, with special emphasis on the Roman soldier.

Leeds
City Museum, Municipal Buildings (weekdays 10–6.30). Collections relating to Yorkshire and Aldborough mosaic pavement showing Romulus and Remus with the she-wolf.

Leicester
Jewry Wall Museum, St Nicholas

Circle (weekdays 10–5.30, Sundays 2–5.30). Finds from the Roman city Jewry Wall site and surrounding area; Roman mosaics *in situ*.

Lincoln
Lincoln City and County Museum, Broadgate (weekdays 10–5.30, Sundays 2.30–5). Large collection from the legionary fortress.

Liverpool
Merseyside County Museums, William Brown Street (weekdays 10–5, Sundays 2–5). Very large collection of prehistoric material from the area; note especially the Celtic Mayer mirror and the Anglo-Saxon jewellery.

Sheffield
Sheffield City Museum, Weston Park (weekdays 10–5, Sundays 2–5). Strong collection of prehistoric material from the area; note especially the Benty Grange Anglo-Saxon helmet, with its unique boar crest.

York
Yorkshire Museum, Museum Gardens (weekdays 10–5, Sundays 1–5). Extensive Roman collection from the legionary fortress; Roman remains in the gardens.

6 WEST OF OFFA'S DYKE
Cardiff
National Museum of Wales, (weekdays 10–5, Sundays 2.30–5). All aspects of Welsh prehistory and the Roman occupation; branch museum at Caerleon relating to the legionary fortress.

Newport
Newport Museum and Art Gallery, John Frost Square (weekdays 10–5.30). Roman material from Caerwent (*Venta Silurum*).

7 THE NORTH
Aberdeen
Aberdeen University Anthropological Museum, Tillydrone Avenue (weekdays 9–5, Sundays 2.30–5.30). Local antiquities and skeletal remains of Bronze Age beaker folk.

Arbroath
St Vigeans Museum, (weekdays 9.30–7). Sculptured monuments of the Celtic Christian period, including the Drosten stone.

Carlisle
Museum and Art Gallery, Tullie House, Castle Street (weekdays 9–8, Sundays 2.30–5). Rich collection of prehistoric finds, Celtic metalwork and Roman remains.

Dundee
Dundee City Museum and Art Galleries, Albert Square (weekdays 10–5.30). Archaeological collection from the region; includes Pictish symbol stones.

Edinburgh
National Museum of Antiquities of Scotland, Queen Street (weekdays 10–5, Sundays 2–5). Contains the major finds relating to Scottish archaeology from prehistoric times; includes many Pictish symbol stones and other sculptured stones.

Glasgow
City of Glasgow Museums and Art Galleries, Kelvingrove (weekdays 10–5, Sundays 2–5). Archaeological gallery covering all periods of Scottish prehistory.
Hunterian Museum, Glasgow University (weekdays 9–5, Saturdays 9–12). Collections include local geological and archaeological material.

Meigle
Meigle Museum, (weekdays 9.30–4). Major collection of 25 sculptured monuments of the Celtic Christian period, plus Dark Age sculpture.

Newcastle
University Museum of Antiquities, The Quadrangle (weekdays 10–5). Large collection of sculpture and inscriptions from Hadrian's Wall; includes full scale reconstruction of Mithras Temple from Carrawburgh and original altars from the site.

South Shields
Roman Fort and Museum, Baring Street (weekdays 10–7.30, Sundays 11–7.30). Unique collection of memorial stones and small finds from the Roman fort.

Acknowledgments

The author and publishers are grateful to the individuals and institutions listed below who have supplied photographs and given permission to reproduce them in this book. In particular they would like to thank Professor J. K. S. St Joseph, OBE, for providing a large number of photographs from the archives of the Cambridge Aerial Survey, and also the Department of the Environment for large numbers of photographs of monuments within its care.

1, 2, 3, 137 courtesy of the Trustees of the British Museum; 4, 5, 8, 10, 11, 15, 16, 20, 21, 24, 26, 28, 29, 32, 34, 36, 40, 41, 42, 43, 50, 52, 54, 55, 56, 58, 62, 63, 64, 69, 73, 95, 103, 110, 118, 147, the author; 6 *Illustrated London News*; 7 Museum of London; 9 Verulamium Museum, St Albans; 12 Ashmolean Museum, Oxford; 13, 14, 18, 22, 30, 31, 59, 76, 78, 84, 91, 92, 97, 99, 105, 106, 112, 121, 122, 131, 132, 133, 134, 135, 139, 140, 141, 142, 143, 144, 145 Department of the Environment (London), Crown Copyright; 17 Ronald Jessup, FSA; 19, 33, 38, 67, 68, 155 Aerofilms Ltd, Boreham Wood; 23, 25, 27, 35, 37, 39, 44, 45, 57, 60, 61, 65, 66, 70, 71, 72, 75, 96, 102, 108, 129, 130, 136, 154, 158, 159 courtesy of Professor J. K. S. St Joseph, Cambridge University Aerial Survey, copyright reserved; 46 Wookey Holes Caves Ltd; 47, 88 James Dyer, FSA; 48 Bath Spa Committee; 49, 53, Alan Saville; 51 A. F. Kersting (National Trust); 74 Professor B. W. Cunliffe, FSA; 77, 107, 115, 116, 120, 128 Peter Chèze-Brown, London; 79, 80, 81, 82, 83, 85, 86, 87, 89, 90 Charles Woolf, MPS, Newquay; 93 F. E. Gibson, Scilly Isles; 94 Colchester Borough Council; 98, 101 Hallam Ashley, FRPS (Norwich Museum); 100, 117 Edwin Smith; 104 Brian Hobley, FSA; 109 Barnaby's Picture Library, London; 111 D. Phillips (York Archaeological Trust); 113, 114 Royal Commission on Historical Monuments (England), Crown Copyright; 119 Gloucester Museum; 123, 124, 125, 126, 127 Royal Commission on Historical Monuments (Wales), Crown Copyright; 138 Warburg Institute, London; 146 Professor R. Birley, FSA; 148, 149 F. S. Cheney, Felixstowe; 151, 152, 153, 156, 157, 160, 161, 162, 163, 164, 165, 166, 167, 168, 171, 172, 173, 174, 175, 176, 177, 178 Department of the Environment (Edinburgh), Crown Copyright; 169 National Museum of Antiquities, Edinburgh.

Map of Roman London and barrow diagrams by Bob Tee.

233

Index